JAN,

IT WAS A PLEASURE TO MEET YOU TODAY. I FEEL WE REALLY CONNECTED AND I THINK YOU ARE A REALLY SWEET PERSON WITH AN UNCOMMON AWARENESS AND A KEEN GRASP OF THE IMPORTANT ELEMENTS OF LIFE. YOUR FAMILY, ESPECIALLY YOUR GRANDKIDS! ARE VERY BLESSED TO HAVE YOU IN THEIR LIFE. FROM ONE STRANGE PERSON TO ANOTHER, KEEP SPREADING THE LOVE AND KNOWLEDGE. THANKS FOR YOUR HOSPITALITY TODAY.

ALL THE BEST,

STAN

# THE JEWISH RECTANGLE

## SIDNEY B. KURTZ

American Literary Press, Inc.
Baltimore, Maryland

# The Jewish Rectangle

Copyright © 1998 Sidney B. Kurtz



Library of Congress
Cataloging in Publication Data
ISBN 1-56167-440-0

Published by

**American Literary Press, Inc.**
8019 Belair Road, Suite 10
Baltimore, Maryland  21236

Manufactured in the United States of America

Itkah Kurtzmann looked at her mule through half-closed eyes as her cart moved slowly along the dirt road leading to her hometown of Lutzin. She was not particularly sleepy, but since Aaron was familiar with this well-travelled route, she could use this time to rest her eyes. Itkah Kurtzmann was not one to waste time.

It had been a busy morning at the market in Rezekne, which was the terminus of the railroad from Riga, and where she was able to buy the fish and vegetables which she brought back and sold to her neighbors in the village.

She looked older than her forty-five years, as did most of the women in Lutzin, a reflection of the severity of life in Latvia in the early 1900's. Her back was slightly bent from years of leaning over washtubs and cooking meals for her family, while wrinkles were making inroads into her once attractive face.

With the morning's work behind her she had time to rest her body and focus a critical eye over Aaron, who had just reached his 14th year – ancient for mules in this part of the world. One day soon he would have to be replaced. David would raise a fuss but it couldn't be helped – she didn't want to be stranded on a snow covered road in the middle of a Russian winter.

Two years earlier the mule had slipped on a patch of ice and fallen heavily to the ground. Everyone was of the opinion that he should be destroyed – everyone but David. He had nursed the animal and said prayers over it as if it was one of their six children, and by some marvel it recovered to the point that it could once again serve Itkah on her excursions to Rezekne.

David was hailed as the miracle worker of Lutzin – the only person known to have brought a crippled mule back from death. As a result of this heroic effort every mule in the village with the slightest ailment was brought to the Kurtzmann household for his professional opinion. Itkah wasn't happy about this. She wanted him to charge for these visits, but David insisted it wasn't the neighborly thing to do.

"Perhaps," she countered, "I shouldn't charge them for the fish I bring back from Rezekne?"

"That's different," he'd say. "That's business."

She knew she would get nowhere in this discussion, but that didn't stop her from getting in the last word. "What do you call treating the town's mules – a hobby?"

David was a good paperhanger but was simply not a businessman. If it wasn't for her regular trips into Rezekne the family would be suffering more privations than they did now, especially with six children needing clothes and insisting on eating every day. She again gave some thought to the Feinwitz family that had emigrated to America in 1906. She wanted to do the same thing. What future was there here for their children, she wondered. Paperhanging, selling fish? Her mind was made up. But she refused to push her husband, even though he didn't object when she casually mentioned it during one of their evening conversations. Or maybe he just wasn't listening.

She felt that her situation as David's second wife precluded her from putting her foot down more than she already did. Only Ellis, the youngest boy, was a product of their bedroom. She loved David and was warmly affectionate toward her adopted family, and she certainly did her share in supporting them with her sales of fish and dried vegetables, but she still resisted the temptation to rule over all. Peace in the family was more important.

All of these things ran through her mind as the cart drew closer to her village.

It was a pleasant autumn day with a hint of chill in the light northerly breeze rustling through the woods that bordered both sides of the road. It was a cool relief after a long, hot. dry summer. The lake, from where those villagers without wells drew their water, was at its lowest level in many years, and it was feared that the unusual number of ill people was a direct result of this condition – only the deepest wells were still bringing up clear water.

Letters from the Feinwitz family spoke of running water inside the houses through a system of pumps and pipes. They also claimed they had a flush toilet in a separate indoor room, eliminating the need for an outhouse and the unpleasantness associated with it, especially in the summer when it was a haven for bees, flies and spiders, and in the winter when it was bitter cold. All of this was difficult to believe. From what she had read in the letters, Philadelphia was a charming city of brick row homes, busy with activity, and where an occasional automobile could be seen chugging along the paved or cobblestone streets. There were few trees, no lakes and it was rather congested. Still, it made her head swim to think of running water, flush toilets, paved streets, and automobiles. She suddenly had the feeling that life was leaving them behind. She wanted to be part of it. She wanted her family to be part of it. She would talk to David after dinner.

The clip-clop of Aaron's hooves was making her drowsy, not unusual at this stage of her journey. Her head began to slump forward when she became aware of another sound – a group of horses fast approaching ahead of her with soldiers riding three abreast. They could have safely passed the cart single file but they expected her to give way before they reached her – nobody in their right mind blocked the road to Russian soldiers on horseback. She snapped up her head and pulled on the reins, but it was a belated effort that proved worse than if she had not turned at all.

Aaron obstructed the right side of the road while the rear end of the cart swung out to the left before following in the new direction. The soldiers tried to manuever their horses through the narrow opening between the cart and the woods that formed the left border of the road. They were only partly successful. The first horseman made it through, but the other two bumped together, the second horse sideswiping the cart harmlessly. The third horse crashed head-on, knocking it over and spilling the driver and contents onto the road. Aaron was pulled off balance and went down with a cry and a heavy thud. The soldier's horse stumbled but managed to remain upright.

He turned and glared at Itkah who was getting up and brushing the dirt from her skirt while surveying her load of fish and vegetables that covered the road from one side to the other. They both looked at each other momentarily. Itkah was furious but did not say anything. With a little effort they could have avoided the cart and passed by without incident. With a little effort she could have stayed awake.

It was too much to expect them to help her right the cart and load her cargo. It would be enough if they went on their way and left her in peace.

"Woman!" he shouted angrily. "Don't you know enough to move out of the way of the Russian Army?"

She knew better than to argue with a soldier. "I'm sorry," she replied. "I was returning from Rezekne and I fell asleep. It has been a long, hard morning."

"It will be longer and harder for you if my horse is hurt. It's time you Jews learned your place in Mother Russia!" He wheeled and rode off to catch up with his fellow horsemen, leaving another cloud of brown dust to settle over the fish and vegetables.

"Filthy beasts," she muttered as she turned towards her mule, fully expecting that poor animal to be beyond saving. To her astonishment Aaron had already struggled to his feet and seemed no worse for the experience. He looked back at the cart which lay on its side, but was still attached to its harness.

"By my God," she exclaimed, "you are a wonderful animal. Fate has decreed a long life for you."

The cart itself was not too heavy without its load of fish and vegetables and Itkah had lost her weariness in all the excitement. She bent down, took a sure grip on the edge with the strength of a woman used to hard work, and with a sudden effort, lifted it and let it drop onto its wheels. With a sigh she stepped back to look things over. It appeared undamaged and Aaron, pawing the ground and anxious to continue, brayed impatiently. She threw her arms around his neck and gave him an affectionate hug.

"You are marvelous," she whispered in his ear. "It's an extra apple for you tonight, my friend." She began reloading the spilled contents before anybody saw what happened. She could have used the help of one of the villagers, but then everybody would learn about her misfortune and wouldn't buy the load. She would have the children wash the vegetables and clean up the fish sufficiently to make them saleable. The mule was well and the cart was in one piece. It could have been worse.


David Kurtzmann was settled in his favorite chair at the end of the dinner table pretending to be reading his bible. He was actually paying more attention to his wife as she bustled to prepare the evening meal, while his two young daughters, Lena and Rhea, set the table.

As he had so often before, he wondered why she had married him, a man with five children – did she love him that much? Who marries a man with five children and then bears him a sixth? Either a very remarkable woman or a very stupid one, and Itkah was far from stupid. It couldn't have been for his money; his paperhanging trade brought in just enough to survive on.

"I love you," she had said, "and I will take care of your family for you."

He had accepted that and never questioned her about it, but that didn't stop him from wondering about it. Nevertheless, without her he would have been at a loss as to what to do. With her the family was whole again. She embraced them emotionally as well as physically and it wasn't long before the children were calling her Mother. Not only did she develop into the cornerstone of the family unit, but she soon showed a resourcefulness that seemed to flourish under the demands of marriage and motherhood.

She cultivated a thriving business by buying fish and produce in Rezekne and selling it in Lutzin. She also, to his horror, began pressing his delinquent customers to settle up longstanding debts. It was all very embarassing.

"But my dear, Itkah," he protested, "these are my neighbors and friends. It's just not good manners to go after them like this."

She stirred the stew impatiently. "Ask your children if they would like a meal of good manners tonight," she answered crisply. Allowing the anger to fall away, she continued in a softer voice. "I'm not faulting you, my husband, but unless we can save more money we won't be in a position to face any real emergencies that might come up."

"What emergencies?" David asked.

She briefly described her unfortunate encounter with the czar's army, omitting the fact that it was mostly due to her falling asleep.

David gasped and put his bible down. "We could have lost our cart and the mule." He hurriedly added, "and you might have been killed."

She accepted his placing her third behind the cart and mule.

"They're beasts," she said as she set the large, steaming bowl of meat, carrots and potatoes in front of him. "Lena, call in the boys for dinner and remind them to wash their hands before they set foot in here. Beasts," she continued, "that's what they are. While I was in

Rezekne I heard that a group of those scum went crazy in Gavry, breaking into barns, stealing pigs and chickens and beating up the people who tried to stop them."

David shook his head. "Terrible," he murmured. "Perhaps they were drunk."

"Drunk with power, you mean, and the officials do nothing about it."

"There's talk of a Red revolution in Moscow," David said. "It's rumored that the communists will take over and put the government back into the hands of the people."

"Rumors, rumors. And when was it ever in the hands of the people? In the meantime Jews are being insulted and their property violated. How long will it be before our village is next?"

"I guess we'll just have to wait and see what happens," David replied. "Maybe everything will just blow away. What else can we do?"

Itkah inhaled deeply. "We can leave here," she said, "and go to America."

David looked sharply at his wife. She had mentioned it before but he had ignored it. "This is our home, Itkah, our roots are here. How can we just pack up, turn our backs on our friends and homeland and leave forever? Life isn't easy, it's true, but things will get better. A new government will put an end to these excesses by the military. Why should they bother us? We've done nothing but to be good citizens and not cause any trouble."

She was about to answer him when four boys ranging from six to nineteen years of age came noisily into the room. They were still wiping their hands on their clothes.

Itkah shook her head. "I don't hang a towel over the wash basin so you can wipe your hands all over your clothes."

"Nathan took the towel and wouldn't share it with us," Jacob complained. At nineteen he was the oldest boy and resembled his father with dark brown hair, dark eyes and a quietly serious manner. He was an intense reader and the most thoughtful of the four.

"He's selfish," Herman added. "He goes everywhere by himself and won't tell us where he's been." Herman was sixteen years old, a clone of his older brother, except for the permanent smile that seemd to forever be planted on his face, and a slightly more prominent nose.

Itkah looked at Nathan, eight years of age and a boy she knew would need watching for a long time. The rebel of the family, he went his own way with a disregard for household rules and regulations. If she said black, he would say white; if she told him to hurry, he would slow down; if he was told to stay near the house, chances were that he would be off somewhere doing his own thing. He tested her patience to the fullest.

Ellis was the youngest and didn't look anything like his brothers. The only child born to Itkah and David, there was no denying his mother. He had not yet established his personality and was content to follow his brothers wherever they went.

They sat down in their customary seats on one side of the heavy wooden table while their mother and two sisters sat opposite to them. David remained at the head of the table and listened to them chattering among themselves. He wondered what the future held for them. Paperhangers? Sellers of fish and vegetables? Not much of a career to look forward to.

Another bowl, filled with tomatoes, peppers and cucumbers fresh from the garden, was set on the table. Other than what they ate, Itkah saved dozens of cucumbers and at the end of the summer, with Lena and Rhea helping her, would peel and cut them up, dump them into a large vessel of vinegar, sugar, spices and an assortment of other condiments, stir the mixture well, allow it to soak for several days and then pack the contents into tightly capped jars. Soon the family was enjoying delicious bread and butter pickles, as Itkah called them, because they tasted so good when eaten with bread heavily coated with butter.

Itkah was amazing. Where she found the time and energy for all this, David couldn't understand. He owed much to her and thought again of her desire to emigrate. He had come to rely on her judgement. Though much of the time it conflicted with his own, their differences usually ended with her convincing him of the logic of her position. This didn't do much for his self-esteem, but he was not a jealous or vindictive person - he just wished he could come out on top occasionally.

"Nathan," Itkah called out. "Please don't handle the stew with your hands. I paid good money for our silverware in Rezekne. Please use it."

That boy, she thought. What is there to do with him? She felt that she could only go so far with her adopted family because she was not their natural mother. She was afraid that one day she might hear, "I don't have to listen to you. You're not my mother." She didn't want that. Better to let Nathan learn most of life's difficult lessons on his own than for her to become the center of dissension in the household. So she held back, hoping that David would pick up on the discipline where she left off.

She put a pitcher of water on the table and sat down at the end, near her husband. She was proud that her family had padded chairs to sit in and silverware with which to eat. Most households boasted only hard benches and wooden utensils. While in Rezekne she had spotted the chairs in a store that was moving to Riga. The owner had put them on the sidewalk and was trying to figure out how to load them onto his already overloaded wagon. Itkah had imagined those chairs around their dinner table. What a luxury they would be - and with padded seats and backs.

"It seems you'll have to leave those chairs behind," she had said, as he scratched his uncombed head. He was a big, heavy man whom Itkah recognized from having passed this way so often. She had never before spoken to him, but the chairs, although scuffed here and there, were beautiful.

"I really don't need them," he said. "I'm expecting a shipment of new chairs when I get to Riga. I thought I'd sell them there."

"Why not sell them here," Itka suggested. "I just bought my fish and vegetables and have very little money left, but how much do you want for them?"

He rubbed his chin at the thought of a sale. "They're good solid chairs - and with arm rests, too."

"I can see that," she answered.

"You won't see chairs like these in any house outside of Rezekne," he asserted.

"They're badly scuffed," she noted.

He looked them over. "Not so bad," he said. "Almost like new. One ruble apiece - six rubles."

"I only have three rubles left." She lied, but she wasn't going to pay him six rubles for used chairs, as much as she wanted them. She decided to appeal to his ego, of which, she was certain, he had an overabundance. "I'm only a woman," she said in a meek voice. "I buy my goods here and sell them to my neighbors so my family may live a little better."

"Very enterprising, I'm sure. Six rubles," he insisted, "or the chairs go on the wagon with me today."

She wanted those chairs. "I'll give you three rubles today and the rest when I come back to Rezekne on Monday," knowing he would be gone and wouldn't come back for three rubles.

"That will do me no good," he said impatiently. "I'm leaving Rezekne forever."

"Then it's hopeless," she said sadly. "We'll have to continue sitting on those cursed hard benches when we eat." She turned to go.

"Hold on, woman," he shouted. "I can get more money for them in Riga, but the load is already too much for my horse. You may have these chairs for your family. Three rubles and you're stealing them from me."

It was a steal, she thought as she loaded them on top of her fish and vegetables and slapped the reins on Aaron's rump.

When the children had seen Aaron laboring under this heavy load with six padded chairs on top, their eyes had opened wide. The benches were swiftly relegated to the outdoors and became firewood the following winter, giving off a warm heat that only hard, seasoned wood can.

A question to her husband from Jacob brought her mind back to the dinner table.

"Poppa, what is a pogrom?"

David and Itkah exchanged sharp glances and then David continued to eat calmly, not showing the inner excitement that the dreaded word generated.

"Why do you wish to know?" he asked.

"A boy in school said that we're going to have one and we should watch out for it."

"Which boy told you that?" David asked, trying to collect his thoughts. So it's beginning, he thought, just as it had years ago with past generations and in other countries. He had hoped it was over, that the government would see that it accomplished nothing in other countries and would cause nothing but misery here.

"Michael," Jacob said.

"And where did he hear this news?"

"From his father, Mr. Ostrov."

That figures, David thought. Ostrov is friendly with that radical swine Voroncovo who knows everything that is going on. He knew that Ostrov, who was very cooperative with the local politicians, was allowed to attend political meetings and had access to the latest news. As much as he wanted to minimize the importance of this latest development, his heart ached with this new burden. He tried to speak in his most casual manner.

"What does Ostrov know – he hears rumors from Rezekne, where they hear them from Vilnius, where some fool who wishes to seem more important than he is whispers them to someone else."

"But what does the word mean?" Jacob persisted.

David usually kept his troubles to himself, at least as far as his children were concerned. There was no use filling their heads with things they didn't understand and that they might blow up out of all proportion. But they are getting older, he thought, and Jacob is the oldest, almost of bar-mitzvah age. Sooner or later they will have to learn where their family stands in the scheme of things; better that they hear it from their father than from an outsider. He looked at Itkah to see if there was any expression of opposition on her face. Seeing none he stroked his well-trimmed beard, took a long breath, and began.

"Children, Jacob has asked me a question and I'm going to answer it to the best of my ability. You will discover one day that we do not live in a perfect world. There is much injustice in one form or another that people must bear throughout their lives, and we, as Jewish people, have to face a particular type of injustice that, as far as I know, seems to exist everywhere."

The children's eyes were fastened upon their father as he spoke and they ate their dinner more slowly. His manner was grave, and he seemed suddenly tired and older. The dinner table was the setting for many conversations, usually about their behavior, their garden,

Itkah's activities in Rezekne, or the health of their mule. This was the first time he had spoken to them about what it meant to be Jewish in Russia.

"Do you remember the story we read every year at Passover about the Israelites and their being driven out of Egypt?"

Everyone shook their heads in unison. They couldn't forget their father conducting the long service without omitting a word while the odor of the gefilte fish and horseradish drifted tantalizingly under their noses.

"They left Egypt to get away from the Pharoah's cruelties, his persecution of the Jews."

"But why the Jews?" Jacob asked.

"Why anybody?" David answered. "It seems to be a tradition. Things aren't going right, so blame it on the Jews – enemies of the people – traitors – stir up the masses. The same thing is happening today. Our country has many problems – crop failures, hunger, civil uprisings against living and working conditions, the list is long. People want to live comfortably, in freedom, but the government doesn't allow it, so there is all kind of trouble. By planting the idea that a certain group of individuals of a particular religion, in this case the Jews, are responsible for the country's problems, they take attention away from the government and focus it on somebody else."

He paused for a moment to give them time to absorb what he had said. The room was quiet. Only the occasional crackling of dying embers in the stove and the far off crow of a neighbor's rooster interrupted the silence at the Kurtzmann dinner table.

"Is that what a pogrom is, Poppa?" Rhea asked, her hazel eyes and long, brown hair framing her pale face.

"That's as simple as I can say it," he answered. It wasn't fair that children should grow up with such a weight around their necks, a weight that could affect them for years to come.

Lena, who was squirming in her chair, raised her hand for permission to speak as if she was in a classroom. "Is this the only village they'll bother?"

"No. There are hundreds of towns and villages where thousands of our people live. They're scattered all over the country."

"If there are so many of us, why can't we do something about it?

Fight back?"

"No matter how many we are, thousands, millions perhaps, we cannot fight the army. They are too strong and we are too weak. The army obeys the government, and we have nobody in the government to speak for us - to plead our cause."

"You could, Poppa," she continued. "You could tell them what you told us. What have we done to be treated badly?"

Bless you, he thought, in your youth and innocence to think that the problems of Russian Jews can be solved so easily. His voice would be like a grain of sand on the beach.

David was not enjoying this. Another father might revel in the glory of expounding his views to his young children, showing them how clever he was, the wisdom he possessed. His heart went out to them. Their lives would never be the same. They would no longer be carefree youngsters unaware of what was going on around them. They would look at themselves differently - an unwanted people of an invisible government they had never seen, except for those hated soldiers who sometimes rode through their lovely garden, stopping long enough to help themselves to some vegetables and then ride off down the road, laughing and making insulting remarks.

"Whatever you think of your father," he answered, "I'm not Moses and this is not Egypt. Every family must fend for itself and find its own way. To try to fight them would be fatal."

A hand rested on his arm. "Enough politics for one day," Itkah said. "Let's finish our dinner and rest a bit. So much knowledge absorbed in one day will make them dizzy. Children, eat! That's an order."

After a few giggles they ate, and after clearing the table and helping Itkah wash the dishes, they went outside to check on their goat and pull some weeds from the garden. Then they joined some of their friends for a subdued game of run, hide and tag.

Itkah watched them through the window as she took out her ledger to tally the past week's receipts.

"Children forget quickly," she said. "God gave them that much."

"They don't forget, my dear wife," David replied. "They put things aside. At the moment, playing with their friends is more important than worrying about the czar. What do you think of the information that Jacob brought home?"

"I shivered when I heard it. We are far away from Moscow, but the arms of evil men are long – they reach everywhere – even as far as Lutzin."

## 2

It was a long night. Neither David nor Itkah slept well. They talked until midnight. She once again expressed her desire to emigrate, but David held back, saying that things would change, the government would relent in their abuse of the people.

"With it all," he said, "we are doing fairly well. My trade doesn't bring in much money but, to your credit, you've developed a profitable business travelling between Krezekne and Lutzin. The children are all clothed. Thanks to your industrious hands our home is comfortable – our garden supplies us with generous amounts of food – we have two goats for milk, a mule and a cart – and we're respected, if not envied, by most people in our village. Let us wait a little longer before we make any hasty decisions we might be sorry for."

They closed their eyes, but despite their exhaustion, lay awake for two more hours before their heavy breathing indicated that sleep had finally overcome them. The house was quiet.

It was about daybreak, as the first of the sun's rays touched the tops of the trees that they were suddenly awakened by a horrible sound, like a tortured animal, inhuman, spine-chilling. It penetrated the walls of the house, lifting David and Itkah upright in their beds, and bringing the children rushing out of their bedroom, terrified and huddling together for comfort.

"Stay here with the children," David ordered his wife with a shaking voice while throwing on some clothes. "I'll see what that unearthly noise was all about."

"Don't go out," Itkah pleaded. "It's too dangerous."

"It's all right," he answered, maintaining his composure. "Whoever it was is leaving. I hear horses galloping down the road. But don't come out until I tell you."

When David left, the children assaulted her with questions and it took all of her effort to calm them down.

"Was it the soldiers?"

"What was that terrible noise?"

"It sounded like a scream."

"Are we going to die?"

Their imaginations were running wild. "What's taking Poppa so long? Maybe we should go help him." Itkah was thinking the same thing when David reentered the house, his face pale against his dark beard. He slumped heavily into his chair at the table.

"They've killed our goats and raided the henhouse, then rode their horses back and forth through the garden – it's destroyed."

"My mule!" Itkah shrieked. "What about my mule?"

"No sign of him." David sighed. "Stolen, driven away or killed. The sound we heard was either him or the goats. I'm afraid it has begun."

The children still clung to Itkah, frightened as much by the sight of their discouraged father as the excitement that awakened them. They had never seen him like this before, shaken and dejected. Itkah gently moved them aside and stood beside him. She put her hand on his shoulder and he looked up at her.

"I can't fool myself any longer. This was no drunken revelry. The district has seen too much of it. The Feinwitz family was smart. Remember when Rebecca was knocked over and almost killed? They didn't wait for it to happen again. I hoped these things would subside, but instead it's getting worse – and we're helpless."

"Don't despair, David," she said as calmly as possible. "We're all still alive."

He placed his hand on hers as the children watched quietly. They normally did not display affection in front of them. He looked up at her.

"Yes, we're alive, but for what purpose? To wait for them to come back? To awaken us again, if indeed we can sleep at all? To witness the destruction of all that's dear to us? To frighten the children out of their wits so that never again will they play outside without looking over their shoulders at the first sound of horse's hooves? We're alive, if one can call it that. I hoped the government would leave us in peace, but it's not to be. You were right, Itkah, it's time to go. Tomorrow I travel to Riga and apply for exit visas so we can escape this cursed land while we are still in one piece."

The room was quiet as his words took effect. Itkah sat down beside him and motioned the children to do the same.

"It's strange, David. I've been hoping to hear these words from you for some time. Now that I've heard them I find myself sad, not happy. I know what giving up all that you have worked for means. Our home, our garden, our animals, our neighbors – all of it melting away. Like snow in the spring, melting away to nothing, disappearing before our eyes. It isn't fair."

She struggled to hold back the tears that were filling her eyes, but they came with a rush, ran down her face and fell on her apron. She made no attempt to stop them.

The children stared, wide-eyed. This was more frightening to them than the soldiers – their mother was crying. It was too much. Lena and Rhea burst into tears and rushed to Itkah, kneeling on either side of her and burying their faces in her lap.

The boys watched nervously, at a loss as what to do. They were trembling inside. They instinctively knew their lives would never be the same. They knew nothing of that far-off country called America except that the Feinwitz family lived there.

A loud knock on the door shook their already badly frayed nerves.

"They're back!" little Rhea screamed, clinging tighter to her mother's skirt.

"Nonsense," Itkah said. "Soldiers don't knock on doors. Jacob, see who it is."

Jacob slowly opened the door revealing their neighbor's son, Joshua Martinova, a young man of about 30 years. He was of average height and weight, but broad in the shoulders from years of hard work on his parent's small farm. His face was thin, out of proportion to his body making him seem taller than his 5 ft. 8 inches. An uncombed mop of dark, unruly hair made his face seem thinner still. He walked with a pronounced limp, the result of a farm accident that severed his left leg just below the knee. When the wound healed a wooden leg was fashioned for him at the small hospital in Riga. His long working trousers hid it from view, but the noise of it on the wooden floor told the entire story.

"Come in, Joshua," David said warmly, glad to focus his attention elsewhere. "Sit down, you look exhausted. Itkah, it's time for breakfast. Have the girls help you. We'll all feel better after a good meal. Tell us how your family has fared through this nightmare."

Joshua sat down and looked around him. "Good, I see that you're all well. I wish it were the same with me." He began sobbing. "God help me! I'm now a thirty year old orphan!"

Itkah clapped her hand to her mouth. "No, Joshua, No! Not your parents! Not both of your parents?"

"Yes," he said in a low voice. "Father was knocked over and trampled as he ran from the house. When she heard him cry out, Mother rushed out, took one look at his body and breathed her last. It's unbelievable that such a thing could happen. I wish I'd wake up and find it was all a bad dream – a nightmare – a glimpse of hell. I can't comprehend it. What have we done to deserve this?"

The room fell silent and Itkah's face was once again tear-stained. She put her hand on his shoulder. "Stay and eat with us. We'll talk and decide what to do."

"I have already decided," David said. "I'm going to Riga for whatever papers we need to leave this unhappy country."

Joshua raised his shaggy head. "Where will you go?"

"Where we should have gone six years ago when the Feinwitz's asked us to join them – to America."

Joshua seized David's arm. "Take me with you," he pleaded. "I can't stay here."

"We'll be overjoyed to have you. But we'll need transportation into Rezekne to take the train to Riga. Do you still have your mule? Ours is gone."

"We have no animals left, but I have some good news for you. While searching for our own beasts I found Aaron hiding in the woods munching on tree berries."

Itkah sprang out of her chair. "He's alive? I can't believe it. Where is he?"

"Outside. I brought him with me, cart and all."

Itkah rushed to the door followed by David and the children. Sure enough, standing calmly in the early morning mist was their blessed animal. He pawed the earth with a foreleg. Itkah gave him a thankful hug while everybody else patted him on various parts of his body, forgetting their other losses for the time being.

"Did I not tell you," Itkah said, her mouth near his ear, "that you lead a charmed life? How will I be able to leave you behind when we go, you magnificent creature?"

"We'll get a good price for him in Rezekne," David said. "Other mules come and go but Aaron lives on year after year. Wait until the people hear that he escaped the wrath of those maniacs on horseback – he'll be immortal."


After the Martinovas were buried in the village's small cemetery, and with a plea from Itkah to be careful, she deposited David and Joshua at the train station in Rezekne, then continued to the market to purchase her usual load of fish and vegetables.

Wherever she went, everyone crowded around to hear her story, expressing sympathy for their losses and shock at the news of the death of Joshua's parents. People spat on the ground at the mention of the soldiers, and marvelled at Aaron's survival. She could have sold him on the spot, but knowing how slowly the beauracracy can move, and that it might be months, if ever, before their visas were granted, she refused all offers.

She returned home as quickly as she could and was relieved to see everything as she had left it. Jacob and Herman were attempting to re-grade the garden, and Ellis and Nathan were rounding up stray chickens and putting them behind the repaired wire fence where the coop had been.

Satisfied that some sense of order had returned and the children had calmed down enough to go about their chores, although she knew they would carry that horrible morning with them for the remainder of their lives, she sat down to write to her former neighbors in America.

"My dear friends," she began. "The Devil is once again casting a shadow over our unhappy land. It is with a combination of sorrow, joy and regret that I must tell you of our decision to join you on the other side of the ocean. We fear that a concerted campaign against our people will soon be a reality." She related all of the details of the previous day. "But my heart aches to tell you that our neighbors, Mr. and Mrs. Martinova, died at the hands of those unfeeling monsters. Their son, Joshua, who I'm sure you remember, survived and is going with us. He has grown into a fine young man despite the loss of a leg in a farm accident. Knowing from your letters that we will need a sponsor, I ask you to fill that need for us and also to find us a place to live.

I hope that you will supply us with good news in as short a time as possible.

As ever, your good friend, Itkah Kurtzmann."

She neatly folded the letter, melted some candle wax to seal the envelope, and sat back with a deep sigh. The enormity of their decision began to take effect. Despite her outward enthusiasm in front of her family, it wouldn't be easy to leave their home, their neighbors, her business acquaintances in Rezekne.

She had dreamed of opening a store in Lutzin. The villagers shouldn't have to travel to Rezekne to buy their food and clothes. They could walk into her store at their leisure and buy whatever they needed – not only fish and vegetables, but ready-made clothes, farm tools, rope, wire fencing, lumber – her store would carry everything. It would have worked well, she thought sadly. The children could have helped, and David would have worked right alongside her, giving up that wretched paperhanging job. He could have run the store during her shopping trips to Rezekne and even to Riga, where ships came from all over Europe. She would be on the dock, waiting. Her store would carry items never before seen in the countryside. Word would spread to nearby towns that the Kurtzmann store was the place to go for whatever was needed.

It was a good dream, she thought, and it would have worked. But at the moment that's all it was – a dream – shattered by the government. She wondered what their leaders were thinking when they sanctioned such violence. Were they afraid that the Jews would take over Russia? We barely have the means to travel from one town to the next, she thought, let alone throw out the czar.

It was too much for her to understand. Suddenly her head ached. She went into the bedroom, left the door open to make herself visible to her children, and lay down. She fell asleep immediately.


The next day David and Joshua returned, sleepless and tired. The government offices in Riga were understaffed and overcrowded with people applying for visas. They had slept in a park like street tramps.

"You look terrible," Itkah told them as she greeted them with a hug and a kiss on the cheek. "You had me worried when·you didn't return last night, but I half expected that. How did it go?"

"Every Jewish family in Russia wants to leave the country. The office was overwhelmed."

"Did you get the papers?"

"The applications, yes, but that's only the first step. We need somebody in America who will vouch for us and guarantee us a place to live when we get there. This is an American law. If it was up to our government we'd be on a ship this minute. They'd be glad to wish us good riddance, the dirty scum."

"I have already written to the Feinwitz family," she said. "I'm certain they'll be more than happy to give us whatever we need. Joshua, did you get your papers, too?"

"Yes," he replied, "but I must be more careful. While standing in line someone told me that if they saw me limping they wouldn't let me go. The Americans are sending back those not physically fit. I borrowed a shoe, tied it around my stump and walked as softly and straight as I could. They didn't question me."

"Wonderful! That was good thinking."

David sat down at the table and shared a snack of bread and meat with Joshua. "I'd forgotten how hungry I was. I wonder how long before we'll be able to go?"

"It took the Feinwitz's a year," Itkah said. "But I don't think we'll have to wait that long if the authorities want us out of the country. Our letter is on the way, and you have the applications. It shouldn't take that long."

## 3

True to Itkah's prophecy, in 10 weeks a thick envelope arrived intact from America. The Feinwitz's had come through. The information was forwarded to Riga and in another 6 weeks they received their visas.

"Amazing," David said. "The beauracracy can be efficient when they want to get rid of you."

The next communication from Riga informed them that no vessels were going directly to America for six months, but sailings to England, from where ships to the United States left on a regular basis, were scheduled once a month. They would then have to take a train to Liverpool and make arrangements there.

Although David and Itkah preferred a nonstop trip, the thought of waiting another six months, and all that might happen in that time, was not inviting.

"We can't wait that long," Itkah said. "We might be dead by then. It's a miracle that we're alive today. We've gone too far to turn back. The Feinwitz's tell us that they live peacefully, there are no government sanctions against any religion, and there is work to be found.

Among the visitors was a gentile merchant from Krezekne, Mr. Krushenko, with whom she had become friendly through her business dealings there. He was a tall, husky man with the wide cheekbones found in those Russians whose ancestors migrated from the eastern part of the country and from Siberia many years ago. His brown hair was resistant to combing, giving him a rough, wild appearance, when in reality he was a rather gentle person. But he was a fine businessman and he explained to David and Itkah the purpose of his visit – he had heard of their misfortune and their decision to move, and wished to buy their property as well as that of the Martinova's.

As they sat at the table drinking the tea that Itkah had served, he spoke of the conditions that were forcing people to make the decision to move away.

"I'm ashamed of my government for permitting such things to happen. I have lived and associated with your people most of my life. There is nothing wrong with them that isn't wrong with anybody else.

It is Russia's loss."

David and Itkah nodded in agreement, then got down to the business at hand, selling their home. Itkah looked around her.

"It's difficult," she said in a subdued voice. "Now that the actual moment is here, the ordinary things that I've taken for granted every day stand out so clearly. This table and the chairs that I purchased in Rezekne, our small bedrooms, the garden – our whole way of life has been violated by the very people who are supposed to protect us. Do you wish to buy Aaron also?"

"More than anything else. He's a living legend."

"That will be the final break," she said, her eyes moistening. "That will be the end. It will be like selling a faithful servant. I love that animal."

"I'll give him a good home," Mr. Krushenko promised.

They talked for some time and finally reached a price that David and Itkah felt was too low and Krushenko insisted was too high. He would go no higher and since they didn't have time to haggle, and felt fortunate to have a buyer at all, they agreed. The money, when added to their savings, would pay for their voyage and leave them enough left over to help gain a foothold in their new country.

"I'll draw up the papers and return in several days."

"Be quick," David said, "Our resolve is still strong and the memory of those soldiers is still fresh in my mind. Would you be interested in the Martinova farm, too?"

"I spoke to young Joshua on my way here. We reached an agreeable price without too much trouble. Quite a tragedy, to lose one's parents in such a violent manner. You're all travelling together?"

David nodded. "They were good friends and would have done the same for us. We're happy to have him."

"Well, that's it then." He held up his empty cup. "A toast to your future."

"Not with an empty cup," David said. "It's bad luck. Itkah, our holiday wine and three clean glasses. That's better." He poured the wine. "This is too important to trust to empty cups."

They held up their glasses and touched them in a solemn gesture.

"To the future," said Krushenko.

David put out his hand and Itkah took it. "To the future," he said.

## 4

The children and Joshua shared the back of the cart which held the large trunk that Krushenko had given them for a farewell gift. It contained all of their clothes and whatever other valuables they wished to keep out of sight. The trunk had metal straps, and it even had small wheels on the bottom making it easier to maneuver. At the bottom, under their clothes, was their perena, a feather filled mattress. Next to Aaron, this was the most important possession they owned.

Itkah and David had shared this mattress while the children had the use of harder mattresses filled with paper and old clothes in the second bedroom. The beds, which they could not take with them, consisted of wood frames with ropes tied tightly across them as supports. This was a luxury in a Russian village where most peasants had only one bedroom, and in some cases, only one room, and where the top of the massive wood-burning stove was used as a bed at night.

As Aaron pulled them along the familiar path, groaning under the load, Itkah found it difficult to keep her mind from wandering back to Lutzin where they had lived and worked so hard. As they entered Rezekne and waved here and there to someone they knew her head began to throb again. With an effort she concentrated her attention upon the train station which they were slowly approaching.

The children and Joshua had been quiet during the entire ride, perhaps realizing after all that this was not a dream – they were really leaving. A loud whistle startled them and caused Aaron to leap to one side. The children perked up at the their first sight of a steam engine. They had seen drawings of trains in books but had never seen one of these iron monsters close up, belching black smoke and trailing many cars loaded with passengers and freight. A mood of excitement replaced their nervous anxiety.

They stopped at the stationmaster's shed and unloaded the trunk and the rest of their belongings onto the wooden platform. The children gawked at the strange surroundings. Nathan wandered over to the tracks and stood between the rails, looking up at the engine. Jacob, Herman, Ellis, Lena and Rhea politely said their goodbyes and then joined Nathan on the tracks. David, Itkah and Joshua shook Krushenko's hand. With a final pat on Aaron's neck they watched the cart turn and head back to Lutzin.

Itkah turned her back to avoid the receding figures of the cart and their beloved mule. She shouted at her children to get off the tracks. As much as she attempted not to, she finally stole one last glance backward. They were gone.


The train ride to Riga, normally no more than two hours, stretched out to a seemingly interminable six hours. A broken wheel on the rear car and an engine breakdown delayed them. The passengers and their luggage were transferred to the cars ahead, making an already crowded trip somewhat overcrowded. The cars were nothing more than cattle cars with no windows. Temporary benches had been installed along the sides and down the center. Those who could not find seats sat on the floor, blocking any attempts at walking. The heat, while moderate at first, became intolerable.

As the afternoon dragged on, the lingering odor of the last shipment of cattle created additional discomfort. The lack of any sort of bathroom became a serious problem to the many children and older people on board. Fortunately, the long delays allowed those in need to get off the train and disappear into the nearby woods. Those who procrastinated and tarried too long were in danger of being left behind, and more than one person was seen running out of the woods adjusting their clothing as the train pulled away. The slow runners were forced to find their way to Riga as best they could.

Aside from people from their village, David and Itkah recognized some families from Rezekne: the Steiners, the Grossmans, the Liebermans and the Bermans.

"At least we are travelling with friends," David said. "We all have much in common."

The children's initial excitement was dulled by their inability to move around and the lack of windows to look out at the passing countryside. Little Ellis clutched his mother's arm.

"I want to go home," he complained. "I don't like it here."

"We cannot go home – ever. Don't ask me that again. We're going to a new home and a new land," Itkah said firmly, loud enough for the rest of the family to hear. "Soldiers will not raid our house or steal from us. We won't have to worry about pogroms. You will enter school there and learn English. You'll get an education, work hard and make yourselves useful members of society. For us Lutzin no longer exists. Soon it will be nothing but a memory:"

They all fell silent again with their own thoughts and the only sounds in the packed car were subdued conversations and the engine up ahead, struggling to reach its destination.

Joshua found a fairly comfortable place on the floor and didn't bother to get up too often. With his artificial leg he was satisfied to stay where he was until they reached Riga. He studied the faces of those around him, unsmiling, dejected. It seemed like a nightmare. He still had trouble accepting the reality of the situation. He was on a train full of lost souls. In a month they would be starting life again in a new land, a new continent. A second beginning. He hoped God would be with them.

## 5

The immigrants, loaded down with bundles and luggage, stumbled from the train and marched in a ragged mass up the platform towards a large ship docked at the end of a pier.

The children, and many adults too, stared speechless and wide-eyed at the first large boat they had ever seen. It was the Latvia to England passenger ferry, the S.S. Valenikov, about 300 feet long. This was small when compared to ocean-going vessels, but to these peasants, used to nothing larger than the wagons and carts of their towns and villages, it was a marvel to behold.

Soon, it was the Kurtzmann's turn to step onto the ship and produce the necessary papers and answer questions thrown at them by port officials and the ship's officers. Once again Joshua tied a shoe to his stump and held himself straight and tall as his turn approached.

"Your name?" The official sitting at the desk didn't look up. He was tired.

"Joshua Martinova."

"Age?"

"Thirty-one."

"Religion?"

"Jewish.

"Are you travelling alone?"

"I'm travelling with my neighbors, the Kurtzmann family."

"No family of your own?"

"Not anymore," he answered firmly. "My father and mother were killed by Russian soldiers in Lutzin."

The official looked up at the peasant with the unruly hair and broad shoulders. He ran his eyes over his body then again looked down at the papers on his desk. "Very well, Martinova. Move on." Joshua was a step closer to America.

They soon discovered that conditions on the boat were not much improved over those on the train – benches and decks on which to sit or try to sleep, with whatever food they carried for the two day trip to England. There was a toilet, a sort of outhouse indoors with the human waste exiting directly into the sea. Unlike the train, however, they could go out on deck for some fresh air if they could force themselves through the mass of humanity that had squeezed into the hold. Joshua and the children found an uninhabited corner where two benches met at right angles. They spread out their belongings on the deck and settled down to their first voyage at sea. Several portholes were opened by the crew to relieve some of the stuffiness which was building up as the population of the hold steadily increased.

A screeching blast from the ship's horn momentarily frightened the refugees. When they realized the ship was about to leave they all climbed up on deck to have a last look at their homeland.

The lines securing the ship to the dock dropped into the water and the S.S. Valenikov moved slowly away from land and out into the waters of the Gulf of Latvia. It was now early evening and the lingering warm air blowing from the land mixed with the colder air of the gulf producing a swirling fog that quickly enveloped the ship and swallowed up Latvia forever.

Itkah and David gazed solemnly into the mist. "We will never return," she said sadly. David put his arm on her shoulder while Joshua stood with the children near the rail.

Around the deck the scene was repeated a hundred times with tears, regret, anger, joy, and fear. They knew what they were leaving behind – homes, relatives, friends, terror, persecution – and wondered if what lay ahead could be worse. One by one they quietly drifted back down into the hold to reflect on their past and wonder about their future.

Itkah breathed deeply of the salt air. Others have done it, she thought. So could they.


It soon became apparent that the immigrants were not suited for sea travel. By the time they crossed the Gulf of Latvia and entered the Baltic Sea most were seasick. They lay in the hold moaning, using their bundles as pillows, trying to find the most agreeable positions for their bodies, and wishing they were back on solid ground.

The large ferry rolled gently in the swells now rolling in from the Baltic Sea, and dipped just as gently into the troughs. It wasn't rough sailing, merely normal conditions.

When they exited the Baltic and entered the North Sea vomiting was rampant and many a person learned the folly of emptying their stomachs at the windward rail. For most, the first English words they learned were "the lee rail," where the wind would not blow the results of their agony back into their faces.

For three days they lay about, wishing they were anywhere else, where their bodies would not torment them in this unnatural fashion.

As the ferry entered the English channel, and with land on the horizon, the rolling and pitching gradually eased. People began gathering up their belongings and shaking off the effects of their first trip to sea.

Itkah distributed some bread and cookies to her family while Joshua managed to obtain some water from the galley, which they shared between them. It was their first meal since leaving Riga.

Joshua whispered to David, "What will it be like crossing 3,000 miles of ocean?"

David nodded. "It won't be pleasant, but we'll survive – just as others have done."


The ship docked at Dover and the main body of immigrants boarded the train for Liverpool, some scattering across England to stay with relatives and friends.

The train was a contrast to the earlier one. There were seperate compartments that accommodated up to eight passengers, with cushioned seats facing each other and with windows along one side making it easy to observe the passing countryside. The aisle on the other side of the compartments ran the entire length of the passenger cars, and for a minimal cost, tea, coffee and sandwiches were available. To most of the immigrants who had never before slept, or even sat, on a cushioned seat, it was the ultimate in luxury.

The Kurtzmanns and Joshua had an entire compartment to themselves, with their luggage and cloth bags piled on the racks over their heads, and their new trunk in the freight car.

The children kept their faces to the windows, watching the lush British countryside pass by. England, for the most part was a green country, and although in the north and in Ireland famine had been the rule for the past years, here in the south rain was plentiful. Wherever they looked the trees were thick with leaves and the ground was abundant with all manner of undergrowth.

The children kept up a constant chatter about the countryside they passed through. Jacob shouted as they passed a horseless buggy belching smoke and raising dust, then fell silent as a burst of rain blew against the window, obscuring his vision. They passed through small towns and villages where people waved as the train rocketed through at the terrifying speed of 50 miles per hour.

"We'll soon be flying," Itkah commented, as captivated as the children. Any moment she expected the train to leave the rails and rip through the lush farmlands of rural England.

As green as the countryside was, London presented another picture. Gray and gloomy, the smoke of many factory chimneys and fireplaces combining with the ever-present fog cast a pall over the city, and even at high noon the sunlight was unable to reach the ground. The train moved slowly through a factory area and then through the slums that always seem to lie near the railroad tracks. Dirty children in ragged clothes could be seen playing in trash-strewn streets, presenting a kaliedescope of the humanity that was crowded together in the unhealthy environment of the large city.

When they finally jolted to a stop, Joshua left the train and melted into the throngs of people rushing back and forth on the platform. He returned with his arms loaded down with sandwiches and small bottles containing various colored liquids that bubbled and fizzed when the caps were removed.

"It's called soda," he announced proudly.

The children sipped and giggled as the bubbles tickled their tongues. The sandwiches, made mostly of bologna or cheese, quickly disappeared and they soon settled back in their seats, their hunger satisfied and their thirst quenched.

The stress of the voyage from Riga and the excitement of the train ride overwhelmed them. Their eyes slowly closed and they remained asleep as the train continued on its journey.

The 200 mile trip to Liverpool took the tired immigrants through Northampton, historic Coventry and busy Birmingham. England was still a major world power with Canada, Australia and New Zealand flying the Union Jack. India and Burma were allied with Britain, as were a host of far-flung protectorates from the Far East, the South Pacific and the Caribean Sea, all faithful for the moment to the small island empire and overseen by their vast navy.

The setting sun was barely visible through the haze as the train entered the city of Liverpool. David stared through the window but could see very little beyond the rail yards and factories. As he and the others collected their bundles he noticed that Nathan was missing.

"Joshua," he asked, "would you please see if you can find Nathan. He must have wandered off while we were sleeping and is probably roaming around the train somewhere."

As Joshua went off in one direction, the conductor appeared from the other, holding Nathan by the collar.

"This lad belong to you?" he asked.

Without understanding every word, David smiled and shook the conductor's hand in gratitude.

"Keep an eye on 'im," the conductor responded and went about his business.

"Nathan," David said, "you can't go off like this whenever you like. Suppose you were left behind? It's easy to get lost in such a crowd and we would have to go on to America without you."

David was aware that his warning would fall on deaf ears, but he was obligated to appear stern with his son, knowing that this wasn't the last time their little explorer would go sight-seeing on his own.

"The train is very long," Nathan revealed excitedly. "There are five cars filled with people like us, but I wasn't permitted on the cars nearest the engine. They're reserved for rich people dressed in strange clothes and looking very important.

David guessed that the people Nathan described were nothing more than everyday British travellers dressed in everyday British clothes which, next to their own, probably looked elegant.

"I really wanted to see how the engine worked," Nathan continued, "but a man in a blue suit wouldn't let me. It must be very strong to pull all of these cars. How does it do it?"

David had never given it any thought. "I don't know," he answered honestly. "I think it has something to do with heat and pressure. Regardless, stay with us or you'll find yourself with a red bottom. We still have a long way to go and your wandering off doesn't make it any easier. Stay close to your brothers and sisters."

After arriving at the docks, they filed off the train and joined the multitude heading towards the dock.

Several ships, much larger than the S.S. Valenikov, towered over them in the mist. David looked at their names and checked his papers. There it is," he pointed, "the S.S. Dominion."

It looked tremendous, a 650-foot freighter with its hold converted to carry passengers. In addition to tables, benches and chairs bolted to the deck, cots were placed in every open space to serve as beds for the two to three week voyage. It was obviously going to be crowded. No sooner had they set down their belongings and made certain their trunks were aboard when the loudspeaker announced a two day delay in sailing due to the late arrival of fuel and food.

The next morning they decided to stroll around the city, taking care not to venture too far lest they become disoriented. Itkah left Nathan on the ship in the custody of Joshua, who didn't want to walk and thus be too conspicuous. As they and the three children walked hand in hand, still wearing the same clothes with which they left Lutzin, they looked around at the buildings and market stalls set on the paved sidewalk. Their appearances drew little attention. The citizens of the Liverpool dock area were accustomed to the sight of immigrants passing through on their way across the Atlantic.

Itkah was stunned at the volumes of food on display, wondering if it had been prepared just for them. She purchased nine plums, five for them and four to take back for Joshua and the boys. They were delicious.

"What wouldn't the villagers back home give for a taste of these," she said, licking some residue from her lips. "They would pay anything." Among the other items on the stalls was a strange looking fruit, unlike anything she had ever seen before. It was a beautiful yellow color, long, slightly curved and bunched together in groups of four to ten.

"Banana," Itkah slowly read from the sign.

"Right you are," said the lady behind the stall. "Not every bloke gets it right the first time. 'ow many would ya likes, Dearie?"

Itkah, not understanding a word, nevertheless comprehended the meaning and held up one finger. The lady broke off one banana and handed it to her, an expectant smile on her face as she watched her bite into it. Itkah's face screwed up unpleasantly as the woman burst into a fit of laughter as she reached across and retrieved it. "It tastes better without the skin," she said with a broad smile while peeling away the outer layer and giving it back to her. "You all make the same mistake. Don't you feel bad at all, Dearie."

Everybody joined in the laughter as they each tasted a piece of the banana. Itkah pointed to a bunch of them on the stall. "America?" she asked.

The woman looked blankly at her, then smiled. "Bless you, Dearie, 'course you'll see these in the states – and lots more. There ain't nuthin the Yanks ain't got. You're a lucky family t' get away from those Russkies. My hubby says the bloody Yanks'll own the world some day. But we and them's cousins – we 'ave nought t' fear from them. God bless ya and good luck t' ya."

Both David and Itkah caught a word here and there but understood little of what the woman said, accepting her smiles with nods of their heads.

The early morning mist had cleared and it was becoming a pleasant morning for late in the fall. The sun shone down on scattered groups of immigrants, seamen and shoppers as they intermingled on the streets and sidewalks.

David's and Itkah's spirits were high. It was a beautiful day for a new beginning. People were friendly. There was no fear of physical violence, and the mention of America brought agreeable smiles from the merchants. It was good to be alive.

## 6

The ship's horn let out a deafening blast as she moved away from the pier. After finally taking aboard a full load of fuel, food and freight, the S.S. Dominion cast off her lines and headed out of port, the decks packed with immigrants taking their last looks at Europe. Circulars printed in Russian had been passed out informing them that they were allowed on deck during calm weather, but they were to stay below if conditions took a turn for the worse.

The vessel cleared port without incident, and after dropping off the harbor pilot, pointed its bow westward toward the United States. At the rail the Kurtzmann family watched as the coast of England slowly receded, then disappeared completely. Lena tugged at Itkah's sleeve.

"Will we ever come back?"

Itkah looked at the little girl. "Homesick already?"

"I liked our animals and the garden. I miss Aaron. Will we have a mule in America?"

A lump rose in Itkah's throat at the mention of Aaron. "The Feinwitz's never mentioned mules or gardens. We will have to get used to a different life."

Rhea, standing next to Lena, began to cry. "Will we have any friends to play with?"

"I'm sure you will, child. There must be many children your age and you'll meet many more once you start school." She averted her head to avoid seeing their sad faces, and looked at the deck where many boxes and large crates that could not be stored below were lashed down. Destination names were written or stamped on each crate and she ran her eyes over them – Philadelphia, Baltimore, Pittsburgh. Customers in each city were waiting for this cargo. Much money would change hands.

David interrupted her thoughts. "I heard that there are more than two thousand of us on board. "How will they feed such a mob?"

"I don't know," she answered. "Suppose we go down and find out?"

"The large galley was set up in buffet style with long lines of immigrants moving slowly along with their trays, each receiving a bowl of watery soup and a stew-like mixture of meat, potatoes, carrots and assorted vegetables in a thin gravy.

"It looks like the stew that you make for us, Momma," Lena said.

Itkah snorted in disgust. "You call that stew? It's brown water with left over food thrown in, but to feed a bunch like this I guess they must cut corners somewhere. Anyway, it's food, so fill your bellies and don't complain."

It didn't matter – as on the Valenikov the motion of the Dominion was taking its toll on these former farm families, and food was soon the farthest thing from their minds. The first swells sweeping in from the Atlantic were forerunners of worse things to come. As they did on the Baltic and North Seas, the immigrants were soon back at the rails. The waves between Russia and England were nothing compared to the monsters rolling across three thousand miles of ocean.

An Atlantic storm was building, pushing huge amounts of water before it. Although the Dominion was barely on its outer edges masses of salt water were breaking over the bow and rushing down the length of the decks, smashing against bulkheads, continuing on to the stern and then returning to the sea. It soon became dangerous to come on deck for fear of being swept away, but at the moment the suffering souls below didn't much care. Their only concern was how to ease their agony, and drowning seemed an attractive alternative to the misery that was being forced upon them.

The Kurtzmanns fared no better than the rest, with Itkah and the girls trying feebly to find comfortable positions for themselves while David and Joshua attempted the same for the boys. Once their stomachs were emptied they lay more or less in the same place, moving only as the ship shifted.

Outside, the sea was blown into a frenzy as the wind reached full gale force with waves as high as three story buildings crashing over the bow. It was all that the Dominion could do to keep from being driven backwards. Several large crates were broken loose from their lashings by the sheer volumes of water rushing down the decks and were washed overboard, floating astern for several moments before slipping beneath the surface.

Down below, despite their agony, some of the immigrants panicked at the tumult above. Children and adults alike screamed and clung to each other while others tried to maintain a calm exterior.

With every roll it seemed that the Dominion would never recover and there was a struggle by some to escape their watery tomb. But the watertight doors had been sealed and the best they could do was bang uselessly against them with their fists until they exhausted what little strength they had left and staggered back to join their companions, hoping that when the end came it would be mercifully quick.

Dealing with the soldiers back in Lutzin now seemed a blessing compared to this. They lay motionless, their bodies moving to the erratic plunging and swaying of the vessel as it fought valiantly to stay head-on into the wind to keep from being blown over on its side.

For two days and nights the cyclone tore at the Dominion, attacking it with screeching winds and turbulent seas. It seemed impossible that anything could survive the uncontrollable fury of a storm of this magnitude.

On the bridge, Captain Eugene Marston, now without sleep for 48 hours, and with many years at sea behind him, had no intention of losing his ship. A tall, wiry British man, with a leathery face lined by long service at sea, a thin, tailored moustache and thick white hair, he shouted orders to the helmsman.

"Forget the compass heading," he commanded. "Keep her headed into those seas!"

The ocean bottom was littered with those who were not up to the struggle, but Captain Marston was determined that no ship assigned to his command would ever be one of them. Despite his preoccupation on the bridge he wondered momentarily how those poor souls below were holding up. He turned to his second officer who had been with the captain for a number of years.

"Mr. Nolan, take one of your Russian-speaking crewmen down to the hold and see how they're doing. Tell them to save their strength and remain as calm as possible and that the captain promises to see them safely through to America. Get cracking!"

Second officer Nolan was a short, muscular, no-nonsense veteran of the British Merchant Service with just enough intelligence to acquire the stripes of his rank. He was conscientious and devoted to his trade. He had no desire to be master of his own vessel. He was content to obey his captain and see that his orders were carried out promptly and efficiently. Slipshod work met with his menacing stare and a roar that echoed throughout the ship.

He opened a bulkhead door leading to the crew's quarters and called out for one of the sailors, pausing to watch the bulkhead walls of the long passageway twisting noticeably under the strain of the water. A green landlubber would panic at the sight, but Nolan had seen it all before and had come to terms with the sea many years ago. This was one of the worst, but he had confidence in his captain to bring them through. If he couldn't do it, nobody could.

They went along the heaving passageway, Nolan followed by the sailor, a Russian immigrant himself who had decided to go to sea. Nolan carefully unlocked the door to the hold, half expecting a surge of humanity to burst through in a mad dash to the open deck. All was quiet. The odor of vomit rushed up his nostrils before he could put his kerchief to his nose.

"Good God!" he exclaimed. "How do they stand it?" He looked down into the hold. The deck was covered with what at first appeared to be lifeless bodies. As they climbed down for a closer look they could hear low moaning above the noise of the storm, and some movement among the bodies lying close together for whatever comfort that afforded them.

"Poor devils," he said sympathetically. "I'll wager they wished they were back in bloody Russia right now." He instructed the sailor to talk in a loud voice and repeated the captain's instructions.

At the sound of a voice speaking their native tongue, some raised themselves to a sitting position while others just opened their eyes.

"Don't be afraid!" the Russian sailor shouted. "The captain has promised to get you all to your destination alive and well. We have sailed with him many times and through many storms. The weather should improve in a day or two. Do not try to come on deck. You will be washed into the ocean and no lifeboats will be sent to look for you. Neither you nor the lifeboats would last in these seas." The sailor paused and looked at Nolan.

"Tell them that this is the safest place for them and these storms rarely last more than three days. Ask them to have courage a little longer."

After these reassurances some immigrants nodded their heads and then assumed their former positions. Nolan dismissed the sailor after a friendly pat on the back and lunged back onto the bridge where the captain was attempting to see beyond the horizontally driven rain.

"They're layin' on the deck like dead people, sir,.They don't look good."

"How did they take the news?"

"Some shook their heads – that's the only way I knew they was alive, sir, and then they lay down again. The stink down there is awful. Couldn't we keep a bulkhead door open to let in some air?"

"Sorry, Nolan. Some of them might try to go out on deck in spite of what you told them. They wouldn't last a minute. They'll just have to bear it a bit longer. The wind seems to be shifting more northerly and the glass has steadied. The center of the storm must be past us."

Nolan looked at the captain's weary face. "You need some sleep, Captain, if you don't mind my sayin' so. I'll be glad to hold the fort here if you want to lie down for a bit."

"Thank you, Nolan, but I can't sleep when it's like this. I'll see it through to the end."

The end didn't come for another 24 hours. By morning the wind eased a little but the seas were as turbulent as ever. They crashed repeatedly over the bow and against the sides of the hull until it seemed the ship would break in two. Captain Marston remained on the bridge for the third straight night with Nolan beside him. By morning the winds dropped to below gale force, and the seas, though still high, were more regular and not as wild.

Later that day the captain had the hatches and bulkhead doors opened and issued orders allowing the immigrants to go to the galley for food, if they could eat, and also go top-side if they wished. The worst was over. Some of the crew were sent to hose down and mop the decks with water and detergent. As the seas calmed further life on the Dominion improved dramatically. The immigrant's appetites returned and they could walk in the fresh air of the open deck without fear of being swept away. Their spirits rose and their desire for a mercifully quick death faded. Life was again beautiful.

The captain visited them regularly, giving them an opportunity to thank him for saving their lives. They were grateful, and felt that he was a man of great ability and high moral character to bring them through what could have been a disaster.

On November 11, 1912, the S.S. Dominion left the Atlantic behind, rounded Cape May and turned northward up the Delaware Bay toward Philadelphia, 90 miles away.

"Good riddance," David said as he examined the coastline of his new homeland. "I don't ever want to go through that nightmare again."

"Amen to that," Itkah said, standing between her husband and Joshua. "Soon we'll be hugging Sam and Annie Feinwitz. How will they know that the ship has been delayed?"

"They have a wonderful machine called the wireless," Joshua said. "Ships can talk to each other and to the shore, reporting the weather and advising the authorities of their time of arrival."

The children were standing nearby, looking at the coast just several miles distant.

Nathan looked up at Joshua. "You mean that they can really talk to each other? Hear their voices?"

"No, not with voices. The machine sends out signals – tapping noises that represent different letters of the alphabet. In this way they form words and sentences just like we do when we write them down on paper – but wireless sends them through the air in an instant, even if they're hundreds of miles away."

"Joshua," Itkah said. "Surely you're joking? Machines that can be heard many miles away – words in the air? Stop filling the children's heads with these crazy stories. They'll repeat them and everyone will think we're a bunch of fools."

"It's not crazy," Joshua insisted. "While you were strolling around the Liverpool docks, we were strolling about the ship. That Russian-speaking sailor took us on a tour and showed us the small room where they keep this wonderful machine. At that moment a message was coming in warning the captain of the possibility of bad weather at sea. It's truly a remarkable invention."

"Then you knew we were going into a storm," David said. "Why didn't you tell us?"

"Why should I frighten everybody ahead of time? I thought it would be better to just let things happen. Anyway, I was caught up in the excitement of leaving England. Even if you knew, what could you do about it – part the waters? Some things are better left unsaid."

"I'm glad you didn't tell us," little Lena said. "I was scared enough as it was. I thought we were dying."

"So did I," David admitted. "You did the right thing, Joshua. I was never so frightened in my life."


The S.S. Dominion, guided by two tugboats, was nudged gently alongside the Dock St. pier as the immigrants crowded the rails looking for familiar faces far below. Many waved wildly back and forth as they recognized those waiting for them. Screams and shouts of joy echoed from the ship to the pier as many wept openly, thanking God for bringing them safely through an Atlantic crossing.

David and Itkah, after searching for several minutes and not seeing anyone resembling the Feinwitz's, retired below to be processed by immigration authorities who had come on board the minute the ship docked.

Once again Joshua, with the shoe in place, stood straight and tall when his turn came. The official eyed him keenly.

"You seem to be walking with a slight limp," the officer said. "Do you have a physical handicap?"

David and Itkah held their breaths, but Joshua didn't flinch. "It was a rough voyage," he said. "Many were hurt."

"I suppose you're right," the official answered. "I've been told it was very bad. All right then, move on."

It took several hours, but they finally cleared customs and exited the ship. They walked down the gangway to claim their trunk, which was already on the pier.

"David! Itkah!" a woman's voice rang out from among the assortment of wagons, carts and horses that filled the dock area and spilled out onto the cobblestone street beyond. She was standing in her cart with a young girl beside her.

Annie was a short, plump woman compared to Itkah. Her hair was pulled back and covered with a traditional kerchief tied under her chin. Her simple dress reached to her shoes, interrupted only by a belt around her ample waist.

The young girl was about eleven years old, slim, but healthy looking, with a fair complexion, some freckles on her pleasant face. She wore a light blue dress with a flowery design, and she was obviously dressed up for the occasion.

Annie hurriedly stepped down from the cart, and worked her way through the crowd, while Itkah ran to her from the ship. Finally, face to face, they paused for a moment, then rushed into each other's arms. The scene was repeated many times about them. No words were spoken for several seconds as they hugged and pressed their wet faces together. Then they stepped back, wiped their eyes, and appraised each other.

"You look very well, Annie," Itkah said haltingly, her voice choking.

"And you look very tired," Annie responded. "Are you sick?"

"Sick of the ocean," Itkah answered. "I never expected to see you. The sea was like a monster, a devil, trying to drag us down to hell, but we're here now, thank goodness."

"And you're home!" Annie declared. "And look how big your family has grown. And David, how wonderful to see you again. Surely you haven't aged one year since I last saw you."

David responded with an affectionate hug. "Thanks to my beard," he said. "It serves a double purpose. It hides my wrinkles and gives me a dignity I wouldn't otherwise possess."

There was another round of hugs and kisses as the children were reacquainted with Mrs. Feinwitz. "Jacob is now 19, Lea is 17, Herman 16 and Nathan is 11. Rhea is 9 and this is our youngest, Ellis – he's 6 and was born the year you moved away."

"They're beautiful. They'll make fine citizens. But you haven't met my Rachel. The last time you saw her she was having her 5th birthday party. Rachel, don't be shy. Come and meet the Kurtzmann's, our neighbors from Lutzin."

The children eyed each other, smiling awkwardly, then they all piled into the cart sharing the space with their luggage and the trunk. Annie expertly manuevered her horse through the crowd along the pier with a flick of her whip and slowly clattered across the cobblestones.

Jacob looked around in disappointment. "I thought the streets were paved with gold in America. They're only cobblestones."

"Don't believe everything you hear," Annie said. "Only what you see. There is gold in America, but not in the streets."

Itkah looked back at the ship. Captain Marston was on the bridge talking to one of his officers. "Thank you for getting us here," she said softly. The cart turned the corner of a building and the S.S. Dominion disappeared behind them. She looked forward at the rows of brick houses that Annie had described in her letters. She was ready for what lay ahead.

## 8

The Kurtzmann family settled down to life on the third floor of the Feinwitz home at 1301 N. 2nd St., less than two miles from where they had disembarked. Joshua occupied a small room on the 2nd floor.

The house itself was a three story brick row home, similar to thousands of other homes in Philadelphia and close to the specifications as laid down by Benjamin Franklin 200 years before.

Franklin and William Penn, both mindful of the fires that had destroyed London, had decreed that houses be constructed only of brick, assuring that the city would be one of mainly brick homes.

Most houses had their parlors facing the street, except those that had store fronts, with the kitchen in the rear, and sometimes separated from the parlor by a small breakfast room where the meals would be served. Beyond the kitchen was a small yard where the trash cans were kept along with buckets and brooms and anything else that occupied too much space inside.

The second and third floors were exclusively bedrooms, except where a bedroom was converted into a living room, or where a more enterprising owner had installed kitchen facilities to make the floor a separate apartment.

The Feinwitz house had no such luxury. Everybody shared the one kitchen and occasionally took turns cooking for all. The host family, of course, had their choice of meal times, and each family was responsible for keeping their part of the house in order. The busiest room was the lone bathroom located in the center of the second floor and available to all. With the Kurtzmann's eight people, Joshua, and the six people in the Feinwitz family, the bathroom was rarely empty.

It wasn't unusual to find a large fish splashing around in a bathtub full of water. It was the only way to keep a fish fresh after buying it, and if it wasn't cooked immediately it was consigned to the tub for the last few hours of its life.

To the utter delight of the new arrivals there really was hot and cold running water, no outhouse, a gas stove for cooking, and lights that went on at the flick of a switch. The children opened and closed the faucets, repeatedly turned the lights on and off and kept flushing

the toilet regardless of the need to do so. This practice came to an end
when they were told that water and electricity cost money, and the
more they used the more it cost.

"A charge for water?" Jacob asked. "But water is free. At home
we took it from the ground or the lake, as much as we wanted. Why
does it cost money here?"

Annie smiled. "The water comes into the house from pipes in the
ground that bring it from a pumping station where it is cleaned and
made fit to drink. This costs money, somebody has to pay for it.
There is also a gas and electric company that provides electricity to
light up the house at night and gas to cook our meals with. Isn't that
easier than carrying water from the well or lake, and certainly cleaner
than oil lamps or candles for light or chopping wood for an old,
smoky, wood-burning stove?"

"I suppose so," Jacob said slowly. "Still, I think the government
should provide these services for the people free of charge."

"That's not the way it works here. The government is not in
business to make a profit or tell you how to live. Their job is to pass
the laws that make this a better country. You aren't forced to work
here or work there. Everybody's on their own and free to do whatever
work he has the ability for."

"It sounds very confusing," he said. "If everybody does as they
please you could have anarchy."

"You've lived too long in Russia." She laughed. "Here you can
think for yourself. It's a wonderful change, you'll see."

"But the forests and the lakes," Rhea said. "Where are they? All
I see are cobblestones, bricks and cement walks. Where can we have a
vegetable garden?"

Itkah put her arm around Rhea's shoulder. "There will be no
vegetable gardens here," she said as kindly as possible. "We must get
used to a different life. Forget everything we did back in the old
country. For us it no longer exists. We moved here to be free of
persecution, that's the most important thing. There are no pogroms
here. What we make of our lives is up to us. Garden, lakes, wells,
forests, all that's in the past, and the sooner we forget them the better
it will be for our peace of mind. It will be difficult enough to begin
over again without wishing for things we cannot have. Besides, what

was the good of having them if we had to face each day not knowing if we would live or die?"

"Your mother's right, Rhea," Annie said. "Many people here came from Russia and now lead full and productive lives. You young folks must concentrate on school, learn English, make new friends and prepare yourselves for the future. You didn't travel all this way to carry water from a lake or grow vegetables in a garden. Leave that to other people."

David agreed. "Let's enjoy the water that comes miraculously from the faucets, and vegetables we'll buy in the store. No more wood-burning stoves, I've seen the heater in the basement that keeps the house warm in the winter, and the boiler that supplies hot water for the kitchen and the bathroom."

"And that's only the beginning," Annie added. "Every day there are more and more automobiles in the streets. They say that soon horses and buggies will be a thing of the past."

"Impossible!" David exclaimed.

"Not only automobiles, but flying machines are seen in the sky, and trains travel from one end of the country to the other.

Everyone was silent. There was so much to think about – so much to do.

"But no garden," Rhea lamented."

"And the streets are only cobblestones and brick," Jacob added.

"But I saw many children playing outside," Herman said.

"Rachel's pretty," Nathan said.

"They all have opinions," Annie said. "But there's something else we must talk about." Her voice took on a serious tone. "It's the matter of your name."

"What about our name?" asked David.

"You know us as Feinwitz. Here it is Fine."

"I'm amazed, Itkah said. "Your letters were always addressed as Feinwitz."

"I didn't want the authorities in Russia to know that we had given up our name. It could have caused trouble for you."

"But why change it in the first place?" David asked.

Annie sighed, her round pleasant face becoming sad for the moment. "My friends, there is ill feeling against Jews no matter where they live. True, we live at peace here, but I regret to say that even in this wonderful country there are people who dislike us, even hate us. Don't ask me why. It's been like this for years and I suppose that it will be this way for years to come. That's why we shortened our name to Fine. You should do the same – to make it sound less Jewish."

"I don't like that idea," David said stiffly. "We may come from Russia, but Kurtzmann is a fine old German name that has a long history. I don't know how our ancestors ended up in Russia, but to bring the family name to an end with the stroke of a pen. No, it goes against everything I feel."

"I understand," Annie answered, "but your name need not come to an end. It could just be altered slightly, It will make it easier to mix into the society here. Gentile employers look very carefully at the names of those they hire. What's wrong with becoming Kurtz instead of Kurtzmann. Kurtz could be anything."

"That's the point," David replied. "It could be anything. I don't want our name to be just anything. Kurtzmann is a good Jewish name. I find it difficult to understand why we should change it."

Annie looked sympathetically at her friend. "It wasn't easy for us either, but you must face reality. Jews have a rough time today no matter where they live. Perhaps, God willing, the day will come when it doesn't matter what your name sounds like, but for the present, why make things more difficult? Remember, you have the children to think of. They'll be going to school and then into the workplace. We're free here, but people are people everywhere."

David was quiet for a moment as he wrestled with all that she had said.

"David," Itkah said, "there's merit and common sense in what Annie says. Kurtzmann is your name first and mine second, and it's not my place to tell you what to do. It's simply another problem we have to deal with. We can be Kurtz, but our children will always know that their family name was Kurtzmann long before that. At least consider it."

The room was quiet.

"Give me some time to think about it," David finally said.

It didn't take him very long to make up his mind. In the coming days, as he became familiar with the neighborhood, he met many families with new names. Goldberg was now Gold, Greenberg became Green, Dedensky was changed to Dean – generally it was a case of simple subtraction, taking away a syllable or two. Three months later, on a blustery February day, David left the Philadelphia City Hall minus one syllable. So be it, he thought. Anything a Kurtzmann can do, a Kurtz can also accomplish.

That evening at the dinner table, as snow began whitening the sidewalks and streets outside, he gave everyone, even little Ellis, a glass of wine. "Hold up your glasses, everyone, a toast to a new family with a new name in a new country. When times change we must change with them or be left behind. Let us make Kurtz a name that you and your future families will be proud of. But never forget your heritage". He sipped the wine and everybody followed his example. "To Kurtz," he said, "a good American name."

## 9

In Philadelphia, the Kurtz family was enjoying the spring of 1914. Talk of the war that had begun in Europe was kept to a minimum at the dinner table, although David and Itkah couldn't help noticing the increasing number of familiar names appearing in the newspapers as the battles raged back and forth. The myriad of alliances dragged first one country and then another into the spreading conflict.

They scrutinized the Yiddish language newspapers while putting extra effort into reading and speaking English. They could now hold a respectable, if halting, conversation in English, and they tried to make it the language they spoke in the presence of the children, but Yiddish took over when the adults were alone.

The children were taking to their new language rapidly and Nathan was Americanizing quicker than anybody else. He roamed far and wide over the neighborhood and hardly a day passed that he didn't bring home a new word or phrase, some not welcome at the dinner table.

"Nathan," David remarked one evening, "just because you hear these words in the streets does not mean that they belong in the home. Better to practice what you learn in school and not the language you hear from your friends. There are enough words in the English language with which to express yourself without resorting to ugly slang."

He looked around the table at his family. We haven't done badly in three years, he thought. Jacob, who was always good with his hands, was apprenticing with a tailor, and Herman had found a job with a cleaner and dyer. Lena and Rhea, when not doing homework, helped Itkah with the cooking and cleaning, and Ellis and Nathan, along with Annie's daughter, Rachel, attended the Ludlow grade school on 6th St.

David was working in a luggage factory, lining the suitcases and trunks with paper and cardboard. Joshua found a job delivering milk in the morning and ice during the day. With his contribution and the money brought home by Herman and Jacob, they lived fairly comfortably after paying their rent to Annie.

Itkah was fascinated by the system of central heating and she could often be seen prowling about the basement looking at the heater and its ever-present pile of coal. She would open the heater door and throw a few shovels full of coal into it, feeling the warmth of the fire, then she opened the bottom door to remove the ashes that fell to the bottom. She did it every day, saving Annie the job of bending over and lifting a basket of ashes through the cellar window where it was then put by the curb for the trash men to pick up.

She mentioned it to David one evening after the children were in bed. "David, I was looking at the coal in the basement. Every house in Philadelphia uses coal. Do you realize how much money is spent every month on coal?"

"I have no idea," he answered without looking up from his newspaper. "It must be a great deal."

"A great deal," she exclaimed. "It's enormous!"

There was an urgency in her voice that made him put down his paper.

"Do you remember all of those large crates that were lashed to the deck of the ship that brought us here?" she said.

"Remember them? How could I forget them? I still dream of them crashing into each other before being washed into the sea. The very thought gives me the chills. So?"

"So, my dear husband, that was money going into the ocean – merchandise from England being sold to a dealer in America who then sells it to us."

"What do you want to do," David asked, "go out and raise them from the bottom of the sea?"

"I'm talking about business – buying and selling. Why can't we do the same? I did it in Rezekne and Lutzin. We could do the same thing with coal."

David pushed the paper aside. "Coal? How do you propose to do that?"

"That thief who sells everybody the coal – what's his name?" She snapped her fingers loudly. David had always envied the way she snapped her fingers. When he tried it the sound was more like a feather falling on a pillow. He had never been able to master it.

"Johnson," he answered.

"Yes, that's it, Johnson. That thief, Johnson, charges Annie and everybody else $12.00 a ton. We could charge $10.00 and still make a nice profit of $4.50 a ton."

David looked keenly at his wife. She didn't usually engage in idle talk. In Lutzin he had always felt it wasn't a woman's place to be buying and selling, but she had never seemed to be satisfied to do the housework and cooking and looking after the children. Now she was talking about selling coal.

"Itkah," he said, trying not to raise his voice. "Women just don't do these things. What will everybody think of me, allowing my wife to sell coal. I have my self respect."

She brushed his remark aside. She had heard this same argument in Lutzin. "Self respect won't feed and clothe the family. It won't pay the rent. You can't deposit it in the bank. David, we're getting older. While we have the strength let's try to put something away for our old age. If it's successful, after a few years we can sell it. If not, at least we tried. And it doesn't need a big outlay of cash, just enough to buy a wagon with a coal chute, a shovel and a strong animal to pull the load."

David sighed. As usual, when she poured her ideas out to him one at a time, his resistance would melt away. But he wasn't going down without a fight. "We have no customers and no experience. How do you know the coal yard will even sell to us? They may not want to take a chance on losing Johnson – he's a big buyer."

"There are other coal yards," she retorted. "We have enough money to buy a wagon. It must have a gate that pulls up so the coal can slide down into the cellar."

"Who's going to look after the children while you're getting rich delivering coal? Who's going to do the cooking?" It was his last, desperate try, but he knew, even as he said it, it was no use.

"The children are all in school or working and I'll make sure I'm home before school lets out. And Joshua can help me. He's getting peanuts working for that ice house and delivering milk. I'm certain he'd rather help us get started in a business than work for somebody else. Who knows? If we get busy enough we might even pay him a salary."

## 10

Itkah Kurtz looked at her mule as it pulled a wagon-load of coal along Berks St., then waited as the No.3 trolley coming from the opposite direction clattered past and made a left to go south on 2nd St. He's no Aaron, she thought, but he's strong enough to pull a load of coal over bumpy streets. Those fool neighbors of hers, telling her nobody used mules in the city. What did they know?

"Do you see anybody using mules in this entire city?" Sam Katz (formerly Katzman), their next door neighbor, a short, fat, balding man, had asked her. "This country was founded on horses. The Indians were riding horses before we came to this country. Mules are for farmers, not city dwellers."

What did Sam know about farms? she thought. He grew up in Minsk and never worked a day on a farm, if indeed he ever worked at all. His family called farmers peasants, and if they weren't Jewish they would have all been Communist revolutionaries. They may yet be, with the party organizing in New York City. Those idiots, she thought. Instead of working with our government they plot against it. If they're not careful they'll find themselves back in Russia being chased by soldiers and hunted down like animals.

Her thoughts drifted back to that dirt path with the trees on either side and the smell of wild flowers, the snow-covered roads in winter and the mud in the spring. Then she remembered the soldiers, their horses charging, the cart going over, her load all over the road, the Martinovas.

It was better to ride down a bumpy street with a heavy load of coal, between rows of brick houses and not have to worry about things like that. Someday we'll live on a lake again, she thought, in a nice house with a large vegetable garden, not because we'll need the food, but for the simple pleasure of growing things.

"You're quiet, Itkah." Joshua's voice came from beside her.

"I was thinking of the old country," she said.

Joshua looked sideways at her. "With regret?"

"Not exactly. I miss the green of the fields, the wind blowing through the trees, the land around our house, my daily rides from Rezekne to Lutzin."

Joshua allowed the mule to move at its own pace. A wagon loaded with coal was too heavy to force the animal to move any faster, and it would serve them longer if not overworked.

"Do you miss the outhouse too, or dragging water from the lake, or huddling together in the winter because the only heat came from a fireplace and the stove, or chopping and lugging wood?"

She laughed, revealing an even row of teeth beginning to yellow with age. "Of course not. And I don't miss those murdering beasts who killed your parents, either. I guess I'm just not a city woman."

"And I'm not a city man, but here we are pulling a load of coal down 2nd St. Perhaps if we pull enough loads for enough years we might live in the fields again."

"I was thinking along the same lines. One thing about this country, the opportunities are endless. We're going to open a store."

Joshua stared at her. "You should have been a man," he said.

She ignored the remark. "We are. Look where we live – fruit stores, candy stores, grocery stores, haberdashers, many items that the stores don't carry because they must be bought through the mail. Do you like to buy things that you can't see?" She didn't wait for his answer. "I would never buy anything from a picture. What if you ordered something and it wasn't what you thought, then what? But if everything was in one store, under one roof, wouldn't that eliminate all of the ifs, ands, or buts? No more tramping from store to store to get what you want. No more catalogs that promise everything but guarantee nothing. What do you think?"

"I'm breathless," he answered. "And as far as what I think – I think David will have a nervous breakdown."

"He'll get over it," she stated flatly. "That's why I told you first, to get your opinion. I asked you what you think about it."

He was honored that she confided in him like this and that she respected his opinion. "You're a smart woman, Itkah. It's a wonderful idea, but just how do you propose to do it? Where will the money come from? What's going to happen to the coal business? It's thriving but we've only been at it for one year. Who will deliver the coal? Who will work in the store? My head's spinning."

"Now you sound like David with all of your negative questions. But that's fine. Questions are sparks that light up the mind."

"A philosopher also," Joshua said.

"Nevertheless, it's true. I don't mind questions. If I can't answer them, then I know something's wrong with my reasoning."

"When do you plan to do all this? You deliver coal in the morning, a house and children to look after the remainder of the day. You can't be in three different places at one time."

"I don't intend to. The children can work a little harder after school, and if all goes well, David can give up that piddling job of his. He should be paid three times what he gets."

"But why give up the coal business? It's doing fine. You serve 18 customers a week; 72 a month; times $8.00; that's over $500.00 a month, less the generous salary you pay me, and expenses. That still leaves you more than 50% profit. That's more than anybody in the neighborhood earns in five years."

"I have no intention of giving up selling the coal. You're going to do it for me. You know as much about the business as I do. I heard you haggling over the price with that big, red-faced Irishman. I liked the way you held your ground. You know all of the customers and they like you – you can do it without me."

Joshua considered this. "I could still use an extra pair of strong arms. I can't do everything with only one good leg."

"True enough, and I don't expect you to. We'll hire one of the blacks from the other side of 9th St. God knows they can use the work. We'll pay him $5.00 a week. David doesn't make much more than that. He'll work his head off for you."

"For $5.00 a week I'm sure he will. Most of them are working for less than fifty cents a day. That's a good wage, Itkah."

"Pay him a little more and he'll work a little more. We don't want somebody that will work this week and leave the next."

"Do you think David will give up his job to work with you in a store?"

"Eventually. My husband is a proud man, full of principle, and I love him for it. I don't want him to think that he's dependent on me to support the family. He'll come around. We have to take care of men with principle. Someday we may need them very badly."

Dinner that night was alternately quiet and loud. Quiet because Nathan was absent, and loud with speculation as to where he might be.

"I saw him running around with Sol Klein and Mendy Bush," Jacob said as he finished the noodle soup and served himself a helping of beef stew.

"He wasn't running around with them," Herman said. "They were chasing him."

"Chasing him?" David asked. "What for?"

"He owes them money."

"He owes them money?" David put down his fork. "What for?"

"He borrowed it from them," Herman said as he plunged his fork into the stew.

"Why is he borrowing money from them?"

"Who knows?" Herman said with a mouthful of food.

"Herman," Itkah warned, "don't talk when your mouth is full."

"Poppa asked me a question."

"And I would like an answer," David insisted.

Lena giggled. "He gave Rachel a ring," she said.

"A ring!" It was Itkah's turn to put down her fork. "What kind of ring?"

"Momma," Herman said, "don't talk with your mouth full of food."

Itkah ignored the remark. "What kind of ring?"

It was Rhea's turn to contribute to the conversation. "It's the kind of ring you find in grab bags that you buy for a penny. They have candy, bubble gum and prizes in them. I guess that's where it came from. She calls it her 'steady' ring.

"A 'steady' ring," David exclaimed. "This is too much. Everybody knows what's going on but me. I'm going out to find him right now!"

As he opened the front door he was greeted by a policeman holding Nathan by the back of his collar. Officer Thomas Brody was a big, gruff Irishman, as nearly the entire police force was, and his beat included the area where many of the immigrants lived. He also was an immigrant and he could relate to their problems and frustrations. He knew everybody by name and he was a familiar figure walking down 7th St. swinging his night stick.

"This tyke belong to you, Mr. Kurtz?"

"What's the trouble, Officer Brody?" David asked, not wanting to know. He glared at his son, who kept his eyes fixed on the steps.

"The other kids and him was throwin' stones at each other and he broke somebody's window."

David sighed. "Whose window did you break, Nathan?"

"Mr. Dreiser's," he answered wearily.

"Thank you, Mr. Brody. Now, Nathan, I want you to go to Mr. Dreiser's house and apologize for breaking the window and tell him I"m sending over the man from the hardware store to fix it."

Officer Brody still remained on the step. "Ya better count on fixin' their lamp, too," he added.

"Their lamp?"

"Ya see, Mr. Kurtz, when the stone went through the window, it hit the glass lamp on the parlor table."

Itkah could contain herself no longer. She bid the officer goodbye and dragged Nathan inside. "That settles it," she said sternly. "Low marks in school, not attending classes, getting into all kinds of mischief – and now this. And what's this business about you giving a ring to Rachel?"

Nathan looked angrily at his brothers and sisters.

"Joshua," she said. "Forget about hiring that black man. You just got yourself a new coal shoveler. Nathan's going with you from now on. He can work off his energy shovelling coal down the chute. He's not learning anything in school. At least he'll get an education riding behind that mule and coming home with dirty hands and an aching back!"

Everybody stopped eating, except Joshua. He kept his head down over his food waiting for the explosion.

David looked at his wife. "What's this about hiring a black man? What's going on around here? Nathan, do as I told you and tell Mr. Dreiser that the lamp will be paid for also. Now go! And don't stray!"

When Nathan opened the door, Officer Brody was still standing there. "I forgot to tell ya, folks. The lamp knocked over one of them fancy porcelain figures and broke it into a thousand pieces."

"Itkah, after dinner we must talk," David said.

With the children asleep or doing school work in their rooms, David settled into his rocker and looked at Itkah across the table.

"Now that we've all calmed down," he said, "first tell me what made you decide Nathan's punishment without talking it over with me?"

"I apologize for that, David. I was excited and angry. The boy has to be stopped before it's too late. He has no sense of right and wrong."

"Perhaps, and I think your idea has merit. A few months of heavy work may make school more appealing. At worst he'll lose a half grade which he wouldn't pass anyway. But taking him out of school permanently would hurt more than it helps."

"I was a little hasty," she said. "You decide when he's ready to return."

"Very well. For the time being we'll see how it works. Now – am I mistaken or did I hear you say something to Joshua about hiring a black man? What's this all about?"

Itkah hesitated. "I was just airing some thoughts to Joshua – he could use some help, and I'm not getting any younger. I would have told you when the details became clear in my mind."

"Itkah," David said impatiently," you're being evasive. If it's something important let's discuss it. We've never had trouble talking to each other. This is no time to start."

She moved around the table and pulled up a chair beside him.

"It's important," she answered, resting her hand on his arm. "It's about our future. We're doing well with the coal business and have saved more money than all the past years put together."

"True enough," David admitted without hesitation. "You've done a marvelous job, you and Joshua."

"But I can't deliver coal forever," she continued. "You were right when you said it's not a woman's work." She didn't believe it, but if it gave him satisfaction and made him lower his guard, she didn't mind telling a small lie. It might soften the blow that was coming. "I was going to propose to you that we hire a man to help Joshua – we can afford it, but now that Nathan will be with him, we can forget that idea, at least for now."

"That's good," David agreed. "Does that mean you'll be staying home to spend more time with the children and the needs of the house?"

Itkah breathed deeply. "Not exactly," she answered. She repeated her idea of a store exactly as she had related it to Joshua. "It's what I wanted to do in the old country before we were forced to leave. It's just as well. It will work better here. There's a bigger market for a larger variety of goods, and the people here have more money to spend."

David's head spun just as Joshua's had, but her eagerness was contagious. The more she described the operation, the more David was caught up in the excitement.

"It sounds like a big job. But there are only small stores here. You'd need more space than these stores on 2nd St. can provide."

"You're right," she agreed, happy to see his attention was captured. "Girard Avenue has two empty stores available, but only one is large enough for my purpose. It's been vacant for some time." "If it's been empty that long it may mean it's not a good location. There may not be enough foot traffic."

"The street's been torn up for a year. They're putting in new water and sewer lines and should be finished in about two months. It's normally a fairly busy street. Besides, if you give the customers what they want, they'll find you."

David settled back and allowed all of this to sink in. He had faith in her ideas and ability. Look how she worked back in Lutzin, he thought, and what she's done with the coal business. She hadn't cared one bit about the comments made about her as she travelled the streets behind her mule with Joshua next to her. They made fun of her mule while everybody else was driving a horse, but the people at the bank treated this coal-stained woman with the kerchief tied around the top of her head with respect when she and David walked through the front door.

She was their most regular depositor and the store's account was one of the largest in the area. The manager never failed to greet them with a smile and a handshake as he did when they entered the next day. A well-dressed, dapper man with a short moustache and black hair combed straight back, he recognized the ambition in this hard-working, no-nonsense woman.

"Good afternoon, Mr. and Mrs. Kurtz," he said with a slight bow. Itkah liked his politeness, intuitively feeling that it was not artificial.

"Good afternoon, Mr. Polowski. May I have a moment of your time?"

"Of course," he said after shaking their hands warmly. He ushered them to chairs next to his desk.

Her face and hands were still dust covered from the morning's work, her hair held back by the kerchief, the wrinkles around her mouth and eyes not detracting from her strong, still handsome features.

"Now, what can I do for my best customer?" directing his question to Itkah.

"You're very kind, Mr. Polowski. Nothing right now, but I need some free advice."

"Anything within my power."

"The store at 631 Girard Ave. You are familiar with it?"

"Of course. There are two empty stores there. That's the larger of the two."

"Exactly. I want to start a business there."

"What sort of business?"

"I guess you would have to call it a general store, that is, it will carry all kinds of general merchandise."

"Such as?"

"Such as anything you need. Things that you can't get without ordering from a catalogue, in addition to the usual items you expect to see in any half-dozen stores." She repeated her ideas as she had told them to Joshua and David.

Mr. Polowski leaned back and twirled his thin moustache. "A very interesting concept. Everything in one place. Very exciting. It hasn't been tried before, that I know of. And I suppose you want to make a loan to help you get started on this project."

"Not yet," Itkah said.

Mr. Polowski looked disappointed.

"Later perhaps," she added, seeing the look on his face. "I need to know that I can count on you – the bank, that is, if I find it necessary."

"I'll be here when you need me, Mrs. Kurtz. I know a good businessman when I see one."

Itkah smiled. "You mean a good businesswoman, don't you?"

Mr. Polowski's face reddened. "Of course," he stammered. "A thousand apologies, my dear. It was just an expression, a habit."

"Of course," Itkah answered with a half-smile.


If it was up to David, he would be content to continue on as they were. The coal business doing well, his small salary from his job at the luggage factory and what the working children contributed to the household. They were doing all right. Why look for trouble? There was food on the table and a comfortable home in which to live.

"And another thing," Itkah said, as they sat in bed sipping hot chocolate "If all goes well you can leave your job and work in the store, you'll be your own boss. The children can help after school and we can alternate our time so neither of us has to work from morning until late at night. Don't feel bad about making more money, it's become very fashionable here in America. We'll be in good company."

David sighed and took her hand in his. "When we married, we took a vow, for better or for worse. Whatever we do, let's do it together. I guess we'll have to fill the wine glasses again."

## 11

In America the warm spring sun of 1916 was drying out the land after a long, cold winter. The last of the snows had finally melted, the water running down the sewers in dirty torrents and soaking into the farmland in the countryside. Farmers were soon plowing fields and city dwellers were filling their window boxes with colorful flowers.

Itkah and David had opened their store on Girard Avenue. The street and sidewalks were freshly paved and a new movie house had its grand opening, helping to bring customers out in great numbers. The area became a magnet to shoppers. The store couldn't match the catalogs in quantity, there just wasn't enough space, but it stocked much of the most desirable and saleable items, justifying Itkah's assertion that people would rather buy what they can see.

Despite the general poverty of the immigrants who comprised 95% of the area, they still required the necessities – clothes, or cloth with which to make clothes, shoes, boots, hats, stockings, work gloves, clocks and many other items.

The American General Store, as Itkah and David had proudly named it, was able to supply carpeting at $3.00/sq. yd. and cement at 70 cents per 100lb. bag. Itkah had no qualms about underselling merchandise that other nearby stores carried, but David said it wasn't ethical to do business that way.

"My dear husband," she would say, "when we go to shul we can worry about ethics. When we go to the bank, that's business. Profit and ethics do not make good sleeping partners. We aren't cheating anyone. We're able to sell things at a lower price. We're helping more people than we're hurting."

They sold tea at 25 cents per pound – the shoemakers were coming to them for sole at 50 cents per pound. A roll of wire could be had for 6 cents per pound and occasionally, if there was enough demand, they carried a staple like rice for 5 cents per pound, although food products were kept to a minimum because they attracted mice and bugs and were less profitable.

As word passed from mouth to ear, Itkah and David began seeing more unfamiliar faces in the store. Customers came from the Gentile neighborhoods south of Poplar St. and north of Norris St.

Itkah and David paid their bills promptly and salesmen visited them on a regular basis, anxious to add them to their list of clients.

Rhea and Lena, and even Ellis, now 12 years old, helped out after school, and with Nathan now withdrawn from the coal wagon and working reluctantly under the eagle eye of Itkah, they had sufficient help to run the store without having to depend on outside assistance.

Jacob, with a small loan from his parents, opened a small tailor shop near 3rd and Girard Ave., while Herman still worked for a cleaner and dyer, but hoped to soon emulate his brother and go into business for himself. Jacob married a pretty woman by the name of Nettie, and Herman, not long after, married her attractive sister, Tillie.

It was a struggle for both couples, but as the economy improved and more people found jobs, their businesses increased. Though not well off, they managed to create a stable environment for their respective families.

The fertile soil of the free enterprise system during the early years of the war provided the immigrants with opportunities to put down secure roots. Some made the cross-over with relative ease, many struggled for years to learn the system and the language, others never managed it, living out their years speaking mostly Yiddish, learning little English and depending on their family's generosity to help them survive.


As 1917 wore on, the news headlines became more ominous. American vessels were being sunk by German submarines, and it seemed only a matter of time that the war would force its way across the Atlantic. President Wilson announced the beginning of military conscription for single men to age 25, married men being exempt for the time being. This left Nathan, who would turn 18 the following year as the only Kurtz likely to be drafted.

The possibility of being in uniform by 1918 didn't seem to bother Nathan, and he went about his duties in the store with barely enough enthusiasm to get through the day without receiving a sharp reprimand.

His flirtation with Rachel, who was flattered by this attention, continued, but since they were no longer little children it took on a new meaning. Nathan was an exciting young man, adventurous and daring.

"You know what I'm gonna do?" he asked as they strolled up 7th St. with store lights blinking on in the evening dusk. "I'm gonna own this whole block," he said with a sweep of his arm.

Rachel looked at him in admiration.

"Yep," he continued, "everybody will be paying rent to me. The Steiners, Silvers, Wassermans, everybody."

"That's wonderful," Rachel said. "You'll be rich."

"We'll both be rich. You're my girl, aren't you?"

Rachel blushed. "I – I guess so."

"And you're going to marry me, aren't you?"

"Marry you?! Nathan – I don't know what to say."

"Say yes," he urged.

"But, Nathan – I'm so surprised."

He pulled her into a dark doorway and held her close. "I love you," he said, "I want you to marry me." He pressed his lips against hers. Rachel's world was spinning.

"Nathan," she murmured. "Oh, Nathan. But I must talk to my mother first. I can't think."

He kissed her again. "Don't think. Say yes."

"Oh, Nathan," she whispered, "I do love you, but –."

"Say yes," he repeated.

Her young body ached with joy. She put her arms around him. "Yes, Nathan, yes."


David turned the sign on the door so the "closed" side faced the sidewalk, pulled the shade down and locked the door. He walked hand in hand between Rhea and Lena who spent several hours each day after school at the store until it closed at 6:00 in the evening. He and Itkah both agreed that as long as the business was doing well there was no need to stay open from 9:00 in the morning until 9:00 at night merely because all of the other businesses did the same, particularly with colder weather setting in and fewer shoppers out on the streets.

David pulled his coat collar around his neck while the girls huddled close to him. A sharp wind was blowing scattered bits of trash and paper around the sidewalk and street. The children had schoolwork to do, Itkah was preparing dinner after which there were store ledgers and accounts to attend to. With the days getting shorter and the air much colder, he eagerly looked forward to the warmth of a centrally heated house. It was a modern day comfort he would never cease to enjoy.

His thoughts returned to Lutzin and the futile attempts of the fireplace and the kitchen stove to keep their home comfortable against the brutal blasts that swept down out of northern Russia and Siberia. He remembered the deep snows that isolated the villages for weeks at a time, the goats brought inside to keep them from freezing to death and losing the family's supply of milk. He remembered the struggle to exist from one year to the next.

Newspaper reports told of poor crops leading to shortages of food, and riots in the streets of the large cities, with soldiers firing upon civilians and fellow soldiers alike, running wild through the countryside, looting and leaving behind a trail of destruction. Russia was in a state of upheaval. Faced with a menacing German army to the west and anarchy in the east, it was being torn on all sides. David shivered and he held his daughter's hands a little tighter.

He opened the front door and allowed the warm air and the odor of Itkah's freshly-cooked meal to chase away those bleak thoughts.

She had prepared a treat for tonight – sirloin steak with baked potatoes and string beans. Everybody washed their hands and sat down to eat while Rhea and Lena set the table and prepared to help their mother serve. David dropped into his chair with a pleasant sigh. He had been on his feet most of the day and the walk home in the cold air whetted his appetite even more.

"My goodness, sirloin steak," he exclaimed. "What's the occasion?"

"The occasion is that thief, Gross." Itkah called anybody a thief who charged more than she thought was a fair price. "He gets 37 cents a pound for a hen when I can buy sirloin for 2 cents less from Steiner on the next block. And I don't have to pull pin feathers out of sirloin. The hens come from farms just outside the city and the steak from animals raised in the west, so what reason does Gross give for the high prices? We're at war, he says, and with a straight face, too."

David filled his plate with two slices of steak and the hot vegetables. "It's possible," he said. "Much food goes abroad to the military to help fight the Germans."

Itkah joined her family at the table. With Jacob and Herman married only four children were now present at dinner, not counting Joshua, who still lived with them. "All the more reason to have consideration for the steady customers. The war won't last forever, and long after the military comes home people will remember who ripped them off and who treated them fairly."

Itkah was astute enough to know that prices, to a large extent, were dictated by supply and demand, but she would never admit that any hen was worth 37 cents a pound. "When Joshua told Mrs. Gross that coal was up to $9.90 a ton she almost burst her corset. Now coal is really a precious commodity – it supplies the power to drive the ships that carry their precious hens to England and France."

"I guess they're in the same boat," Nathan remarked, but his quip passed unnoticed. "Can you imagine the uproar if I charged her $5.00 for a pair of her shoes instead of the $4.85 that I get now?" Itkah said, "she'd call the police. But there's something more important to talk about than Gross's hens or Steiner's sirloin. Nathan has to sign up for the draft."

This news brought the knives and forks to a standstill as everybody looked up from their plates.

"Yes," she said. "His age group is listed in today's paper."

Nathan looked at her. "You mean I'll have to go into the army?" he asked with a slight tremor in his voice.

"Now, now," David said in an attempt to calm him. "It means you have to register, it doesn't mean you'll be called. Besides, we're not at war yet and may never be."

"No," Nathan said, "but everybody says it won't be long. I can read. German submarines are sinking our ships, and there are demonstrations every day at Independence Hall calling for the government to teach Germany a lesson."

"Some German-owned stores on Market Street had their windows smashed," Lena commented.

"That's bad," David said. "They can't help it if they have German names. I'm sure there are plenty of German-Americans serving in the army and navy right now. Are they traitors because their names happen to be German?"

"Eat," Itkah commanded. "We'll talk about it later."

So they ate, and then they talked. Nathan had to register, there was nothing else to do. The war could be over by the time he was called.

"David," Itkah said after the table was cleared and Lena and Rhea had washed the dishes. "We have to do something about Nathan."

"I thought that was settled," he answered. "He's going to register and that's that."

"No, it's something just as important, maybe more. Annie told me that Nathan asked Rachel to marry him."

"What?" David put down the newspaper. "Rachel? Married to Nathan?"

"That's what I said," Itkah replied. "What do you think?"

David scratched his beard. "He could have said something to us. They're both children."

"You think so? You should see him making eyes at every girl that walks into the store. I respect him as your blood son, but I can't see him as a loving husband sitting quietly at night reading the newspaper and making light conversation with his wife. The truth is, it would be a bad match for both."

"How can you be so sure? It might be good for him. It might settle him down."

"Perhaps," Itkah said, unconvinced. "But Rachel isn't the woman to settle down a restless soul like Nathan. And if somebody requires settling he shouldn't be married. It's difficult enough without putting up extra barriers to climb over. Besides, there's something else you may not have thought of. I think he's doing this to stay out of the army."

"I never thought of that," David said. He was quiet for a moment. "Does she want to marry him?"

"She's crazy about him – she thinks. She's young, infatuated and overwhelmed by his attentions. She can't see beneath the surface. I'd say, first let him go into the army when the government calls him and if they still feel the same way after he gets out then give them your blessing if you wish. Remember, his only income is what we pay him at the store, hardly enough of a foundation for a marriage."

"True enough," David said, "but we can give him more responsibility and pay him a higher wage."

Itkah smiled. "Think of him as a stranger and not your son. Would you say that his work merits more money?"

"He's young and immature, give him time."

"Exactly," Itkah answered. "If, after he comes home, he shows that he really wants to make something of himself and earns your confidence, then do as you please. Until then, I'd go slowly, for his good as well as your own. David, I've never counselled or suggested anything if it wasn't for the welfare of the family. Can you believe that?"

David took her hand in his. "With all my heart," he answered sincerely. "It was a fortunate day for me and our family when you decided to cast your lot with us."

She covered his hand with her own. "I have no regrets," she said simply.


Nathan registered for the draft and in less than a month was notified to straighten out his affairs. After affectionate farewells from his parents, brothers and sisters and Rachel, he reported to the armory on Broad Street from where he was shipped to Indiantown Gap, Pa., one of the many army bases scattered all over the eastern third of the United States.

On April 6, 1917, President Wilson declared war on Germany, and it was now truly a world war, with thousands of American soldiers being sent to Europe.

Nathan, however, was not one of the casualties. After three months he appeared unannounced at the store, his uniform hanging loosely on his thinner body, his face tanned, but haggard.

"I'm finished with the Army," he declared. "I hate it. I'm not going to get killed. It's no use trying to talk me out of it."

Itkah and David stared in amazement. "Nathan," Itkah said,

"What are you talking about? You can't just walk away. You're a soldier now."

"They'll come after you," David added. "They'll throw you in prison. You'll be court-martialled and given a dishonorable discharge. Do you realize what that means?"

"I don't care," he answered.

"Besides the disgrace," Itkah said, "it will plague you the rest of your life. You won't be able to find a job. It's difficult enough as it is. Don't make it worse."

"They've got me cutting hair and giving shaves," Nathan said. "Can you believe it?"

"So?" Itkah questioned. "A trade is a valuable tool these days."

Nathan ignored her statement. "There's only one way I'll go back, if I can marry Rachel. Married men are exempt."

"So far," David said. "But if the war drags on, that won't mean a thing."

"Then I'll have children," he answered defiantly. "There's no way they'll keep fathers in the Army."

Arguing with him was useless. He was determined. Itkah and David reluctantly agreed. A dishonorable discharge was an unacceptable alternative.

## 12

After marrying Rachel just before the war's end, Nathan recieved an early discharge, borrowed some money from his parents, and opened a one chair barbershop at 621 Oxford Street.

The shop was the front parlor of the house, which he converted for his purpose. The building was three stories high with a flight of four marble steps out front. He and the tenants living in the house paid rent to the landlord, Mr. Klein, who operated a shoe store around the corner on 7th Street. With Mr. Klein's permission, Nathan installed a striped barber pole outside showing everybody that if you wanted the best haircut and shave, this was the place to come.

He was a surprisingly good barber and being very personable, soon developed a steady stream of customers.

Rachel, who had become pregnant just prior to the war's end, decorated the two rooms behind the store the best she could, one room being the kitchen and the room next to the store serving as a combination breakfast room and parlor. Rachel was not mistreated, nor was she overly loved. She was Nathan's wife, to keep house, cook and clean. On May 20th, 1919, a cute, little red-haired girl, who they named Edith, was born to Rachel and Nathan. A small crib was placed in their bedroom despite Nathan's protest that it would interfere with his sleep.

"Where do you want me to put her, in the barber shop?"

After Rachel promised to move Edith into the parlor if she was a noisy baby, he relented.


Although the barber shop was busy, Rachel saw very little of the money that went into the register. She depended on Nathan to parcel out whatever she needed for food and other family needs, sitting in a chair between the shop and the parlor waiting until he took notice of her.

"What is it?" he would ask. He never addressed her by name. A statement was uttered and she would answer.

"I need food money, Nathan."

Nathan's generosity and affection both had disappeared after their marriage. When he was ready, he went to the register and removed some money.

"Nathan," she pleaded. "Why can't I have several day's money at one time instead of having to ask you every day? It's a shame to have to sit here in front of the customers until you decide to give me some money."

Nathan returned to his barber chair without comment.

Rachel did the best she could with what he gave her, leaving the house every day with her "allowance" and carefully buying only the basic items needed for that day's meals. She often came home to find Edith crying and unattended.

"It wouldn't hurt," she told Nathan, "if you could take a few minutes to comfort her, then maybe she wouldn't cry so much. You're not that busy."

"The customers are more important," he answered brusquely. "Where do you think the money I give you comes from?"

It was no use arguing with him. Even on Sunday, when the store was closed, he found no time for his daughter. In fact, once he pulled down the shade on the front door and put out the lights, he was rarely home. Where he disappeared to she didn't know. She hoped he wasn't womanizing. She could put up with his card playing and gambling, although that made it more difficult than it already was to squeeze money out of him, but the thought of her husband being unfaithful would be too much to bear.

"The store looks fine," she commented one evening at dinner.

"Customers appreciate a clean store," he answered.

"And business seems to be picking up."

"I'm working on it. My visits to the Orphan's Home, the Hebrew School and the social clubs are paying off. I'm offering them discounts."

"That's smart, Nathan, but it keeps you away from home so much. It's nice when we can sit together and talk – like now."

"I can't help it," he answered. "It takes time to run a business."

"I'm not complaining, Nathan."

"But you are."

"I can't help it. I wish you could spend more time with us. Edith doesn't know she has a father."

"I'm on my feet from morning 'til night," he said. "What spare time I have goes into cultivating customers. There are two other barbershops in the neighborhood that'll steal customers away if I turn my back for a minute."

He was a hard worker, driven more by his desire to succeed than by wanting a more comfortable life for his family. She still found it difficult to extract money from the register though, and hardly a day passed without her sitting by the parlor doorway waiting for her daily handout.

As far as she knew, Nathan had no bank account, and she didn't have the slightest idea where he kept his money or what he did with it.

For the barbershop he couldn't do enough. New linoleum, brighter lights, a mirrored wall. It was the only store in the neighborhood with a red neon sign.

The shop was kept spotless. He swept up after each customer, the mirrors and front window were cleaned every morning, and the spitoons, which gave off a curious musical sound when accurately struck, were washed out regularly and placed at strategic positions around the floor. Ash trays were conveniently placed for those customers waiting their turn, cigarette and cigar smoking being the fashionable habit of the day.

Nathan considered family life a minor annoyance that didn't interfere with his accustomed lifestyle – spending the night hours with his friends, returning only to sleep and force occasional sex on his wife, then starting all over again in the morning. Rachel overlooked his bedroom manners, happy to have him near her, and pretending to enjoy his sweaty body moving back and forth on top of her. She didn't need his occasional sex, but she did want his permanent affection.

Unlike Rachel, the arrangement suited Nathan well. He had comfortable living quarters, thanks to her painstaking use of the meager resources available to her. Breakfast was always ready in the morning. Lunch, if he had time for it, was prepared for him and put in the icebox, making it available to him at his convenience.

She missed the dinner hours of her younger years with everyone sitting around the table involved in lively give and take. But that was in the past. She had taken an oath, "for better or for worse," and she became resigned to the worse. She had her daughter, Edith, and a place to live, and she was determined to hold up her end without complaining and do the best she could with what she had.

When visiting her in-laws at the general store she gave no hint of any problems, but Itkah knew better. The sparkle was gone from Rachel's eyes, she seemed tired and thin, and when questioned she merely said everything was all right.

Poor girl, Itkah thought to herself. Everybody tried to warn her.


There were new faces in the store. Itkah and David were compelled to hire two young boys to replace the girls. Lena had married an apprentice tool and die maker, and Rhea was now the wife of Lou Schwartz, a young man just starting out as an electrician. They had each moved into small two room apartments nearby and were happily planning futures of their own.

The two boys were not as diligent as Lena and Rhea, but with Ellis assisting after school they helped keep the full burden of physical work from overwhelming Itkah and David. They were now in their fifties and beginning to feel the strain of working every day, taking care of the books at night and giving some attention to the coal business being run satisfactorily by Joshua.


"I see in the newspaper," David said after dinner, "that Germany is refusing to pay reparations for war damage."

"How can they pay what they don't have?" Itkah said. "Their industries are not functioning, inflation's running wild, their leaders are fighting with each other. To expect them to pay billions is not realistic."

"But they were our enemy," David insisted.

"Enemy or not, you can't give what you don't have."

"The paper says the war has left England a second rate power behind our country." The word "our" when referring to their adopted country was now a permanent part of their vocabulary.

"War is expensive," Itkah said. "It takes money and manpower. England's been stripped of both. Thank God there's an ocean between

Europe and us. Things are looking better here."

"Especially for those engaged in bootlegging," David said. "Many people are getting wealthy."

"You mean many law breakers are getting wealthy," Itkah said.

"People like to drink. The paper says bartenders in the speakeasies are paid $80.00 a week! Can you believe that? And furthermore, if they're arrested, they get a $50.00 bonus. And they're back on the job the same day."

"The country's going through growing pains," Itkah said. "It will pass."

"Not as long as people are willing to pay for illegal alcohol. It's forbidden fruit."

"I hear our son is getting his share."

"Nathan's drinking?" David asked.

"Stories are circulating about Nathan the great lover."

"He's running around?"

"He hangs out at the Cat and Fiddle at night, fooling with the women and gambling with the men."

"Poor Rachel," David sighed. "What can we do?"

"Not much, I'm afraid. He's too old to spank. But he's not too old to feel the sting of a sharp tongue."

## 13

It was a wild fall day in late September of 1924. The season's first northeaster had struck early and was moving up the Atlantic coast with high winds, heavy rains and temperatures in the 40's. The streets were empty and all horses and wagons had been moved into sheltered areas. Electric trolley cars, with their power lines criss-crossing the city operated independently of the weather and with few passengers on a day like this. Motor vehicles, now a common sight throughout the country, splashed past, defying the elements and representing a sign of things to come.

Itkah and David sat close to the coal stove. The wind was whistling through every small, unsealed opening around the door and rain was streaming down the window like a waterfall. Morris's fruit store was barely visible across Girard Ave.

With few customers venturing out in this weather it gave them a chance to catch up on their paperwork, which they ordinarily did at home. Itkah had a thick shawl over her shoulders to ward off the dampness, and the familiar kerchief pulled down over her head and tied under her chin. David wore a heavy sweater and was going over a long inventory list and preparing merchandise orders for Itkah's approval. Doing this work now would provide them with a few extra hours of leisure later. Ellis was at home today, at 18 the only child still with them.

Suddenly the door opened and amid a blast of wind and rain, Joshua, water running from his storm coat like a faucet, limped into the store and slammed the door behind him.

"Joshua," Itkah cried. "What in the world are you doing out on a day like this? Coal deliveries can wait for better weather. Take off your hat and coat and come over here by the stove. Nobody should be out in this weather."

He pulled up a chair and vigorously rubbed his hands. "As a matter of fact," he said, "I came out for one delivery."

"Only one delivery?" David asked. "What's so important about one delivery to bring you out in this ungodly storm?"

"A family by the name of Tannen. They just moved into the neighborhood yesterday and they didn't have one piece of coal in the basement. Johnson promised them a delivery but I guess he didn't want to come out. I made the delivery and put my suffering horse back in his stall."

Itkah shivered, not from the cold, but from the thought that this fine man might have been left behind in Russia.

"And you walked down here, in this storm?" she asked, examining him closely. He was still the husky Joshua that came with them from the old country 12 years ago. His work on the farm had prepared him well for the work he was now doing. His thick, curly hair was still unkempt, but now she noticed for the first time some grey showing along the temples. They were getting older together.

He took the mug of hot chocolate that David brought to him from their small gas burner in the rear of the store. He sipped it slowly, holding it with both hands to warm them faster.

"Is something wrong to bring you to the store on such a day?" Itkah asked.

Joshua swallowed slowly, allowing it to warm his insides. "Yes and no," he answered. "Something is wrong, but it's a good wrong, if there can be such a thing."

"Relax, Joshua," Itkah said. "There's nothing so wrong that we can't fix together."

He hesitated. "Now that I'm here I feel stupid, not being able to resolve this by myself."

"We've come a long way, Joshua," she said. "You can talk to us about anything. Come, out with it."

He took a deep breath. "It's crazy, it's love! Can you believe it? I'm in love."

David leaned back. "Is that all?"

Itkah poked her pencil through David's sweater, forcing him to grimace painfully. She glared at him. "That's all you can say? Our Joshua is at the crossroads of his life and all you can say is, is that all? You men make me sick sometimes. You know nothing of feelings and emotions. Ignore this old man, Joshua. He's forgotten what love is all about. He has as much understanding of such matters as the man in the moon. Now, tell me, what's this all about and who is she?"

"She lives on Poplar Street. I met her when I was making a delivery to her mother's house. We spoke a little and I couldn't wait until the next month's delivery. Then I visited her several times between deliveries. Her name is Hannah Klein. Perhaps you know the family, the small upholstery store on the corner of 6th and Poplar. Her father died recently, I believe."

"That's right, and they closed up the store and bought a two story house. They live on the first floor and rent out the second," David said.

"I remember the young lady now," Itkah said. "A pretty girl with reddish blond hair and freckles on her nose."

"When you talk to her, please don't mention the freckles," Joshua pleaded. "She's very sensitive about them. Anyway, we both feel the same about each other, but there's a problem."

"What kind of problem?" David asked.

"Our ages," he answered. "She's only 20 years old and I'll be 40 soon. It's too big of a difference."

"Twenty years," David said thoughtfully. "That is a big difference."

"Nonsense!" Itkah declared with a withering glance at her husband. "Twenty years is nothing. When you're 50 she'll be 30 – it won't seem so bad then."

"Perhaps," Joshua said glumly. "I don't think Mrs. Klein is happy about her daughter being courted by a coal delivery man 20 years older than her. I'm closer to Mrs. Klein's age than to Hannah's."

"Then marry Mrs. Klein," David said. He received another jab through his sweater.

"Besides," Joshua said. "There's still another problem. I haven't told them about my leg. My limp is not so pronounced since I had a new one fitted, but sooner or later they'll have to know. I'm afraid that'll end it."

"If Hannah loves you it shouldn't matter. Her witch of a mother is something else, but we must be realistic. No man is ever good enough for a mother's daughter."

"Especially one with a wooden leg," he moaned.

Itkah was silent for a moment. She had come to love this man and felt as if he was her own son. He had shared their adventures from Lutzin to America and now he was in love. Her heart went out to him.

"It would be better if you don't tell them yet. Give me some time to figure something out, and don't have any serious discussions with her mother. Be pleasant, be charming, no matter what. She'll come around. Don't despair, everything will turn out fine. We'll talk about this again in a few days."


That night, with the wind driving the rain against their bedroom window, David and Itkah sat in bed warming themselves with cups of hot chocolate. This was their nightly ritual. Regardless of what kind of day had transpired, they would end it with their favorite drink, a cup of chocolate, and discuss any problems that needed their attention.

"David," Itkah said as she sipped the warm drink. "I've been thinking lately. Why are we working so hard? And who are we working so hard for? Everyone but Ellis is grown and gone. The girls are married, Jacob is tailoring, Herman is in the cleaning and dyeing business and Nathan has a barber shop. They've all done it on their own, except for a small loan to Jacob which he has repaid, and a larger one to Nathan."

"Which he hasn't repaid. He promised it to us within two years," David said. "That was three years ago and we still haven't seen one penny, and we probably never will."

"Perhaps," she said. "But we must be happy that we're in a position to help in an emergency. Anyway, forget about Nathan. What do you think of lightening our work load a little?"

David's ears perked up. Whenever Itkah asked what he thought, it was a sign that she had already decided on a course of action.

"I'm all for that," he said. "Every day the legs bend more slowly and the body tires more quickly. What do you have in mind?"

"I think we should unload the coal business."

"The coal business?"

"Why not? It served its purpose. It made money for us when we needed it. Without it we would never have been able to open the store, and now that we have more money than I ever expected to see in a lifetime, we can sell it and bank the proceeds."

"But you were talking about lightening the load," David

protested. "Joshua and his helper do all of the hard work. The store is our real load."

"True, but one thing at a time. First the coal business, then the store."

"But what about Joshua? The new owner might decide he doesn't need him. Then what? The only thing we will have accomplished is doing Joshua out of a job."

Itkah smiled. "Not if Joshua's the new owner."

David put his cup down on the end table. "Of course. Why didn't I think of that? Who else would we sell it to? Then he wouldn't be just a worker anymore, he would be the boss."

"And being his own boss," Itkah continued, "would make a big impression on that snob, Mrs. Klein. He would no longer merely be a man delivering coal, but the owner of his own business who is more than able to support a wife."

"Itkah, you're a genius! Have you mentioned this to Joshua yet?"

"How could I? We just saw him today. But there's still one more obstacle."

"What's that?"

"His leg. No mother can be overjoyed at having a son-in-law with a wooden leg."

"Does she think their children will be born with one leg, too?"

"Be serious," she said. "But we've cleared one hurdle. I'm sure we can get over another."


By morning the rain was easing and the wind shifted around to the northwest. By late in the day the remaining clouds moved off to the east and the weather turned bright and colder. Shoppers, huddled in their houses the day before, were again out on the streets.

Dave's fruit store was crowded, as it usually was after a delivery of oranges from Florida. They were a favorite with area residents, not only because of the oranges, but for the tissue paper in which each was extravagantly wrapped. It didn't have the softness of today's toilet tissue, but it was less harsh than the newspaper that most people used.

Itkah watched through the store window with amusement.

"Thank goodness we don't have need for that anymore," she said to nobody in particular. She opened the door for a short, stout woman with black hair piled high on her head. It was Mrs. Klein.

"Oh, Mrs. Klein, such a beautiful hairdo," Itkah lied. "Wherever did you get it done?"

Mrs. Klein glowed at this compliment as she eyed Itkah's hair which was always swept back and kept in place by her kerchief. "You'll never guess," she answered. "From your son, Nathan. I had no idea he was so talented."

Itkah was staggered at this news. "Since when is he doing women's hair?"

"Oh, he didn't do it in the store," she answered, delighted to see the consternation on Itah's face. "He did me a special favor and came to my house after hours." There was a scarcely hidden twinkle in her eyes.

Itkah was quietly furious. What special favor did she repay him with?, she thought. Hardly able to control herself, and wanting nothing more than to twist that hairdo out of shape, she took a deep breath and managed to keep her emotions barely beneath the surface.

"My Nathan is talented beyond belief," Itkah said. Shallow wench, she thought, to take pride in helping a man to cheat on his wife, as if she was a pioneer in the field, unable to see that any woman with two legs and no morals could do the same.

"I saw a pair of shoes in the Sears catalog," Mrs. Klein said. "They look very stylish, but they're only available in brown and I want them in black. I wear a lot of black and grey, and I want them to match my clothes. If you have them in size 7 I'll take them. Sears advertises them for $4.25."

"I know what Sears advertises them for, wench," Itkah murmured to herself as she disappeared into the back room and returned with shiny black shoes, size 7. Mrs. Klein tried them on, walking back and forth to test the comfort. She should wear a size 8, Itkah thought, seeing her feet bulging over the tops of the shoes. But she seemed pleased, and size 7 sounded so much more petite than size 8.

"How much are they?" she asked.

"$4.25," Itkah answered.

"But that's what Sears charges," Mrs. Klein protested.

"True enough, but Sears has them only in brown, and even if they had black it would take more than a month to get them. I have them here right in front of you and there are no freight charges."

"I'll give you $4.00 for them."

"$4.25," Itkah repeated. "Not a penny less."

"Well – I don't have time to stand here all day. I'll take them. Do you have rice today? Good, I'll take a pound."

"Fifteen cents," Itkah said.

"That's a lot."

"Since the war it's gotten expensive. It's still less than what Grossman charges."

"Make it two pounds."

"Thirty cents."

"And a five pound bag of sugar."

"Thirty-five cents."

"That will do. Here's five dollars."

Itkah took it and gave her a dime change. "How is your lovely daughter, Hannah?"

"The apple of my eye," Mrs. Klein answered. "But I'll feel better when she stops being silly over your coal delivery man. What's his name?"

"Joshua."

"Yes. What does she see in him? He's practically an old man, much too old for a sweet young girl like my daughter. And to make matters worse," she leaned closer and lowered her voice, "he has a wooden leg. My Hannah, seeing a man with one leg."

"A wooden leg? Really?" Itkah acted surprised. "You would never know it the way he walks. How did you find out?"

"He told her. He said it was the only honest thing to do. Very noble, but no daughter of mine is going to marry a coal delivery man with one leg. Her life would be ruined."

Itkah raged inside. She had told him to keep his mouth shut. Noble, indeed, a lot of good that will do him, she thought. But she loved him all the more for it.

"I understand how you feel," Itkah said. "I'd feel the same way, even if he does own the business now."

"He owns the business? I thought he worked for you."

"He just bought it," Itkah said. She'd have to talk to Joshua today, before this gossip spread the word. "He's ambitious and a sharp businessman. He'll be rich some day."

"You really think so?" Mrs. Klein's demeanor softened somewhat as inner forces struggled with each other. "But his leg?" she insisted. "What about his leg?"

Itkah silently asked God to forgive her. "What about his leg? In his home town he's a hero. When the soldiers came he fought like a Siberian tiger to defend his home and his parents. He rallied the townspeople to stand their ground until the soldiers left, but it cost him his leg. He deserves a medal. I heard they put up a statue of him in Lutzin."

"Really?" Mrs. Klein was agog. "I had no idea. You never know about some people, do you? I always said you should never judge a book by its cover."

Very original, Itkah thought.

"Well, I must go, Mrs. Kurtz. Thank you. It was interesting to talk to you."

I wish I could say the same, you trashy gossip, Itkah thought. Well, I gave her something to think about. A little lying sometimes doesn't hurt. And Nathan, wait until I see him, making house calls to Mrs. Klein. Will I give him a piece of my mind, fooling around with that bum.


Rachel was in her 8th month with her second child and was not having a good time of it. She was still cleaning and cooking and doing the wash, as well as the daily food shopping.

"You shouldn't be working so hard," Annie told her as they sat at the breakfast room table behind the barber shop. "Why don't you get a cleaning woman in once in a while, you can afford it."

"You mean Nathan can afford it," she said.

"Won't he give you the money? My God, you're ready to have a baby. You should have some help. You can't take care of a three story house and do all of your other work while you're in this condition."

"Don't say anything to him," Rachel pleaded. "I don't want to make him angry."

"Angry? You're the one who should be angry! How can he treat you like this? If you were paupers it would be different. But he has a nice business going here and can easily put out a couple of dollars to help his wife."

"Why make trouble?" Rachel said. "The baby will be here soon and things will get back to normal"

"Some normal," Annie said. "You bear the children and feed them, bathe them, change them, cook for your husband, clean and do the shopping – you call that normal?"

"I'm not complaining."

"Well, you should."

"Please, Momma, don't make trouble."

"You already have trouble. I won't make any more for you if you promise to speak up."

"I will, Momma, when the time is right."

Annie kissed her daughter on the cheek and walked through the store, giving her son-in-law a frosty goodnight.

Several minutes later, as Nathan swept up the floor, David and Itkah walked in. David went into the parlor and engaged Rachel in conversation as Itkah sat down in the store and waited for her son to finish his end of the day routine, cleaning his tools, washing the mirrors and emptying the ash trays and spittoons.

"How's business, Nathan?"

"Pretty good," he said. "I just picked up the Hebrew Orphan Home's children. They used to go to Ikey Trust's place, but they're not happy with how he cuts hair. Did you ever see a customer after he left that store? He should have been a butcher the way he chops up people's heads."

"That's fine," Itkah answered. "Now maybe you can bring in a woman to help Rachel. Don't you ever look at your wife? She looks exhausted. Don't you have any feelings for her?"

"You've been talking to Annie."

"What if I have? We're all concerned about her."

Nathan lit a cigarette. "Lena comes in now and then to help her."

"Lena has a family of her own to look after, two children and a house. You can't expect her to be your housecleaner too. For a couple dollars you can get somebody to clean the house from top to bottom. What do you do with all of your money, anyway?"

He blew some smoke toward the ceiling. "That's my concern. Rachel gets enough money for food and clothes. She has a nice place to live in and nobody's going hungry. What else do you want me to do?"

"A little affection wouldn't hurt, Nathan. Love is food also. What happened to that romantic fellow who courted Rachel and told her all the wonderful things every girl wants to hear?"

Nathan looked out of the store window as a #65 trolley clattered noisily up 7th St. "It's not what I thought it would be," he said. "But I'm here working and I'm not going anywhere."

"Except to Mrs. Klein's," Itkah said, lowering her voice.

He inhaled deeply on his cigarette, blowing another cloud of smoke toward the ceiling. "What about Mrs. Klein?"

"That was a gorgeous hairdo she was sporting when she came into the store recently. What did you charge her for it?"

He didn't answer.

"Nathan, if you're not happy in your marriage, that's one thing, but don't disgrace the family with this fooling around. What can you possibly get out of it but trouble?"

Nathan turned to face her. "I do what I have to do," he answered. "My family will never go hungry or unclothed, I promise you."

"Nathan, that's not enough to sustain a marriage over a long time."

"Mama, I'm on my feet from 9:00 in the morning until closing at night, six days a week. A man needs – recreation after working all those hours."

"Some recreation," she said, her voice rising. "Take your family out to Fairmount Park on Sunday. You'll get all the recreation you need."

He pushed his cigarette into a freshly cleaned ash tray, but again didn't answer.

David came into the store, closing the parlor door behind him.

"Keep your voices down. You want Rachel to hear you?"

"It wouldn't be so terrible if she did," Itkah declared. "What are we protecting her from?" Itkah was losing her patience. "And while we're talking, what about the money we loaned you? You said it would be paid back in two years. Your two years were up three years ago."

"It'll take a little longer," Nathan said. "I'm buying a car."

"A car?" David exclaimed. "What do you need a car for? You're in the store all week."

"For one thing," Nathan answered, "I can take the family out on Sundays like you want me to. We can spend the day in the park or drive out into the country, we could even take the ferry over to Jersey and drive down to the shore."

"Not a bad idea," David said. "How much will this car cost you?"

"Ford just came out with a Model T. It has room for three people in the front seat and three in the rumble seat when it is opened."

Itkah wasn't impressed. "Big deal. And if I may ask, just what is a rumble seat?"

"It's outside the car. When it's closed it's nothing; when it's open it has room for three people. It's like having a buggy in the back, but instead of a horse out front there's a motor."

Itkah snorted. "How much is this wonderful toy going to cost you?"

"Three hundred dollars."

"What?" Itkah shrieked. "Three hundred dollars! That's almost the amount of money that you owe us. You can buy a horse and buggy for $175.00 and still be able to go out to the park."

"Times are changing," Nathan said. "Automobiles are the way to go today. Horses will soon be obsolete."

To this, Itkah had no answer. "Very well, Nathan, do as you see fit. I talk to you like this because you're family and I have your best interests at heart."

"I believe that, Momma, and I promise you'll get your money when I have it."

"As a business man," David added, "nobody will trust you if you don't pay your debts. Your mother knows what she's talking about. You can't survive in business without good credit."

"I'll remember that," Nathan said indifferently.

"I hope you mean that," Itkah said. She gave him a reluctant hug, as did David, and they left.

"What do you think?" Itkah asked her husband as they walked down Oxford St.

"He's a tough one," David answered. "He promises one thing and does another."

"Exactly," Itkah agreed. They walked silently for a while, arm in arm. She had no faith in her stepson and knew they would never see their money again. She didn't like him, but she would never say that to her husband. She despised unkept promises and had little time for those who didn't keep their word.

"Rumble seat, indeed," she finally said. "Who needs a rumble seat anyway?"

## 14

On Columbus Day, October 12th, 1924, a little red-haired boy was born to Nathan and Rachel, and was named Sidney Bernard. Somewhere back in the Kurtzmann family there must have been somebody with red hair, because Edith and Sidney both had an abundance of it.

As Nathan had prophesied, times were changing, and America was the catalyst. Technological innovations in the movement of information enabled people, business and government to communicate rapidly with each other. Revolutionary changes in the manufacture of goods provided consumers with a diversity unknown in human history.

But for most of the millions of immigrants and their children, family and neighborhood were still most important. They formed their own enclaves within cities and towns, and their shared race, language, religions, customs and even their foods, served as insulation against the discrimination with which they were commonly regarded.


Nathan, true to his word, at least in this instance, took his family on Sunday outings in their new Model T Ford. They traveled to the park and picnicked on the grassy slopes adjacent to the Schuylkill River. Occasionally they went to Atlantic City where they spread their blankets on the beach, bathed in the ocean, and returned home with fiery sunburns which left them "untouchable" for days.

Their most satisfying times, at least to Rachel and the children, were in the countryside, in towns like Collegeville, Pa., where they stayed at Krekstein's farm, drank fresh milk and played in the fields. Days like these gave Rachel hope that her marriage would now be more pleasant. Away from the city and the barber shop, Nathan was almost a different person, sitting with his family at meals and joining in the conversation, chatting with Mr. and Mrs. Krekstein, and seeming to find enjoyment with her and the children.

Once returning to Philadelphia, however, he was again his normal self, remote from those closest to him and parcelling out daily funds to his patient wife for the needs of the household. The images of the rare days they spent by the river and on the farm became memories to be cherished all the more by Rachel as she struggled to make life as comfortable as possible for her difficult husband and her children.

Nathan continued working throughout the day, eating meals between customers, then cleaning up the store after closing and disappearing into the night, not returning until everyone had been asleep for hours.

Early in their marriage Rachel had angrily questioned him about why he left and where he went, but her anger was soon hidden by a reluctant passivity. He was a man who never should have married. His restless nature brought him in contact with men of similar interests, and together they caroused, played cards, flirted with women, and engaged in various other activities. With a magnetic personality and a smooth tongue, he attracted and cultivated friends easily, both male and female. He gambled with them, losing more often than winning. He drank at speakeasies and soon gathered around him a wide circle of assorted characters.

Nathan was happy leading this type of life, having adjusted rapidly to the American way. He lived in two worlds, the daytime world of his store, and the night-time world of back rooms and speakeasies. He moved in and out of each without losing a step, satisfied with the convenience of having a woman to look after his personal needs during the day and the excitement of the night.

If nothing else, this arrangement increased his business dramatically. His companions needed haircuts and shaves eventually, as did their friends and families, necessitating the installation of another barber chair and another barber to keep up with the constant flow of customers. Being a good barber, and proud of it, he impressed strict standards that his new employee must follow. No customers were allowed to leave the store unsatisfied, no matter what, and once, when the new man accidently nicked a customer's face when someone bumped his arm, and they had difficulty in staunching the blood, Nathan refused to charge him. He extended free haircuts not only to him, but to his entire family on their next visit. As stories like this spread throughout the area, it merely served to add to his reputation as a quality barber.

By now the three story house at 641 Oxford Street was bulging with Nathan's and Rachel's relatives and tenants. In addition to Rachel's parents was Rebecca Dean, who was almost trampled to death by Russian horsemen back in Lutzin, and her two daughters, Jean and Sylvia, and a family of four by the name of Cantor. With so many people filling the house at 641 Oxford Street, Rachel now had plenty of company with whom to share conversation and activities. This made life still easier for Nathan. With his wife more occupied and her attention not always focused on him, he was freer than ever in his night life, cementing his relationships and forming new ones. Joshua expressed an interest in renting a room there but Itkah and David would not hear of it, insisting he stay with them for as long as necessary.

"Over my dead body," Itkah exclaimed when he told her. "Where we live, you live. This is your home until you marry, and even then you and your wife will be welcome here."

"Then I wish you would charge me more rent," Joshua protested. "I feel guilty paying what you charge me."

"I wouldn't charge you anything if I thought you wouldn't move out. There are some things that aren't measured in money, and our relationship is one of them. I can just imagine what would happen if the shoe was on the other foot and David and I needed a place to stay. You wouldn't take a penny from us."

"You think not?" Joshua answered. "I'd bleed you for every dollar you have. I'd have you cooking, cleaning and washing my clothes until you couldn't stand up."

Itkah laughed. "Your wife perhaps, not me." She gave him a firm hug.

He never told her how much he looked forward to her putting her arms around him and holding him close. It was the most comforting feeling he ever experienced. Even having Hannah close to him was not the same. She was soft and tender and stirred his passions. Itkah was wiry and hard. When she held him he knew that nothing in the world could hurt him. In any crisis he knew that she would be there with her strength and love. No mother could mean more to him than this beautiful woman with her graying hair swept back and held in place by her kerchief. Additional wrinkles lined her firm face but her eyes remained alert and her body was still erect. May she live forever, he thought.


At the American General Store on Girard Avenue, David and Itkah, contrary to their decision to cut back, took over the property next door, knocked down the dividing wall and immediately doubled the size of their business. With the availability of inexpensive merchandise made possible by the mass production of the 20's, they stocked their shelves and filled the floor space with goods never seen outside of a catalog.

On the 2nd and 3rd floors they created two apartments, installing a kitchen in each one, and renting the upper apartment to a newly arrived family from New York, anxious to flee the congestion of the crowded tenements. Hannah's mother, with a sudden change of heart, showered her new son-in-law with praises and welcomed him into her family with open arms, whereupon Joshua and Hannah moved into the 2nd floor above the general store, to the delight of Itkah and David and the consternation of Mrs. Klein. Her daughter deserved better, she thought, but she was certain that Joshua would one day be a rich man and buy a mansion in the suburbs where she would join them.

Joshua had sold his horse and wagon and invested in a truck. It functioned in any weather, carried three times the load, which allowed him to make more deliveries per trip, and didn't get sick when left out in the rain and snow.

Several months after enlarging their store, now busier than ever, David and Itkah accepted an invitation from Nathan and Rachel to take an automobile ride up to Collegeville. It was their first ride in a car and they sat in the rumble seat, straight and formal, David holding on to his yarmulke with Edith between them and Sidney on Itkah's lap. Aside from visiting local manufacturers and one train trip to New York to assure some suppliers of their good credit, they had never left the North Philadelphia area in which they settled, less than two miles from the Dock Street landing where the S.S. Dominion had deposited them in 1912.

Block after block of brick row homes passed by as they drove. The brick houses were soon left behind, replaced by brownstone mansions separated by colorful gardens with neatly dressed men and women sitting under umbrellas enjoying the pleasant weather. Farms appeared on all sides with cows munching on the lush grass, horses running untethered and giving an occasional glance toward the noisy intruder that interrupted their pastoral pleasures. Except for the car and its occupants there was no sign of humanity – only the farmhouses that sat alone in the fields.

Itkah found her thoughts returning to her homeland and the countryside around Lutzin, her daily trips into Rezekne with her faithful mule Aaron. It seemed so long ago. She thought of the forces that drove them to leave, to face unknown dangers, to cross 3,000 miles of wild ocean to a strange world, obliged to learn a new language and new ways of living.

She shook herself out of her dream. No reason to look back. She had no regrets. We've done very well in our new homeland, she thought. She was grateful to her new motherland and despised the old. This was now their home and Russia was a foreign country. They had left a land of persecution and violence in order to be safe and free, to work in the city and enjoy an automobile ride into the beautiful farmlands of rural Pennsylvania. What problems they did have seemed small and far away. Even Nathan's indifference towards his family, his wanderings, his debt, it didn't matter. It was a lovely day. She was happy. This was her home. Her eyes filled with tears as she turned to her husband.

"David," she said softly. "It's time for us to become citizens."

## 15

In the eastern United States the winter of 1927-28 was relatively mild, just enough bad weather to show that nature followed its own path regardless of the Farmer's Almanac. That esteemed and widely read publication had forecast an extremely cold and snowy winter for two years running. The unexpectedly mild weather was welcome. Shoppers were not confined to their houses as in many past years and as a result business was above normal for the cold months of the year.

The entire shopping district along Girard Avenue was able to look forward to spring and summer with their bills paid and a little left over.

The American General Store was thriving despite the opening of a Woolworth's 5 & 10 cent store at Broad and Girard. Although many of their products were available at Woolworth's, some at even lower prices, the one mile separating the two stores kept people from walking the extra distance to save a penny or two. Thus, each store managed to keep its own following without seriously affecting the business of the other.

One day in late winter, David was finishing with a customer when Itkah returned from a pricing trip to Woolworth's.

"Well?" he asked.

She removed her coat and hung it on a wall hook.

"I don't know how they do it," she exclaimed. "They sell shoes and boots for $4.00 a pair and cotton for 30 cents a yard. It's lucky they're so far away."

" $4.00 a pair," David repeated. "That's a good price."

"It must be the quantities they buy. They're opening stores all over the country and the manufacturers and wholesalers give them a better price than they give to us."

"So?"

"So nothing. As long as they're a mile away it's no problem. We'll just have to carry enough variety to offset some of their lower prices. In fact, they could help us."

"How?"

"I think people will be faithful to a neighborhood store rather than to a chain like Woolworth's where they don't know their customer's names. But we'll have to stay on our toes, especially with transportation making it easier for people to get around. Let's continue to compete with the catalogs rather than with Woolworth's. We're doing fine just the way we are."

And they were. They had more than made up the cost of expanding the store, were able to afford two full-time workers, and had instituted a credit system, allowing select customers to purchase any item with a deposit that covered the cost, followed by monthly payments with interest. It was Itkah's idea and was a hit from the start, although it did create extra paperwork for them.


Ellis had married Martha Crystal and opened a small watch repair and jewelry shop under their apartment in the brownstone area of 26th and Girard, reasoning that it was more prestigious and would be more lucrative than the old immigrant neighborhood. Itkah and David looked down on this snobbishness, but admitted from a business viewpoint it had merit.

At 641 Oxford Street, Nathan added hair shampooing and hot towel after-shave applications to his list of services and was becoming adept at cutting women's hair. Behind the scenes stormy weather was brewing. His extra-curricular activities were setting the entire household against him, particularly Rachel's mother, Annie. She ordered her to take the two children and leave, but Rachel refused, saying the children still needed two parents. As long as the household was relatively peaceful she was willing to tolerate her spouse's wanderings.

As congested as it was in their home, it was more the rule rather than the exception in the "Jewish Rectangle." Immigrants tended to be clannish and were most comfortable living amongst their own people, sharing customs and traditions. Being so close it was convenient to visit and converse in the language they knew so well, discussing the day's happenings. They supported each other, if not financially, then emotionally and morally. They alternately praised and criticized their country, taking delight in criticizing because they wouldn't have dared to do so in their former homeland. They cried when someone died and rejoiced at every new birth. They watched their sons reach Bar

Mitzvah, they danced and laughed at weddings, and they prayed together at Ohel Jacob at 7th and Columbia Avenue. Families formed mishpochas and met monthly, usually on Sunday evenings to share conversation, coffee, tea and homemade cakes and pies.

And many became citizens. Learning english from books and the people around them, they stood at the Customs House at 2nd and Chestnut before a federal judge and swore allegiance to the flag of the United States of America, hugging each other with tears in their eyes, eager to vote in the next election. They no longer had illusions of America and its streets being paved with gold, but they instinctively knew it was the best place to be in a turbulent world. The immigrants understood its faults and cherished its benefits. Most were working and laying plans for the future – homes of their own and college for their children. They saw that education was the key. Without it they would follow their parent's fate and become shopkeepers. There was no disgrace in it, but it was nothing like being a professional person. Without exception, every immigrant dreamed of a college education for the children. It didn't always work out, but that was their dream. This would be the obsession for the next generations – education.


On a December night in 1928 as the first snowflakes of the winter drifted down, David put aside the store ledger and picked up the newspaper, taking a cup of hot chocolate from his wife. He read the English paper as often as possible, alternating with the Yiddish Forward. It helped him to improve his english and gave him different opinions about what was going on in the world. He peered over his glasses at Itkah, who was examining Woolworth's newspaper ads.

"Business was down again this month," he stated.

"It's nothing," she answered. "It always slows down when the weather gets colder."

"The summer was slower, too, compared to last year."

"You told me before."

"We can't blame it on any new stores opening up because none did. The financial page says that even Woolworth's announced a decline in sales. In fact, they let some people go."

"I heard," she said again. "It can't be busy all the time. It goes down, it goes up, that's business."

David was quiet for a moment. "Some analyst in the paper says that people are saving too much and not spending enough."

Itkah sipped her hot chocolate and turned the page. "So, what's wrong with saving all of a sudden?"

"Nothing, I guess, but he says if people save too much and spend too little it affects business. Stores sell less and order less, industry gets less orders, they cut down on production and lay off workers. The less people working, the less money being spent. It goes around in circles."

"Perhaps," she said. "We save money. We also spend money."

"We're in business. We have to spend. Most people can't do both."

"We've had slow seasons before."

"Not two in a row."

Itkah pulled her shawl tighter and sipped more of the chocolate. "What's bothering you, David?"

"I'm not sure. Too many articles in the papers these days predicting a letdown, after so many good years the economy has to take a rest."

Itkah snorted. "A rest? Who are these so-called experts? There are just as many expecting another ten busy years."

"That's true. But have you heard the latest game they're playing on Wall Street?"

"I can't be bothered with Wall Street, only Girard Avenue. We sell our merchandise, we order more. It's as simple as that. I admit we've had to cut back our orders for next year but that's only normal when things slow down. Next year is another year.

"Itkah, I've always had faith in your judgement, but it doesn't hurt to look beyond Girard Avenue once in a while. Have you ever heard of buying on margin?"

She didn't look up from the paper. "Suddenly you're a stock market expert."

"Of course not, but I've been reading. You can buy stock in a company without paying the full price."

Itkah sniffed impatiently. She knew her store. She understood the law of supply and demand without the help of a course in business or economics. But she had no idea of how the stock market worked or why it even existed. She didn't need the stock market to teach her how to deliver coal, nor to help her open their store. They had more money than they ever expected to see in their lifetime. And they did it without the help of the stock market.

"What about buying on margin?" she finally asked. "What is it?"

"Well, it goes something like this – if you want to buy a share in a company, let's use Woolworth's for example, and you don't have all the maney to pay for it you could put up 10% of the value. Suppose 100 shares cost $10.00 apiece. That's $1,000.00. You put up 10% – $100.00 – and you own $1,000.00 of Woolworth stock."

"How can that be?" Itkah asked. "What happens to the other $900.00?"

"The broker pays it."

Itkah thought about this for a moment. "Why would he pay $900.00 for you? He doesn't do it out of the goodness of his heart."

"Of course not," David answered. "It's like our credit business. Customers leave a deposit and pay off the balance in monthly installments. If they stop making payments we take back the merchandise."

"Which you never want to do," she commented with some irritation.

"But most pay eventually." David said. "That's why we charge interest on the payments, for the privilege of buying something they need and to cover costs and any losses from nonpayment."

"Yes." Itkah answered impatiently. "I know all that. But how does the broker make money by putting up the balance of the cost of the stock?"

"First, the buyer takes a risk that the value of the stock increases, then he can sell it if he wishes and pay the broker the $900.00 balance plus interest of maybe 5% to 10%."

"That makes sense," she said. "A plain business deal. But you depend on the stock going up. What if it goes down?"

"You can hold it, hoping conditions change, or sell it at a loss."

"Does he charge anything for selling it?"

"He gets a percentage of the sale."

"Smart man," Itkah commented. "He gets you coming and

going. Thank God we don't have to depend on shenanigans like that. Better to be in control than deal in dreams and fairy-tales."

"Oh, I don't know," David continued, holding up his newspaper. "There's a story in here about a man who bought Radio Corporation of America stock at $85.00 a share."

"That's a high price."

"They're a big company. He put $10.00 a share down and his broker put up the remaining $75.00. This year he sold it for $420.00 a share."

"$420.00," she gasped.

"$420.00," David repeated with pride, as if he was the buyer. "His $10.00 per share investment made him $410.00 per share profit, less what he owed the broker. Can you believe that?"

"Amazing," Itkah said. "It seems too good to be true."

"Well, this is probably the exception rather than the rule. They all don't make killings like that."

"But what happens if the whole market slumps and all those stocks go down in value?"

"I guess a lot of people will lose a lot of money."

"You may be sure," she stated. "Better to buy leather sole at .50/lb. and sell it for .75/lb. without worrying about brokers rushing over to take it back. I'll deal with things that I can see. What does the stock market mean to men like Jacob sitting and tailoring all day in his store? Or to Nathan standing on his feet from nine in the morning to eight at night, or to Joshua, up early every day delivering loads of coal around the neighborhood? I don't trust what I can't see and feel." She waved her hand and pointed at the wall. "This I have faith in, this home, the store, you and me and our ability to create with our own hands and think with our own minds. Not the promises of brokers who make a profit when you buy and a profit when you sell. A fair profit at a fair cost. That's all I ask. At least we know what to expect today and are reasonably certain what will be tomorrow. Our money is safe in the bank where it belongs and where we can take it or leave it as we choose."

David had no reply to that. "I was only telling you what I saw in the newspaper. I thought it might be an idea to put part of our money, not all of it, into stocks and see what happens."

"You meant no harm, David. Perhaps someday we will, but we shouldn't rush into something we know so little about."

"Very well," he answered, dropping the subject. "It was only a thought."

**16**

The winter of 1928 slipped into the spring of 1929 and memories of the Old Country faded as the immigrants of North Philadelphia continued their efforts to strengthen their roots in America. The brick row homes were well cared for, notwithstanding the widespread poverty among the residents, and every morning women were seen sweeping their sidewalks and streets or scrubbing the front steps. The wooden doors and window frames were neatly painted, and in some instances where families could afford it, wrought iron railings were installed on the steps.

Trees planted along the curb line ten years ago were now 20 to 30 feet tall, adding a touch of shady green to the unrelieved stretch of brick walls and paved streets. People went to their jobs, such as they were, opened their stores every morning, attended synagogue services on Friday evening or Saturday morning. On Sunday, except for the occasional trolley or automobile rumbling by, the city was quiet.

For the most part, the immigrants accepted the changes in their lifestyles since arriving in America. Their customs and ethnicity were retained due to their physical closeness within the enclave in which they settled. Considering that the greater majority of them came from rural areas of Europe and Russia and found themselves herded together in the congestion of large cities, they adapted with surprising resilience. Bound together by their heritage and past history and speaking mostly Yiddish, they retained the old world flavor and atmosphere which stood them apart from the rest of the population. They lived and died within arm's length of each other, as they did in the old country, and expected their children to do the same.

Few had the means to travel very far, and the idea of somebody moving to another city or state was preposterous to them. There was no reason for it. Everything they needed was nearby. If a need arose to get to another section of the city, the trolley car system was available.

An occasional trip to the seashore without a car was an involved undertaking requiring a ferry ride across the Delaware River to the Reading Railroad Lines in Camden and a smoky, smelly, ash-filled 60 mile ride to Atlantic City behind the big coal burning engine.

Nathan was one of the few automobile owners in the neighborhood. He never tired of displaying his Model T to other members of the family and taking them for a ride around the city with the children chattering excitedly in the rumble seat and a few adults squeezed into the front. He inserted the crank-handle into the front of the engine, turned it clockwise as fast as possible, then he jumped into the car before it stalled out. They putt-putted down the street to the consternation of any horses that were in the way and the attention of any interested neighbors.

Train trips to other parts of the nation were luxuries that only the rich could afford, while passenger planes, for the most part, were still in the future.

This was the world in which the Kurtz's lived, worked and met at monthly family meetings to be known in later years as the David Kurtz Mishpochah.


The first mishpochah meeting was in Nathan's barber shop, the largest room in the house. Tables and chairs were carried from all parts of the house. David, Jacob, Herman, Nathan and Ellis sat around one table with Lena's husband, Dave Kuhr and Rhea's husband, Lou Schwartz. Itkah, Jacob's wife, Nettie, Herman's wife, Tillie, Rhea, Lena and Rachel occupied the other table.

"How's the cleaning and dyeing business these days?" Jacob asked Herman. Jacob was now 36, the oldest of David's children.

Herman, 28, looked at his older brother, knowing that the conversation would soon turn political no matter what the subject was now. "Making a living," he answered. "There's a store available near that hotel at Broad and Girard. I'm thinking of giving it a try."

"You're leaving your job?" Jacob asked.

"I'll have to, I guess. We've saved enough money to put a down payment on the equipment and I'm looking to the hotel to provide most of the business. People that stay at hotels need their clothes cleaned and the hotel manager likes the idea of having a valet service that will pick up and deliver."

"So you'll have to pay off your equipment," Jacob said. "Pay rent and utility bills in the store and at home and probably give the hotel a piece of the action, too."

"If I have to," Herman said.

Jacob snorted. "You'll be a slave to five different people who can put you out of business with the snap of a finger – two landlords, the company you rent the equipment from, the utility company and the hotel manager."

"That's free enterprise," Herman said, knowing where his brother was headed.

"Free? You call that free? You're a prisoner of your own ambition."

"Who isn't?" Herman replied. "In Russia it's dangerous to have ambition. It's against the law. Here a man can go as far as his ambition will take him."

"And how far will that be?" Jacob asked. "Do you think you can match wits with those who wield the power? They're hungry, greedy people who will take what they want and then toss you in the gutter. They suck the blood out of working men like us."

"I don't see it that way," Herman answered, becoming irritated. "I'm not trying to match wits with anybody. I'm just trying to make a better living for my family. What's wrong with that? If I have to pay for the equipment and the rent and electric bills, so what? Ask Nathan. He bought the barber chairs, makes mortgage payments, owns a car. What do you think, Nathan?"

Nathan was listening with only one ear; he was thinking about introducing a new feature that might increase business in the barber shop, but he heard enough to come up with an answer.

"Herman's right, Jake," he said. "What are you complaining about? There are always some men with more money and influence than the next guy. They had to start somewhere, too."

"That's right," David added. "They were all poor at one time. If they weren't, then somebody further back in their family was."

Jacob was not deterred. "True, and as soon as they made their fortunes from the sweat of the average worker's brow they forgot where they came from."

"You're exaggerating," Herman said. "A man makes more money, he lives differently. It doesn't mean he forgot where he came from."

Jacob swept this aside. "Ask the people working in sweat shops or the coal mines. I think they'd disagree with you."

"We can't all be empire builders and queen bees," David said. "Somebody has to do the work. Working conditions in some places are terrible, but things will get better. Everything takes time."

"Easy for you to say, Father," Jacob replied. "You own your own business."

"And I'm proud of it. Does that make me a criminal? We treat our help very well, thank you. Not all owners are tyrants. And your mother and I have never forgotten our past, nor will we. We didn't hurt anybody."

"You're the exception."

"Jacob, don't try to alter the whole world. Remember, the faster a tree grows, the more brittle its branches."

"I heard that the garment workers and coal miners are re-organizing their unions," Herman said. "Making them stronger. That should help."

"Maybe," Jacob conceded. "They'll probably succeed in getting their heads knocked together"

"Nothing is ever gained without a little sacrifice," David said.

Jacob would not surrender without a fight. "Too much sacrifice and too little gain. Do you know how many Americans live in sub-standard conditions? It's a disgrace."

It was David's turn to be impatient. "In Russia, people like us are hounded and persecuted. We're lucky to be alive. Here, at least, we're only asked to work a little harder."

"Overworked is more like it," Jacob said. "But things will change in Russia, too. The Communist Party has instituted a five year plan to build up their industry."

"According to our Yiddish newspapers, it's mostly for the military. There's very little in the way of products for its citizens. Better to focus our energies on the positive of the here and now rather than what might be in the land of Stalin and Lenin. What they do there shouldn't concern us."

At the other table, Itkah was listening to the women, but had one ear cocked towards the men. It was a happy evening for her. The entire family was alive and well and enjoying the pleasure of each other's company. Even Nathan was joining in the conversation and his occasional laughter gave her some hope that family getherings such as this might provide the spark that would keep him closer to his wife and children.

She listened to Jacob and Herman debating the good and bad of capitalism and her thoughts returned to those years when criticism of the government was mentioned in cautious whispers, even in the privacy of their home. David was right, she mused. We shouldn't waste our time worrying about five year plans and collective farms.

Tillie's voice interrupted her reflections; "Did you see John Boles at the Gem last week? Wasn't he marvelous?"

"He's my favorite," Rachel said, as she brought in a fresh pot of coffee. "He's so handsome, the way he holds a woman. And to think they pay those actresses to make love to him. I'd do it for nothing."

"Don't worry, nobody's asking you," Lena said.

"I like John Barrymore," Rhea said. "Such a face. And he's got a nice Jewish nose."

"Don't tell him that," Nettie said. "How many dishes have you collected so far?"

"I've got six saucers and two cups," Rachel answered. "Four more Tuesday night movies and I'll have a set of six."

"I'll be glad when my set is complete," Lena said. "That Gem, it's like sitting in a closet. Don't they ever air the place out? They shouldn't allow people to take their shoes off in there."

"Or eat those baloney and onion sandwiches with sour pickles," Rachel said. "I swear between the odor of feet and the pickles I could find my way there blindfolded." Everybody laughed.

"I heard," Itkah joined in, "that they're going to build a new movie house at Franklin and Girard."

"It's about time," Rachel said.

"It's going to have plush seats, according to Mr. Heller, whose bakery will be next door to it. They're even installing equipment to show the new sound motion pictures."

"Sound movies," Rhea exclaimed.

"How exciting," Rachel said. "I wonder what John Bole's voice sounds like?"

"Or John Barrymore's?"

Rhea lowered her voice to a whisper. "Now maybe we'll be able to hear every sound when they make love." The women looked at each other and giggled.

"Sidney!" Rachel shouted. "Stop pumping that barber chair up and down. You'll break it. Your father paid good money for it."

Lena looked at her sister-in-law. Poor woman, dragged half-way around the world to end up in an unhappy marriage. Thank goodness Rhea and she have stable, hard-working husbands. Not that Nathan wasn't a hard worker. If anything, he worked harder than the rest of them. If only he would stay home at night instead of running around with his friends and flirting with any woman that looked at him. I'll have to talk to him soon, she thought.

"Each family handles their troubles in their own way," her husband, Dave, had told her. "Keep your nose out of their business. We can't tell them how to live." But Lena wanted to see everybody happy. And it was her business regardless of what Dave said. She'd sit them down and talk things over in private, just the three of them. When she explained to Nathan how his actions were affecting his family, how the other men were handling their home lives, and that the children needed more time from their father, he might come to his senses.


Itkah looked around the table at these silly, adorable women. How they loved the movies, and how they loved to collect those dishes, one every week. And why not? They all worked hard and were entitled to some diversion, and movies filled the need perfectly. So, every Tuesday night, off they went to the Gem with the other neighborhood women who were willing to invest fifteen cents to collect a dish, watch Movietone News, assorted short subjects and the main feature, a good night's entertainment for the money.

At the men's table the conversation was still travelling from politics to business and back again.

"What does everybody think about Hoover?" Ellis asked after listening quietly all night.

Herman wanted to kick his younger brother in the seat of his pants. He finally opens his mouth and look what comes out. He was tired of arguing politics with Jacob and this would start it all over again. To his surprise and relief, Jacob had nothing but compliments for their 31st president. The entire family had voted for him chiefly because he was a product of a poor environment, was orphaned at an early age and struggled through college earning a degree in engineering.

"A self-made man," Jacob announced. "He worked his way up from nothing, did a good job as Secretary of Commerce and fed and clothed many people as head of the Belgian Relief after World War I."

"I feel the same way," Herman replied. " The newspapers say he supervised the feeding of over 9,000,000 people in Belgium and France."

"And held the cost of the entire operation to 1% of the money available to him," Jacob added.

"Quite an accomplishment," David remarked. "I wish I could say the same about the store."

Jacob wasn't finished with his praises. "And his record in agricultural production is amazing. They call him "the man who can make miracles happen."

"We can use somebody like that," Herman said, happy that his brother was finished with his political tirades against the government.

"He's got liberal ideas," Jacob continued. "He believes in taxing the rich at a higher rate and not taxing the lower classes at all."

"A noble thought," David said. "If the government can afford to operate without taxing all workers more power to it. Sooner or later every working person will have to pay taxes. Government is a business and it takes money to run a business."

"It's not that simple, Papa," Jacob said. "It may not work for you, but the government isn't in the retail business. It's there to provide a comfortable environment for its citizens, and on a non-profit basis."

"What's wrong with the government making a profit? They could put the money away for a rainy day, just like any business."

Jacob shook his head, putting his fingers together in a thoughtful pose. "Hoover believes government should keep its nose out of business affairs. He feels there's too much reliance on government to solve problems. It's bad for progress and is less efficient."

"He has a point there," Herman said. "Keep the beauracracy out of business and this country will grow like crazy."

"Ah, the political beauracracy," Jacob said. "If anything can impede a president's goals, it's the beauracracy and the opposition party. Nobody likes to see their opponent do a good job, regardless of its merit, so they do their best to obstruct and confuse."

"The stock market seems to like him," David said. "It's jumped up 50 points since he was elected."

Itkah heard her husband's remarks. Maybe she was wrong in discouraging him from putting some of their savings into the stock market. Others had done it. She filed the thought away for future discussion and gave her full attention to the women.

"I was in Shuster's fruit store yesterday," Rhea was saying. "I still can't believe the amount of food available to people in our country. Why do citizens of foreign countries go hungry when there's so much here? How do we do it?"

"We live in a very large country," Itkah answered. "Thousands of miles of good soil and favorable climate."

"But Russia is a large country, too, larger than ours. Why was there never enough to feed everybody?"

"Different systems," Itkah said. "They call it private enterprise. People own the farms and businesses. When you own your own business, like David and I do, you make sure you run it as efficiently as possible in order to increase profits. The less waste, the more profit – more money available to spend means a healthier economy. The government can't control waste as well as a private business owner. He's in the middle of his investment day after day and has a personal financial stake in how efficiently it operates."

Rhea thought about this for a moment. "And in Russia the government has its hands in everything, is that it?"

"Probably," Itkah answered. "They kill your incentive. I can't think of any other reason."

There was a knock on the door and Itkah went to the front and raised the window shade. "Joshua and Hannah," she called out.

They came in to a noisy welcome with hand-shaking and hugging all around, while their bushy-haired little four year old son,

Joseph, scurried past and jumped into a barber chair. Soon, he and Sidney were spinning themselves in circles to see who got dizzy first. Rachel immediately stopped them and they were sent off to a corner of the store to play with a building-block set.

"Sit down and eat," Rachel said to Joshua and Hannah. "There's coffee, tea, hot chocolate and cakes and cookies."

"How's the coal business?" Herman called from the next table.

"I had a good winter," Joshua answered.

Itkah looked at him. His usually unruly hair, showing some streaks of gray, was now combed neatly back and his new turtleneck sweater showed Hannah's influence.

"Very smart looking," Itkah said approvingly, running her hand affectionately over his hair. "Whatever happened to that dirty, uncombed man with the torn pants that used to work for me?"

"He got a better job," Joshua said and smiled. "The rest is Hannah's touch. She says a man who owns his own business must make a nice appearance. And to think when she married me she said she loved me just as I was." Everybody laughed.

"I did," Hannah said, "and I love him this way, too."

Itkah glowed in the reflected contentment of her blushing face and sparkling eyes framed by her dark hair that she let fall to her shoulders. She was happy for them.

"We just saw the most wonderful motion picture," Hannah said. "Ben Hur."

"Wasn't that great?" Rachel exclaimed. "But where did you see it? It's not at the Gem anymore."

"We walked over to the Diamond on 6th Street."

"Pretty risky," Lena said, "venturing into Goyisha territory. Some of the Irish there haven't been the friendliest."

"No," Joshua said, "but we have customers there and many people know me. Besides, we wanted to see the movie."

"Isn't Ramon Navarro great?" Rachel said. "And that Francis X. Bushman! They were all so good. And that chariot race."

"That was thrilling," Hannah agreed. "It was so exciting. I don't know how they filmed it. Wings is coming soon," she added. "They call it the best airplane picture ever made."

"If Hannah wants to see it, I'll go," Joshua said. "But it's a war movie and I don't like to see people getting killed, even if it is just a movie."

"Amen to that," Itkah declared. "There's enough misery in the world without glorifying it in a motion picture."

"Yes," Rhea agreed. "Let's talk about happy things."

Hannah took hold of Joshua's hand. "Yes," she said, "like somebody expecting their second child."

For a second all was quiet, then everyone erupted into more hand shakes and hugs. Joshua's back was slapped and Hannah ran the gauntlet of tears and kisses. Having a baby was always cause for celebrating and Rachel asked Nathan to bring out a bottle of wine and glasses.

David filled his glass, waited for the room to quiet down, and stood up.

"My dear family," he began. "It seems like yesterday that I drank a toast and asked God to be with our decision to come to America. It's a miracle that we're all here, still healthy and still together as a family. We've grown in numbers since then and with His blessing, this will continue. I drink to Joshua and Hannah and to the entire family. May the sun continue to shine down on us."


Later, after most of the family left and the remaining children had gone to bed. David, Nathan and Joshua sat at one table, while Itkah, Rachel and Hannah sat talking quietly at the other.

"David," Joshua asked, "Do you have any money invested in the stock market?"

"No," David answered. "We've talked about it but Itkah doesn't like the idea."

"Why not?"

"I think the main reason is, she wants our money where she can see it, and get it right away if necessary. I trust her judgement."

"So do I," Joshua said sincerely. "Is that her only objection?"

"As far as I can tell. Itkah" he called. "Come and join us for a few moments." She came over to their table. "Joshua is asking about the stock market and what you have against investing in it, besides not having your money available whenever you want it."

Itkah poured herself a cup of hot water and stirred some chocolate into it. "That's one reason," she said, enjoying the warmth of the chocolate. "I don't fully understand it, and what I don't understand I stay away from, unless it concerns us directly."

"Well, it does in a way," Joshua said. "The stock market is a reflection of the public's confidence in our economy. It goes up and down accordingly."

"I don't like elevator economics," she answered. "Our money is in the business, in our merchandise; the rest is in the bank. Why complicate things?"

"It's not as complicated as it sounds," Joshua said. "Companies offer shares of stock to the public for what they think is a fair price, in return for which they pay you a dividend on that stock if the business prospers. The more a company prospers, the higher the dividend, much higher than the 2% the bank pays."

"And what if the company goes kablooey?" Itkah asked.

"Then, of course, they can't afford to pay you your dividend."

"And the value of the stock goes kablooey as well."

"It happens," Joshua admitted, "but not often. The trick is to invest in solid companies, not just one, but several. Spread your money around so that the chances of making money are better, and losing money is kept to a minimum. The whole idea is to let your money work for you. People are making a lot of money in the market."

"The advice is," Joshua continued, "don't put all your eggs in one basket."

"Sound enough," Itkah agreed. "And I suppose that's what you've done?"

"Not yet. I wanted to hear what you and David thought about it."

"What do you think, Joshua?" she asked.

"We've got $10,000 saved in the bank – more money than I ever expected to see in one place in my life."

"Quite a bit of money," Itkah commented. "I'm proud of you."

Joshua's face flushed with satisfaction at her words. "We were considering investing half of it in a variety of companies, all established and dependable, with a little going into some risk stock, maybe a new company on the way up. The rest would remain in the bank."

Itkah thought about this. It sounded conservative enough. Invest some, hold some. At the very worst, half their money could be lost or not grow as expected, she thought. At best, over a few years, a substantial profit could be realized.

"What do you think, David?" she asked. "This man has tied his life to us for almost 20 years. Would you like to share his enthusiasm?"

It didn't take long for David to answer. "Why not? We can't let Joshua make more money than us. It's a matter of principle. It wouldn't look good for a former employee to be wealthier than his ex-employer. Just imagine what might happen? We could be working for him some day. Such a disgrace." Everybody laughed. "Another toast," he said, holding up a cup of chocolate. "To the future capitalists of America. Long may they prosper."

David and Itkah, with all of the children now married, devoted full time to their store, bringing in new merchandise, eliminating the old slow movers, and trying to stay one step ahead of increasing competition by placing an occasional ad in both the English and Yiddish language newspapers.

Jacob had opened a small tailoring store at 3rd and Girard Avenue. Herman had rented that empty store at Broad and Girard to start a clothes cleaning business, and Nathan's two chair barber shop was always busy.

Rhea's husband, Lou Schwartz, had answered an ad from a small construction company and was now working full-time as an electrician, while Lena's husband, Dave Kuhr, was employed as a machinist at the Philadelphia Naval Shipyard.

Ellis was developing his watch repair and jewelry trade in the small store at 26th and Girard.

On October 3rd, 1929, the stock market began to decline and continued its fall for the next two weeks. David and Itkah called their broker on their recently installed store phone.

"It's a readjustment," he assured them. "The market's been going up for so long it was only a matter of time before it took a breather. It'll start up again. Your stock is still higher than when you bought it."

Feeling better, they returned to their customers and tried to put it out of their minds.

Later that day, Joshua came into the store. "I'm getting nervous," he said. "Half of my money is in stocks."

"Ours, too," David said. "The broker just told us it's a readjustment from having gone up for so long."

"I got the same story. He said it should start up again in a week or two. What do you think?"

"I think we should wait," David said, with a glance at Itkah. "We've only had it several months. Let's wait a little longer and see what happens."

But the decline rapidly became a free fall as a wave of selling soon developed into a financial panic. The value of stocks fell drastically and those who managed to unload without suffering too great a loss were few and far between. David, Itkah, Joshua, and many other first time investors, not familiar with the paper world into which they had entered, hung on in the hope that things would turn around.

On October 26th, David and Itkah were in the store when Joshua rushed in.

"We can't wait any longer," he shouted breathlessly. "The market's going crazy. We must get rid of our stock before it's worthless."

David, clenching his fists, stared at Joshua. "I don't understand. How could this happen?"

"I don't understand either" Joshua exclaimed. "All I know is half of what I own is going down the drain while we're standing here looking at each other."

Itkah rushed to the phone and dialed their broker. She tried twice, three times, then hung up. "I can't get through. Everybody in the world must be on the phone. What do we do?"

It wasn't often that Itkah was at a loss for a solution. Joshua took the phone from her.

"We've got to keep trying," he said, a tremor in his voice. After a few minutes, he gave the phone back to Itkah.

"Don't stop calling," he instructed. "While you're on the phone, I'll drive over to his office. I'll get in if I have to break down the door!" He rushed out as quickly as he entered and was off down the street.

David fell heavily into a chair and rested his head between his hands. "This is a bad day," he murmured.

Itkah tried to console him. "We've been through bad days before," she said, with her hand on his.

That evening as Itkah prepared dinner and David sat disconsolately, making a brave attempt to interest himself in the paper, Joshua entered and sat down at the table, exhausted from the nervous excitement.

"He said he would do the best he could, but didn't hold out much hope. Everybody's selling everything. The only people buying are the very rich, and they want it for nothing. We can kiss our money good-bye."

Itkah turned quietly back to the range, fussing with the food and moving pots around.

David put his paper aside and stared straight ahead. Joshua looked down at the floor.

"Joshua," Itkah finally said, "have a bit of dinner and keep us company for a while."

Joshua looked up at her face. A tear ran down her cheek, her lips quivered. The person who lifted him up when he was down, the woman who took him in when he had nobody, and was like a second mother to him, was asking him for help.

"I'll get Hannah and the boy," he said. "We'll spend the night with you."


But it was not over. On October 28th, everything fell apart. The Great Depression was underway.

For David, Itkah and Joshua, it went from bad to worse. Without warning, thousands lined up at banks hoping to retrieve their savings. Large member banks supported their smaller branches whenever they could, but for many, it was too late. There simply wasn't enough to go around.

Among those who lost everything were David and Itkah Kurtz and Joshua. Within weeks every dollar they had worked for and saved was gone, swept away by a tidal wave of panic selling and bank runs. The modest success they had achieved was returned to nothing.

Both workers were let go and in six months the store was closed.

## 18

In 1932, Franklin D. Roosevelt was elected president of a disillusioned nation. As he took office, he inspired a new hope in the American people. The country was paralyzed, and so had been the president, but he had not given up. He had fought back to triumph over his illness. Perhaps he could lead America to do the same. Scant as this hope was, it was all the country had as winter gave way to the spring of 1933.

A late March snowstorm had changed to a cold, windy rain that rattled the windows as David and Itkah sat down with Joshua and Hannah to listen to the first radio broadcast by their new President, Franklin D. Roosevelt. David and Itkah had moved in with Joshua and Hannah to pool their resources until everybody was back on their feet.

It was Joshua who was the principal source of income, having been able to keep one of his two vehicles after the truck company reclaimed the other for not keeping up with the payments.

Fortunately, people still needed coal to heat their houses. Working alone, Joshua labored long days and into the night to supply his customers. Both he and the truck were overworked and overtired. Hannah hid the keys in a drawer amongst her undergarments and wouldn't give them back until he promised to take a day off from his work and rest. Today was that day.

Itkah made hot chocolate and tea, and after Hannah made certain the children were asleep, they pulled chairs up into a semi-circle.

"My fellow Americans," came a soothing voice from the radio. His words were in tune to the spirit of the times. His phrases spoke of moral stimulation, and the mad chase for profits. He pleaded to his listeners to "minister to ourselves and to our fellow man." He judged the temper of the people correctly when he said, "we now realize as we have never realized before our interdependence on each other; that we cannot always take, but we must give as well."

When he finished, Itkah was the first to speak. "I like his voice," she said. "It makes me feel better."

"It will take more than words," Joshua said.

David, his hair still dark but his beard growing whiter, spoke up.

"It won't happen overnight. We must be patient."

"Do we have a choice?" Hannah asked.

"Don't listen to those radicals preaching revolution and violence," David said. "Have those fools forgotten so quickly what they left behind that they would foster the same madness here?"

"When people are hungry," Itkah said, "they are vulnerable to any promise, no matter how wild."

"True," David said. "These are times when even madmen seem to make sense, when everybody is troubled and confused."

"That's enough," Hannah said. "Enough bad news. I can't bear it any longer. Let's talk about good things."

"Very well," David said. "Mr. Myers at the wallpaper store has just landed a contract with a real estate firm to help furnish some expensive homes on the Main Line. He promised me at least three months work starting in April."

"That's wonderful," Joshua said. "I'm so happy for you. That's a good sign. Maybe things are turning around."

"Perhaps," David said. "It seems that there are always people building homes and having their walls papered. Every little bit helps."

"That's not all," Itkah said. "I'm going back on the streets again. I'm borrowing a horse and wagon and going back to my roots, selling vegetables and assorted foods from the streets."

"Marvelous." Hannah exclaimed. "But where were you able to borrow a horse and wagon?"

"From the milk company. They're starting to use trucks and are phasing out their horses, so they agreed to lend one to me rather than send the poor animal to a glue factory. If it works out, I'll pay them what they would have sold him for."

"But where will you get the stuff to sell?" Joshua asked.

"From the market down on Washington Avenue, where the wholesalers buy their produce before selling it to the stores. I'll be able to sell it cheaper and go into whatever neighborhoods I please. I'm ashamed I didn't think of it before."

"But, Itkah," Hannah said, "won't it be too much work for you? You're not 25 years old any more."

"I'm not 55 any more, but I should manage. The worst part is getting down there at 5 o'clock in the morning. That's when all of the business is done."

"Five o'clock," Hannah shouted. "Oh, Itkah, that's too much. You shouldn't be working so hard anymore. If I didn't have two children to look after, I'd go with you. You deserve some rest, you've earned it."

"I've had too much rest these last few years and I'm tired of taking advantage of your generosity. It's time to get moving again. I'm not ready for the cemetery yet."

"And when you get too feeble to work you'll stay here with us for the rest of your days. I don't want us separated anymore. We've been through too much together."

Itkah's eyes clouded over and a flood of emotion poured from her body. She threw herself into Joshua's arms and cried as never before. Her body shook, her hands trembled. David had never seen her like this, and he put his arms around her and Joshua, as did Hannah. They stood holding each other close for several moments, enveloped in happiness.

**19**

At 641 Oxford Street, a different type of storm was brewing. Dissention caused by Nathan's borrowing money from various members of the household, and his inability or reluctance to pay it back was creating a crisis.

"Nathan," Rachel said, "what do you do with the money from the store? You shouldn't have to borrow money from the family."

"It's none of your business what I do with the money. I give you enough for food and you shouldn't need anymore," he said.

Rachel knew well enough what he did with his money. Between playing big shot to his politician friends, treating them to cigars, drinks and food at the Cat and Fiddle, gambling with them until late into the night, and feeding his ego on the attention any woman who was willing to look in his direction, it was no surprise that he was always running short.

As more people left the house to live on their own, the entire burden of expenses fell heavily upon his undependable shoulders. It wasn't long before he was overwhelmed, and being unwilling to give up his extra-curricular activities, he lost money. Soon the bank closed up the shop and he moved his family and the barbering equipment to a smaller location at 705 W. Columbia Avenue.

The two-story row house and small store was one city block north of the old address and more suited to his financial condition. They rented the building, and he installed both barber chairs, which he had removed before the bank could get their hands on them. There was a kitchen and breakfast-living room behind the store and three bedrooms and a bathroom on the 2nd floor, one bedroom each for Edith, who was now 16 and Sidney who was 11 and Nathan and Rachel, who still shared the same bed but little else.

Outside, in front of the store, Nathan installed a barber pole.

Columbia Avenue was a wider street than Oxford, with paved sidewalks on the barbering side and red brick making up the south side.

As on Oxford Street, a store occupied each corner where 7th Street crossed Columbia. Grocery stores were situated on the northwest and southeast corners. As on many streets, trolley tracks ran up the center of 7th Street.

The grocery store closest to the barbershop, at 701 Columbia Avenue, was owned by Mr. and Mrs. Goldberg, a middle aged couple who lived quietly and unobtrusively and rarely ventured outside. Upstairs lived the Goldberg's daughter, Rose and her husband, Ralph Estrin, and their 12-year-old son, Joseph.

With dark hair, a fair complexion, and inquiring hazel eyes, Joseph was a quiet, introspective youngster and he and Sidney hit it off immediately. If it wasn't for Sid's red hair and freckles, they could have passed for brothers. They both attended Ferguson Grammar School at 7th and Norris, where Edith had gone several years earlier.

With five years difference between them, Edith and Sidney had little in common, but it didn't prevent their having a reasonably amicable relationship despite some hair pulling and shin-kicking.

The altercations usually ended with Edith having to comb her hair and apply a soothing lotion to her shins. Sidney's shoes were hard and his aim was good. She eventually learned to keep both her head and legs beyond his reach, but not before she lost some hair and suffered discolored and scarred shins.

After one of these incidents, as she pulled him through the store and into the dining room, they found their mother and Aunt Lena sitting together, talking in subdued tones. They stopped when the children came in, Sidney angry, Edith breathless.

"Look at my legs!" she said exasperated. "Every time I have to bring him in, it's the same thing – chasing, pulling, kicking. I'm not going to run after him anymore. He can stay outside all night for all I care!"

Lena was horrified. "Sidney," she scolded, "you kick your sister? When it's time to come in, no more arguments. You come in! Rachel, what are you doing about this? Why is he allowed to get away with this?"

"He's really a good boy," Rachel said. I've asked Nathan to talk to him, but he never does anything."

"Well, I will," Lena said sternly. "If I hear about this again, I'll come down and give you a licking you've never had before. I'll take your pants off in front of everybody and spank your hide with one of your father's razor straps. Is that clear? Now tell your sister that you're sorry and you won't do it again."

"I'm sorry," he whispered, barely audible.

"Say it louder, like you mean it."

"I'm sorry," he repeated.

"That's better," Lena said. "I don't want to hear about this happening again. Now go up to your rooms and do your homework. Both of you. I want to talk to your mother for a while."

They disappeared up the stairs and Lena turned again to Rachel just as Nathan came into the room.

"Nathan," Lena said, "please sit down for a minute so we can talk."

Nathan knew what was coming. The great negotiator was here. He'd been through it all before and wished that Lena would stay home. He knew what the problem was better than she did, but he sat down anyway.

"Make it quick," he said, "before a customer comes in."

"This is more important than customers, Nathan, it's about your family."

"Lena," he said, "I know all about my family. I work for them. I support them. They have enough to eat and they have clothes on their backs. What else do you want?"

She looked at her brother. "There's more to a family than food and clothes. Look at Sidney. Have you ever talked to him about the way he treats Edith? Do you ever talk to him about anything?"

Nathan sighed. "What's there to talk about? He's just a boy growing up and wants to play outside. Besides, I have the store to take care of. Without the store, we have nothing – no food, no clothes, no house to live in. That's important."

"Of course the store is important, but it's also important for the family to know there's a man around who cares about them, who cares about what they do, who cares enough to reward them when they're good, or punish them when they're bad."

"Reward them," Nathan said, "with what, money?"

"I don't mean that kind of reward. I'm talking about a kind word, a little attention and affection, a little guidance, make them feel important, and I mean Rachel too. She cooks meals for you, makes the bed, cleans the house. Acknowledge her," Lena paused before saying the next words. "Love her – it will be good for you, too."

Nathan kept his eyes on the table and was relieved to hear a customer come into the store. "You can't manufacture feelings," he said. "I do the best I can. If it doesn't measure up to your rules and regulations, I can't help it." He stood up. "Give my regards to Dave."


Sidney finished his homework and asked his mother if he could go out and watch the older boys playing ball on 7th Street.

She allowed him to go out if he promised to come home to dinner as soon as he was called. Promising to do so, he bounded outside and ran around the corner to 7th Street. He ran across the street and sat down on the steps of the Ohel Jacob Synagogue to watch a game of wallball now in progress.

Four boys in their teens were playing, two in the field, two batting. The street was the infield. The sidewalk and row homes opposite the synagogue were the outfield.

"Okay, Bobby," shouted the boy in the street. "Let's go."

Bobby, thin and tall for his 14 years, aimed the ball at a horizontal angular projection that ran across the synagogue wall. It struck the upper slope of the projection and rebounded high into the air. The infielder caught it for an easy out. The second batter aimed and let loose. This time the ball hit the point of the projection and shot past the infielder's outstretched hand. It went directly to the outfielder who pocketed it for the second out.

"You'll have to do better than that," he shouted.

"Okay," answered Bobby. "How about this?" The ball hit below the point and bounced into the street. It evaded the infielder's grasp for a single.

"Man on first," Bobby yelled. "Come on, Sammy," he urged his partner. "Keep it rolling." But Sammy grounded to the infielder for the third out.

"Samuel Gold!" A woman's head protruded from a 2nd floor window down the street. "I need you here right now."

Sammy kicked the sidewalk. "Can't it wait 'til after the game, Mom?"

"I need you right now!"

"Damn it," he murmured. "Okay, I'm coming. See you guys later."

Bobby looked at Sidney. "Hey, Reds, you wanna play?"

Sidney was the only redhead around. "Sure," he replied, looking both ways before stepping out into the street. "Where do you want me to play, infield or outfield?"

"Ya ever play before?"

"No."

"Then play the outfield. Not too many get that far. I'll take care of the tough drives. My name's Bobby, what's yours?"

"Sidney."

"I like Reds better," he said.

Sidney stationed himself on the far sidewalk, happy to be out of the street should his mother or Edith come looking for him.

The game was held up as a No. 65 trolley car rattled past, along with two or three automobiles behind it. A horse and wagon rounded the corner of 7th and Columbia, but it was moving slowly and the game resumed.

The first ball came off the wall low and to the right. Bobby lunged but couldn't get it. Sidney moved alertly to the right, leaned as far as possible while running and snared the ball in his right hand on the third bounce.

Bobby cheered ecstatically. "Great catch, Reds. That was a good back-up job."

Sidney's face flushed with pride and he tried to contain his excitement. He felt exhilarated. This was a new experience for him. He felt like one of the guys.

The second batter improved his aim somewhat and the ball flew off the top of the angle, higher than the first ball. It maintained this path, sailing over Bobby's outstretched hands and was still climbing when it reached the outfield. Sidney leaped as high as he could, stretched up with his left hand and came down with the ball. Bobby jumped up and down.

"You're my man, Reds," he yelled. "Yes, you are. Two in a row! Boy, you can play with me anytime."

"Beginner's luck!" shouted the player whose ball Sidney had just caught. "Just plain beginner's luck."

"I'll take that kinda luck every day," Bobby answered. "Stop complainin' and play ball!"

The third ball was a high pop-up that Bobby caught easily for the third out. They changed places with the other team.

Bobby took the ball and threw it as hard as he could at the angular projection. It hit the wall a little low, ricocheted off the sidewalk, and took an odd bounce off the trolley tracks, hitting the fielder in the chest and bouncing away.

"Man on first," Bobby shouted. "O.K., Reds, let's see what you can do."

Sidney held the ball in his right hand and studied the wall. From what he had seen while watching the game earlier, he theorized that one point of contact, and only one point, would give the maximum distance for energy expended. Any place else could be used effectively for line drives or tricky grounders, but if a player wanted to go for all the marbles, the lower part of the angle where it met the point was the spot to be targeted.

Sidney stared at the wall as the horse and wagon prodded slowly past.

"Come on, Reds," shouted the infielder. "I'm falling asleep out here."

Sidney's arm whipped around in a sideways motion and the ball hit the target exactly, taking off on a flight that left no doubt about where it was going.

The fielders watched as the ball soared over their heads, hit the brick wall of the house behind them at the second story level and rebounded into the street and back to Sidney who was as surprised as anybody else.

Bobby was beside himself. "What a shot!" he shouted. "That's one of the best hits I ever saw. You sure you never played this game before?"

"Honest," Sidney answered. "This is my first time. Lucky, I guess."

"Lucky or not, we're ahead 3-0."

Bobby was next and lined one to the outfielder for the first out.

"O.K., Reds," he said, "let's see ya do it again."

"Lottsa luck," yelled the outfielder, as he threw the ball in to Sid.

"He shot his load last time. He's finished."

Sidney was being taunted and he loved it. He was playing the game and was willing to accept all remarks, both friendly and otherwise. It was the mark of a professional to stay calm under pressure.

With the ball in his hand, he again studied the wall, concentrating on the target.

"Bobby," the infielder shouted impatiently, "Would ya kick him in the ass or something? We ain't got all day!"

Sidney's arm again whipped around in a graceful sideways motion. The ball flew from the wall and followed the same general route as the first one. Bobby was cheering and clapping while the players in the field watched the ball zip over their heads. But this time, the ball didn't rebound onto the sidewalk after it reached the house behind them. There was an unpleasant sound of glass breaking as the ball crashed through the second floor window and disappeared inside. Bobby's cheering abruptly ceased. There was silence. The three boys fled up 7th Street and vanished across Columbia. Sidney was paralyzed, frozen to the spot, too frightened to run. He had broken his first window.

A large man with a menacing look on his face came out of the house, crossed the street and confronted him. "Did you break that window?" he shouted, looking down at the terrified little 12 year old.

Tears were running down Sidney's face and loud sobs rose up from his throat. He couldn't answer. He hadn't moved one inch from where he was standing. He was thinking that this was where his life would end. He would die here. Edith would not have to chase him anymore. It was an inglorious end to his brief wallball career. His luck had already run out.


An unusual event occurred that evening at 705 Columbia Avenue. The four members of the Kurtz family were having dinner together. It was rare for all four to be at the table simultaneously, Nathan either busy with a customer or preferring to eat alone later. The crisis of the broken window, as moments of trial will do, had brought them together momentarily.

"Sonny," Nathan said. He had developed the habit of addressing him by that affectionate title, but it was never followed by any affection. Nathan was neither affectionate nor cruel. He never punished him and never praised him either.

"Sonny," his father repeated. "Do you know how many haircuts I have to give to pay for a broken window?"

Sidney had never thought of it, but now that it was brought to his attention, he hazarded a guess. At twenty-five cents a haircut, and the window costing about a dollar, it was simple mathematics.

"Four," he volunteered.

His father looked up from his soup. "That's exactly right," he said, and went back to eating. Sidney watched as his father took great gulps of the noodle soup his mother had made. His father pushed aside the bowl and took a helping of goulash.

"The window was bad enough," he added, "but the ball broke a figurine that was on a table next to the window. So now we're talking a lot of money. That figurine cost Mr. Beren three dollars." Sidney multiplied rapidly; twelve haircuts – sixteen haircuts altogether, he thought. "That's twelve haircuts," Nathan continued, "a total of sixteen haircuts because you threw a ball into a window."

"I didn't do it on purpose," Sidney said. "Once the ball hits that point, it's pretty tough to tell where it's gonna go." He went on to describe the mechanics of wallball.

"Very interesting," Nathan said, "but that's no excuse."

"It was an accident," Rachel said. "The boy was playing an innocent game. I'm sure it won't happen again."

Nathan was attacking the goulash when the tinkle of a bell announced the arrival of a customer. After several rapid swallows of food, he gulped down a cup of coffee, stood up, let out a loud belch and went into the store. The discussion was over. Rachel sighed.

"Sid, please be more careful in the future," she said. "Now let's finish our dinner."

I'll be more careful, Sidney thought. Next time, I won't stand there like a jerk. I'll run as fast as the other guys did. He helped himself to some goulash.

At 705 W. Columbia Avenue, the barber shop flourished as it had at 641 W. Oxford. Nathan's customers from Oxford Street followed him to Columbia Avenue, and the additional patrons kept him busier than ever.

Whatever else he might have been, Nathan was a good barber and an idea man, constantly looking for new ways to bring in more money. His ego demanded it and his lifestyle couldn't be maintained without it. For Rachel, the difficulty remained the same – getting enough money from him for food and clothes. And now she had to face him with still another problem.

Sidney was approaching 13 years of age. That meant a bar mitzvah, which required studying the Hebrew Torah. This couldn't be done without a teacher, and teachers wanted to be paid. Nathan wasn't exactly philanthropic.

She cornered him one evening while serving a late dinner.

"Teachers are expensive," he said. "Couldn't he just go to Hebrew school a couple of times a week?"

"He won't learn enough that way. It would take too long. Rabbi Landers said he needs at least 4 hours of concentrated tutoring each week if he's going to be ready for bar mitzvah."

"How much does our wonderful rabbi want for this?"

"He said he would do it for a dollar an hour. Four dollars a week."

"Four dollars!" Nathan shouted. "I thought rabbis do these things out of the goodness of their heart, like priests."

"Nathan, priests and rabbis are human, too. They have to eat just like us. Besides, it's a once in a lifetime thing. We would be the disgrace of the Kurtz family if our son wasn't bar mitzvah. What would everybody think?"

"Okay," he agreed. "I'll pay him at the end of each week. Tell him to do a good job."


After that disastrous wallball game, Sidney was hooked on sports. When his new friends saw that he could catch, throw and hit a tireball as good as any of them, he never lacked for a spot on the team.

A whole new world, from touch football to wireball, opened up for him, becoming an escape from the boringly long hours in school and the antiseptic life at home. His street name was changed from "Reds" to "Rusty," and "Sidney" was heard only from the family.

After school, he zipped hurriedly through his homework, if he looked at it at all, stopped for Yussel, then they both went dashing up 7th Street to take part in whatever games were going on. On weekends, weather permitting, he was out most of the day, returning only for lunch and to satisfy his thirst.

Then came the rabbi. Twice a week, rain or shine, usually after school, heedless of the game in which he was involved, Rabbi Landers would approach him steadfastly. He would stand on the sidewalk, stalking his prey, unwavering in purpose, until Sidney caved in to embarrassment.

"Why do you always come when I'm in the middle of a game?" he protested as the rabbi marched him up the street.

"There will be plenty of games," the rabbi would say, "but only one bar mitzvah."

Always adept in English class, he learned his Hebrew just as quickly, chanting his portion of the Torah over and over, accenting some phrases, lowering his voice on others. Rabbi Landers was a stern teacher, a young man in his mid-thirties and clean shaven. A sensitive, well-educated man, he was experienced in making friends with young students who felt that reading and chanting Hebrew stories infringed upon their play time.

It wasn't long before Sidney voluntarily left whatever game he was taking part in when he saw Rabbi Landers approach. After two months, the rabbi nodded his approval. After four months, he complimented him on his progress. After six months, Rachel was told that Sidney was ready, and on a predetermined Sabbath in October of 1937, Sidney Kurtz stood on the Bema at the Orthodox Ohel Jacob Synagogue, the same building where he was thrust into the world of sports, and with his father, mother and sister, aunts and uncles, and grandparents smiling from the congregation, he, in the eyes of God and his people, became a man.

**20**

The autumn of 1937 was mild, and the winter was no different. No prolonged cold spells nor heavy snowstorms plagued the eastern half of the country. In early February, temperatures climbed into the 50s and people were talking about an early spring. Sidney, Yussel and two friends were playing in the Ferguson school yard. The yard gates were usually closed and locked after classes ended and any youngsters wanting to play in it were forced to climb a six foot iron fence with sharp tips on each post. After several children received nasty gashes, the school board voted to leave the yard open after school and during daylight hours on weekends. This provided a place for the kids to play without them worrying about getting hit by a trolley car or an automobile. Although it wasn't enough space to accommodate a fraction of the children in the area, sometimes there was room enough for a touch football game.

They were throwing and kicking a football around with Charley Rosen, a slender, dark-haired boy with bushy eyebrows, and Danny Long, a fair-skinned, blond youngster and one of the few gentile boys in the neighborhood. Charley wasn't endowed with any particular athletic ability, but he was the fastest runner in school. Danny was always ready to play, but had a history of injuries due to his insistence of bucking against interference head on.

Four boys, three to four years older, approached and challenged them to a game of touch football. Rusty and Yussel exchanged glances with Charley and Danny, then looked back at the challengers. Each had at least six to ten inches in height over them and twenty to thirty pounds per man.

They were familiar faces to them, but the age difference shut off any social contact. They had their own gang and Rusty and Yussel hung with their own age group.

"They must be feeling a little bullyish today," Charley said.

"I'm no coward," Yussel offered, "but this could be suicide."

"Look at those big gorillas grinning," Danny said. "I'd like to wipe those smiles off their faces."

"Me, too," Rusty said. "If we don't get murdered first."

"I saw them playing the other day," Yussel said. "They're big,

126

but not too fast. Maybe we can work around them. Head to head contact with that bunch is out of the question. Should we take a vote on it?"

"Ya can't live forever," Charley said. "Let's give it a try."

"Yeah," Danny added. "I'm gettin' mad. Listen to them snickering to each other."

"That's what they want," Rusty said, "to goad us into playing. Okay, but let's play it cool and not take any chances. Let's talk about what we want to do before each play. We've got to outsmart them or we may never see our homes again."

After winning the toss and electing to receive, they huddled at their end of the school yard. It was to be touch football, no tackling, no rushing the quarterback and no unnecessary roughness, although who would be the judge of that was unclear.

"Now," Yussel said in the huddle. "Let's try to surprise them with a pass on kick-off. If you don't take a step after catching the ball you're allowed to pass."

"Good idea," Rusty said. "You've got the best arm, Yussel. You let loose and we'll try to outrun them. They won't expect a pass so soon. Don't anybody try to block, you'll get run over."

"Come on, big shots!" came a voice from the other end of the field. "You're not playing in Franklin Field"

"The gorillas are getting restless," Rusty said. "Okay!" he shouted. "We're ready! Now as soon as they throw the ball, spread out and tear down the field."

And that's what they did. Sidestepping the oncoming horde, they burst through into the clear. The ball was thrown straight and true and was gobbled up by Charley who leisurely stepped across the goal line – score, 6-0. They were jubilant.

"That was beautiful," Danny bubbled, slapping Charley on the back. "They're not laughing so hard anymore."

"No," Yussel agreed, "but they'll probably go crazy now."

"Ya think they'll try a pass, too?" Charles asked.

"Could be," Rusty answered. "After we throw to them, let's hold back and see what develops. If they run, we'll just have to slow down the interference the best we can, then maybe one of us can sneak in for the tag."

The three biggest bruisers surrounded the man with the ball and powered their way through to the goal line – score, 6–6.

"That was rugged," Danny said. "My ribs will be sore for a month. These guys are all bone and muscle."

"Yeah," Sidney agreed. "If they keep that up we'll all wind up in the hospital."

"Should we try another pass?" Charley asked, rubbing his bruised arm.

"They'll be looking for it," Yussel said. "What they won't expect is our trying to run it through. Let's pretend a run. We'll all go down the left side. That should pull them all over. Charley, you're the fastest runner. Break away to the right side and we'll try a long lateral."

"When are you guys gonna break up that huddle?" came the cry from the far end of the field.

Yussel again took the kickoff and ran down the left side of the field close behind his interference. Charley, as planned, broke away to the right while Sidney and Danny tried valiantly to give Yussel time to throw, getting knocked down in the process. At the last second, he threw a long lateral off to where Charley was waiting. The pass was complete. Charley nimbly side-stepped an opponent who came rushing at him and again leisurely crossed the goal line – score, 12–6. They were delirious. But they were paying the price. Rusty was rubbing his backside and Danny was examining a scraped knee.

"This isn't funny anymore," he said.

"It's their turn to receive," Charley said. "They'll probably run through us again."

"Tell you what," Rusty said. "Yussel, throw the ball high and deep. That might give one of us a chance to get around them before the interference forms up."

"Okay," Yussel agreed. "Everybody spread out."

The throw was high and far. Charley managed to outflank the interference while Rusty, Danny and Yussel did their best to slow them down, being roughly knocked aside and sent sprawling. This time Charley was able to get to the ball carrier and tag him.

"That was great," Yussel said, massaging his arm. "Now let's play them one on one on passes. Stick to your man like glue. Make it tough to complete a pass unless it's thrown perfectly."

"And if they run?" Rusty asked, flexing his aching arms.

"We'll do what we did before. Charley's the fastest. It's up to him to get in there for the tag."

The opposition was waiting impatiently. "Is that all you guys do is talk? Play ball!"

Their first play was a rush. Again Charley managed to get around them for the tag. Again Yussel, Danny and Rusty picked themselves up off the ground.

"I've got a terrific headache," Rusty complained.

"I hurt all over," Danny added. "We can't take much more of this."

"We can't quit now," Yussel said. "Besides, we're ahead 12–6."

The opposition then tried two passes. Only one was completed, but no touchdown. On fourth down they ran, barreling through a courageous defense, but again Charley raced around and tagged the ball carrier from behind. The gorillas had been stopped. It was first down. They huddled.

"They won't expect a run," Yussel said, "so let's fake one to the right. Rusty, you carry the ball. I'll fade off to the left for a lateral, then I'll throw a pass. Charley and Danny, criss-cross down the field. One of you will get the ball. If you're too well covered, move up for a short pass."

The short pass wasn't necessary. Charley was pushed around by two defenders, allowing Danny to break out into the open. Yussel put the ball right in his arms. Score, 18–6.

"They're getting rough," Charley said. "You're not supposed to push a receiver."

"They're frustrated," Rusty said. "It's gonna get worse."

"How much worse can it get?" Danny asked. "Every bone in my body hurts."

This time the big guys tried a pass on receiving, but the throw wasn't accurate and Danny picked it off and ran up the field behind Rusty who went head on with a gorilla rushing over to stop them. Rusty bounced off as if he hit a stone wall, but it gave Danny time to scoot across for another touchdown. Score, 24–6.

Rusty was slow getting up. Yussel looked at his friend and called the game. They were all in need of medical care.

"You're not quitting while you're ahead?" a gorilla taunted.

"No," Yussel answered, "while we're still alive. You guys are just too big for us."

"What're you complainin' about? You're ahead, ain't you?"

"Yeah," Yussel answered, helping his friend to his feet. "But look at the cost."

One of the gorillas came forward. "Good game, you guys. Ya did okay." He held out his hand to Yussel.

"Thanks," Yussel answered. "Maybe we'll do it again some day."

They limped out of the school yard and headed for home. They looked like losers rather than winners.

"That was something," Yussel said with a laugh. "Those big guys thought they were going to beat us today."

"They should've," Rusty said. "Most of them were about 17 or 18 and outweighed us about 30 pounds to the man."

"What they should've done and what happened are two different things. They counted on size and power. We out-thought them, out-ran them, out-maneuvered them. They didn't know if they were coming or going."

"You can say that again," Rusty said.

"They didn't know if they were coming or going."

Both of them burst out laughing.

"I'm glad we stopped while we were ahead," Rusty said. "I was getting tired."

"Yeah," Yussel agreed. "They were knocking us around pretty good."

"I guess they were getting mad," Rusty said. "How about coming out after dinner. It's not cold. We can sit on your uncle's bread box and talk some more about the game."

"Sure, see ya later."


Itkah looked Sidney up and down when he came into the dining room. "What on earth happened to you?" she asked. "Your face is scratched, your hands are dirty, your pants are torn."

"Just a football game, Grandmom."

"No kiss for Grandmom today?"

He came over and pecked her on the cheek.

"You call that a kiss, young man? Don't they kiss you around here?"

"Sure they do," Sidney lied. "All the time. Hi, Grandpa."

David came down the steps and hugged his grandson.

"What happened to you?" he asked.

"Football. It was a rough game."

"Good," David said. "It will make you strong. Did you win or lose?"

"We won against guys who were older and bigger. We had a ball."

David smiled. "We had a ball, eh? Where do you get such phrases? What does it mean - You had a ball?"

"We had a good time," Sidney answered. "You stayin' for dinner, Grandpa?"

"We are. Go wash your hands and tell us about how you beat those older, bigger guys."

It was an outwardly pleasant dinner with Sidney and Edith on one side of the table, David and Itkah on the other, and Rachel and Nathan occupying the end seats. Itkah helped Rachel serve the soup and then sat down to eat brisket and potatoes.

"How's business on the street?" Nathan asked Itkah, after Sidney related in detail the strategy that had brought them victory.

"About the same," Itkah answered. "I can only cover so much ground by myself. If I was 20 years younger, I would buy another horse and wagon and hire somebody to visit neighborhoods I can't reach, but I'm getting too old for that. Every day it's tougher to climb up and down that wagon, and I'm out in all kinds of weather. In fact, I want to get out of this business altogether. We looked at a small store at Franklin and Berks. We're going to open a general store, like the one we had before, but much smaller, something that David and I can handle on our own without worrying about the hired help."

"You're going to move?" Rachel asked.

"Yes," David said. "It's got three rooms and a bathroom in addition to the store. I'm looking forward to it. It's time we stopped running around and settled in one place. God willing, we'll spend the rest of our lives there."

"You'll be right around the corner," Edith said. "That's only two blocks away."

"And you can visit us whenever you want," Itkah answered.

"And one block from the school yard," Rusty said.

"Yes," David said, "Maybe we'll come up and watch you beat those older, bigger guys."

Everybody laughed. "How's the barber business?" Itkah asked, with a view to asking Nathan for some of the money he owed them.

"Could be better," Nathan replied. "You may have us as a neighbor. There's a larger store at 7th and Berks that I've been looking at. I have some ideas that will need more space and it looks perfect."

Rachel looked up in surprise. "When did you decide this?"

"I've been thinking about it for a while. It's a three story house with an apartment on the third floor. We'll use the first two floors and the rent from the family living on the third floor will help pay expenses."

"Thanks for letting me know," Rachel said. "It would have been nice if you talked things over with me."

"It's a good opportunity," he answered. "There's nothing to talk about."

"You could have told me," Rachel said. "I'm your wife. Don't you think I'm entitled to know what you're planning to do?"

"She's right," Itkah said. "You should talk things over. Rachel's not a stranger."

"What's there to talk about?" Nathan said. "I know the barber business. What can she say – that it's not a good idea and I shouldn't do it?"

"She's entitled to an opinion," David added. "Don't make her feel like an outsider. Itkah and I have always discussed things like this before making a decision."

"That's you and Itkah," Nathan said, his voice rising. "I don't need any advice or anybody telling me what to do. It's a good chance to make more money."

"Money that I never see," Rachel said.

Edith and Sidney were forgotten for the moment, both becoming uncomfortable and embarrassed by the turn the conversation had taken.

"Speaking of money," Itkah said, "You've never paid one cent towards the loan we gave you."

Nathan stood up. "I was wondering how long it would take you to get around to that. You don't trust your own son?"

"Nathan," David said, "it's because you're our son that we loaned you the money, but that doesn't absolve you from paying it back. It's only reasonable to expect a debt to be repaid. You've been doing very well as a barber."

"How do you know how well I've been doing? Are you here every day? Do you take care of my finances?"

David was about to tell Nathan that he wasn't doing too good of a job at it, but forced himself to be quiet. This was leading nowhere but to an argument. He suddenly realized the children were still at the table.

"All right, Nathan," he said, "have it your own way."

"That's what I intend to do," he said loudly, leaving the room and going into the store. Several moments later the front door slammed shut.

It was quiet around the table as they poked awkwardly at their meals.

Itkah looked at the children. "I'm sorry you had to hear this. We don't have any right to argue in front of you. Families argue all the time."

Rachel dabbed at her eyes and blew her nose. "Do your homework or go out for some air," she said.

Edith went upstairs and Sidney left to go to Yussel's house.

"I apologize, Rachel," Itkah said. "We've ruined a good dinner and exposed you and the children to unnecessary abuse."

"It's nothing new," Rachel answered. "It's always there just under the surface. This just brought it out. He doesn't care about anybody but himself."

"Again, I'm sorry," Itkah said. "I won't mention the money again. We'll just write it off as a bad investment. What do you think, David?"

"It's all right by me. I don't want the family turned upside down because of money. We've survived without it. We just won't give him any more."

"I'm the one who's sorry," Rachel said. "You don't deserve to be treated that way."

"Neither do you," Itkah replied.

"Look at it like this," David said, "out of six children, he's the only one that gives us trouble. That's not a bad average."

"Except that Rachel and the children are the victims."

"We'll be okay." Rachel said. "Please, I don't want you upset over me. We have a house to live in, clothes on our bodies, and food on the table. It could be worse."

"It can always be worse," Itkah said.


Sidney found Yussel sitting on the large bread box in front of his uncle's grocery store on the corner. It was a clear, mild evening. All the stores were closed with lights showing at windows up and down the street.

"My grandfather and grandmother are moving into the neighborhood soon," Sidney said as he sat down next his friend. "They're opening a small general store about two blocks from here."

"What's a general store?"

"I don't know. I think it's a store that sells a little bit of this and a little bit of that. They had one on Girard Avenue when I was smaller. My mother used to go there and I remember her taking me."

"That was some game today, wasn't it?" Yussell said.

"I was talking about it at dinner. My grandfather said he wants to come up and watch us beat those older and bigger guys. I never thought we would win."

"Hell, they thought they would run right over us. They won't be so confident next time. I mentioned it at dinner, too. My father wanted to know how we did it? Did your father ask you, too?"

Sidney hesitated. His father never talked to him about anything. He couldn't remember when his father spoke to him at all. It was the first time he had ever thought of it. How come Mr. Estrin talks to his son and my father doesn't talk to me, he wondered. Maybe I did something long ago to make him angry, he thought. He was suddenly envious of his friend who could talk in a casual manner about the conversation he held with his father.

"Sure, he asked me," Sidney lied. "He kept questioning me about all the plays and strategy we used. He said it was wonderful."

"That it was," Yussell said.

They were silent for a moment.

"Look at that full moon," Yussel said. "Isn't it beautiful?"

"Yeah," Sidney agreed. "How come sometimes it's only half full or one-quarter full?"

"It has to do with the sun. My cousin, Elmer, has an astronomy book and it says that the moon doesn't have light of its own. It reflects the light of the sun, and the moon and the earth revolve around the sun at different speeds. If the earth, sun and moon were always lined up in a row, we would always see a full moon, but that's not the case."

"That's pretty smart," Sidney said. "Maybe I can borrow that book."

"I'll get it for you. I'm sure he wouldn't mind."

"What about the stars? I guess they shine from reflected light, too."

"Wrong," Yussell said. "The stars are all suns and have light of their own. They look so small because they're so far away."

"How far?"

"Very far. It takes their light years and years to reach us."

"Years and years!?"

"Yep. They're so far that the distance is measured in light years."

"What's a light year?"

"How long it takes light to travel in one year."

"One year?" Sidney was amazed. "That's far! Is all of this in Elmer's book?"

"Uh-huh. You'll read it yourself. There are all kinds of stars, large ones, small ones. One group of stars is called the Great Dipper because of its shape."

"Where is it? Can we see it tonight?"

"I don't know. The moon is so bright and the street lights don't help. Let's go over to that empty lot between Charley's Print Shop and the synagogue, where it's dark. Maybe we'll be able to see it from there."

They slid off the bread box and walked across 7th Street.

"It's dark here, all right," Sidney said when they arrived.

Yussell was looking up at the sky. "There it is," he shouted. "Look straight up and to the right a little bit. There are four stars that form a big square and four or five stars running down in a curve. The square is the bowl and the others are the handle."

For several minutes Sidney could not locate it, then suddenly the Dipper appeared just as Yussell predicted.

"I see it," he yelled. "It looks like the ladel my mother serves soup with."

"Great," Yussell exclaimed dramatically. "This will go down in history. You've just renamed the Big Dipper. It's now the Soup Ladle in the Sky."

They laughed until their stomachs hurt.

"Now, I'll show you something else I learned from the book. See the top stars of the bowl? Now, measure five times the distance between them to the left and that's the North Star."

"What's the North Star?"

"It's a star that stays in the same place all the time. Sailors use it to help them navigate. Columbus probably used it to discover America."

Sidney, using his forefinger and thumb measured the distance off to the left, and sure enough, there was the North Star. It was exciting.

"The world's a big place," he said softly, looking up at the universe around him. "It makes me feel small. I don't like that."

"Not much you can do about it."

"But where'd it all come from. How'd it all happen?"

"I don't know," Yussell said. "The Bible says that God created Heaven and Earth in six days and on the seventh he rested. That's good enough for me."

They were both quiet, thinking.

"It's so big," Sidney said. "Do you think God had any help?"

Yussell shook his head. "Nope, all by himself."

They looked up at the sky again. Thousands of twinkling lights looking like so many fireflies at distances beyond their comprehension, dimly aware that the flickering light they were looking at had traveled thousands of years to get here.

They walked slowly back to the breadbox.

"Quite a day," Sidney said. "A football lesson this afternoon and an astronomy lesson at night. Which did ya like better, beating those loudmouths or learning about the stars?"

"I'd have to pick beating the loudmouths."

"Me, too. The stars will still be there tomorrow."

At 14 years of age, Sidney was now allowed to go to the movies on Saturday with his friends if he told his mother which theater he was going to and approximately what time he would return. The Saturday matinee was designed to attract every child for blocks around, and the Astor Theatre, opened some years earlier, was 20 times the size of the Gem. With two balconies extending the full width of the building and halfway to the screen, the Astor was able to accommodate over 1200 people when full.

On this particular Saturday, the place was filled for a return of King Kong. All the children who were not old enough to see it in 1933 were packed into the Astor this day.

Sidney had walked with Bobby and Yussel to Franklin and Girard Avenue, a distance of five city blocks. It was a very warm, humid afternoon. Occasional raindrops splattered down from heavy skies, and lightning flashed on the horizon.

They each paid 15 cents for admission and were forced to find seats on the top balcony. The Astor was crowded with children running around and eating sandwiches brought from home. It was a noisy place, particularly in the upper balcony where the hot air from below remained uncirculated, inhaled and exhaled many times over. After some foot-stomping and whistling the matinee opened with a coming attraction, an "Our Gang" short featurette, a travelogue of the best amusement parks in the United States showing the steepest, longest, scariest chute-the-chutes in the entire world. Next was the 15 minute mini-story, fast becoming the most popular piece of programming in the country – the Saturday Matinee Serial.

By the time King Kong began, perspiration covered everybody's faces and travelled down their backs, soaking their shirts. The heat was not the only cause of damp faces and wet shirts. A family of bats had established residence in the rafters above the second balcony and their occasional, high pitched shrieks did not make the youngsters any more comfortable. Most children still believed the old fairy tale that if a bat landed on your head you would lose all of your hair, so it wasn't surprising to see many kids still wearing their caps, heat or no heat.

Finally, the dramatic musical score introduced the beginning of the movie and Sidney and his friends, as well as the rest of the audience, moved nervously to the edge of their seats. Several of the bats lent an eerie realism to the scene by flying around the theater. Nerves were already near the breaking point as their shadows flitted across Fay Wray as she hung, wide-eyed and limp with fear, on "Kong's" altar. Suddenly, there was a crashing noise in the jungle as something noisily approached.

Fay Wray's terror-filled screams resounded throughout the theater as the huge, hairy body of King Kong, towering three stories above her, pushed the trees aside to get a better look at his latest gift.

Up in the balcony, Sidney and his friends were shivering and shaking. A loud explosion sounded outside the theater as a furious thunderstorm broke out, and successive claps of thunder rocked the building. The screen momentarily went blank and when it came back on, the close-up of Kong's brute face staring greedily at his prize, Fay Wray's hysterical screams, the shadows of bats swooping across the screen, the booming thunder, and the shouting from around the theater, was more than this young audience could take.

Exit doors flew open and a mass of humanity burst out into the drenched streets. Sidney, Yussel and Bobby did everything but jump off the balcony. It was panic. They ran all the way home to the safety of their respective homes.

Sidney sped through the barber shop, received a surprised glance from his father, ran past startled customers waiting their turn, and stopped abruptly in the parlor where his Grandmother, Aunt Lena and his mother looked up at him with eyes opened wide. His hair was plastered to his head, he gasped for breath, and water ran freely from his body, quickly collecting into a puddle about his feet.

The women were shocked.

"What in the world?" Itkah exclaimed.

Lena was speechless.

Rachel finally found words. "Sidney, what are you doing here? You're supposed to be at the movies?"

His mouth opened but nothing came out. He couldn't say that King Kong scared them out of the Astor. No self-respecting American boy would admit to that.

"The film broke in the middle of the picture so they canceled the show," he lied.

"Did they give you your money back?" Itkah asked.

"Uh, oh sure," he lied again.

"Good," Rachel said. "Give it to me and I'll hold it for you for next Saturday."

Now what do I do, Sidney thought. He reached into his pocket while his brain worked furiously. "Oh, I forgot. This guy, Bobby, the same one I played wallball with, well, he bet me that he could beat me in a race home."

"So?" Lena asked.

"So," he continued, taking his hands out of his pockets and holding them palms up, "he won."

Rachel stood up. "You mean to tell me that you took a quarter from your father and bet it on a foot race?"

He shook his head. "But the movie would've gotten it anyway, so what's the difference?"

"The difference is," Lena said, "you threw a quarter away on a silly race. Do you think they grow on trees today?"

"Go upstairs," Rachel said. "Put your clothes in the wash and stay in the rest of the day. I don't know what your father will say about this."

Sidney started up the stairs, his feet sloshing in his sneaks. "Do ya have to tell him?"

"Go upstairs," she repeated.

When he was out of earshot, Itkah leaned forward and said in a low voice, "He doesn't have to know, Rachel."

"Yes," Lena agreed. "It might be better that way."


Dinner passed without further comment about the quarter, for which Sidney was grateful. After the store closed and his father left, he spent the evening reading. He sat in the corner of the store next to the table radio. It being Saturday with no school the next day, he was allowed to stay up until 10 o'clock, so from 8 until 10 he listened to some of the regular Saturday night programs. It was quiet in the store. The darkness surrounded him like a warm blanket, his eyes slowly closed. He awoke to his mother tapping him on the shoulder.

"It's time to go up to bed," she said softly.

He shut off the radio, went upstairs and fell into bed. Even in sleep, his dreams gave him no rest. There were gorillas and bats, storms and floods, family pointing accusing fingers at him. It was a fitful sleep that ended when he awoke to the sound of the front door closing. He jumped out of bed and looked at the clock in the window of the drug store across the street – 2 o'clock. Rubbing his eyes, he carefully opened his door and saw his father climbing shakily up the steps. Sidney closed the door and silently returned to bed. His father lurched past the door and went into the adjoining bedroom. Sidney turned his back and pulled the light cover over himself. His mother's hushed voice came through the latticed transom at the top of the wall, installed when the house was built to allow free air circulation from room to room. It was not designed for privacy. He turned his head. An urgent tone to her voice captured his attention.

"Please, Nathan, – drunk. Don't – the boy's – next door – hear everything."

Sidney's eyes were open wide. He was now fully awake. The rustling of clothes and the slight squeak of bed springs told of a not-so-silent struggle between his mother and father. Sidney knew little about how babies were created. He knew it required a man and woman. Beyond that he was as ignorant of the sexual act as he was of the Great Depression. Both were all around him. Neither was ever explained.

"Please, Nathan," his mother's voice pleaded. "Not like this."

He suddenly wished he was far away. Away from adults who hurt each other, who spit, who stayed out late and came home drunk.

"Nathan, for God's sake – think of the boy."

Sidney pulled the cover over his head, closed his eyes tightly and put his hands over his ears to shut out the sounds. He didn't understand what was happening. His father was doing something to his mother. Something bad. Why didn't God stop him?

He dug his head into the pillow. Soon the sounds ceased and it was quiet. Whatever it was, it was over. He tried to go to sleep.

It took a long time, but he slept and dreamed of football, wallball and the stars, of Yussel and his uncle's breadbox. They were talking about their parents, what they did when they were in bed. He dreamed of a house where his bedroom was separate, alone, with soundproof walls, and no transom. Then he slept soundly.

## 21

In the spring of 1939 Nathan moved his business and family to yet another site two blocks north to 7th and Berks Streets. It was his largest store to date, occupying the northwest corner. The second floor had three bedrooms, a bathroom and a glass enclosed porch in the rear overlooking the backyard and providing a good view of 7th Street which bordered the eastern side of the building.

The store dominated the first floor, and its large glass windows made it look larger and brighter. As on Columbia Avenue, the room next to the store was a combination eating room and parlor, with an ample kitchen next to it. Beyond that was the 10 ft. x 12 ft. fenced-in yard that had a small shed for storage. The rooms were larger than on Columbia Avenue and the Kurtz family soon settled down into a routine which, if not substantially different from that which preceded it, was at least infused with new energy by the fresh surroundings.

Nathan brought in three barber chairs, installed large mirrors that covered the entire wall facing the chairs, and laid new oil cloth down on the floor. He placed brass spittoons and ash trays at the usual strategic locations, a row of chairs along the window side of the store for waiting customers, and set down the familiar humpback radio on a small table against the end wall. It was his most ambitious effort so far and succeeded beyond even his own expectations. Not only did most of his steady customers follow him to Berks Street, but new customers were drawn by the size and cheerful ambience of the place.

The two experienced barbers he hired wore neat, white jackets, were required to wear bow ties, except during the heat of summer, and were instructed to be polite to everybody. Customers, no matter their social standing, were treated royally and responded accordingly. It seemed a bit too fancy for a working class neighborhood, but the people loved it. It wasn't long before men could be seen driving to "Nate's Barber Shop" from out of the area to be fussed over and pampered.

As the quality of his clientele improved, he installed a manicurist for both male and female customers in a far corner of the store, a luxury unheard of in neighborhood barber shops.

This was climaxed by the latest in hair growing systems, comprised of special shampoo, hair cream developed exclusively by a

New York manufacturer, and scalp energizer machines that clamped over the head, fastened around the forehead, and when turned on, massaged and drew on the scalp, creating a greater flow of blood, thus stimulating new hair to grow and dead hair to come alive.

As word spread that there was a barber who could grow hair at 7th and Berks Streets, his clientele soon included men from Wynnefield and other suburban areas.

The fact that Nathan's hairline was obviously going in the wrong direction did not discourage the hopeful enthusiasm of his customers. He rigorously applied the treatment to his own head, and after several months pointed proudly for anybody who would look, to the new hairs beginning to grow. This brought a chorus of amazement from the onlookers who agreed that fuzz was indeed growing where there had been none before. It was contagious. Some customers were reporting the same thing and the news spread like a prairie fire. The system was working.

Nathan gleefully added a fourth chair and another barber to handle the increase in business. He taught his three workers the art of the system and renamed them "hair specialists."

He loved being the focus of all this attention. Customers called for appointments. He opened an hour earlier and closed an hour later. Everybody was happy. The "hair specialists" were making more money than they had ever seen, the customers were happy, Nathan was delirious, caught up in his own creation and actually convinced he was growing hair.

Only behind the scenes did life remain the same. Rachel saw a little more money now, but still had to ask for it. After hours Nathan still left the house, usually returning after midnight.


The dimly lit back room of the Cat and Fiddle Cafe was just large enough to accommodate a card table, four chairs and a cot along one wall. The cot was for any customer who wanted to sleep it off before going home. Tonight it was empty, but at the card table a hot poker game was going full blast. A pile of bills filled the center of the table. It was late, 4:00 a.m. and Nathan would soon be opening his store. But he couldn't leave. He was $1,200.00 ahead and had another good hand, three sixes. Throwing down two cards, he received two in return, another six and a deuce. Deuces were wild. A dream hand, five sixes.

He bet $600.00, half of his winnings. Two players dropped out. The man opposite remained. His unshaven face was blank, his bloodshot eyes focusing alternately on his cards and then on the pile of bills on the table. He had lost heavily, but here was an opportunity to recoup all his losses and then some. But $600.00. He had started the game with $2,000.00 and now had only $700.00 remaining. He should leave, he thought, but not with this hand. Peeling off $600.00, he added it to the pile. "And another $100.00." He threw down his last bills.

Nathan hesitated. Is it possible, he thought, that this guy has a better hand? It can't be. Maybe it's a bluff. No. Guys around here don't bluff $700.00 worth. Anyway, the cards have been mine all night. This'll top it off. "I raise $500.00," he said.

The two dropouts sat frozen in their seats.

"Have a heart, Nate," the man said. "I'm out of money."

"You shouldn't be playing if you don't have enough money."

"I lost a bundle tonight. This is my last hand. If you push me, I'll have to borrow from somebody."

"I could pick up the whole works," Nathan said. But he couldn't afford to appear heartless. These were his customers. They spoke to other customers. Better to be the benevelant benefactor than a heartless scrooge. "Okay," he said, "open up."

The man laid down four threes.

Nathan smiled. "Five sixes," he announced triumphantly and reached for the pile.

Suddenly the door flew open and two uniformed policemen burst into the room. "Don't move, boys!" one ordered. "And leave that money alone."

Nathan recognized them. He knew every cop on the beat and they knew him. "Wait a minute, Johnson. What's this all about? You never bother us."

Johnson collected the money. "Not as long as we're taken care of. The Cat and Fiddle shouldn't miss any payments."

"But, Johnson, that's the biggest pot we've ever had. There must be two grand there."

"Yeah," the officer said. "Ain't we lucky?"


One summer day during a lull, Nathan left the store and returned driving a brand new Studebaker automobile. The Studebaker was part of a new breed of streamlined cars that were coming off the drawing boards in Detroit. Everybody crowded around to see it and touch it. It was a much better symbol of his store than the old barber pole that he had trashed, saying it was too old fashioned for modern times.

To walk from the store into the parlor was to step into another world, a world where Rachel and her children lived. She continued to cook and iron clothes and clean the house. They lived in the backwash of something they couldn't comprehend. Rachel had given up seeking affection, although Lena still made her regular therapy visits, counseling Rachel, trying to talk to Nathan, attempting to keep them from drifting further apart.

A product of the old country, where people were born, lived, married, raised families, and died without straying too far from home, Lena could not understand her brother's actions. He alone was the only Kurtz to be so Americanized.

He bore no resemblance to the youngster who came from Lutzin. His accent was gone, and his lifestyle was contrary to that of his brothers. He was completely wrapped up in a world they could not understand and didn't care to be a part of. They had brought their customs and lifestyles and family closeness with them. These were the first things Nathan had thrown aside.

Edith, meanwhile, had graduated from Girls High School and was sharpening her skills at typing and shorthand with a view to obtaining secretarial work. Sidney moved into the 9th grade at Northeast High School at 8th and Lehigh Avenue, walking the one mile to school and back home every day with Yussel and whoever else was walking up 7th Street at the same time.


In the Spring of 1939, with Europe ready to boil over and America emerging from the Depression, Sidney's prime concern was baseball. His friends were interested in the Fairmount Park Baseball League, and several teams were already forming from nearby neighborhoods. They decided to hold a meeting to see if enough boys were interested, then an application had to be sent to the League Commission. Scrounging money from their parents and using their weekly allowances, they purchased used uniforms, gloves, bats and baseballs from pawn shops or sporting good stores. They practiced at the school despite the ban on hardball playing, travelled out to Fairmount Park to play on a real baseball diamond, and were ready to start league play by June 1st.

The team needed a name as required by the League Commission and there was no lack of ideas. The usual animal names were submitted and were eventually turned down. "Jewish Bombers" was a courageous try but even at that young age they knew it wasn't a good idea to advertise your Jewishness.

At the eleventh hour, they received a donation from Bloom's Candy Store at 7th and Montgomery and the problem was solved. On June 1st, the Bloomers took the field against the first black baseball team any of them had ever seen – The Philly Movers.

It wasn't even close. The Movers, well coached and aggressive, stomped all over the Bloomers, 10-0. The Bloomers had a quiet trolley ride back home. They had a lot of work to do, and not much time to do it. That first season was a disaster, no wins, 12 losses, but there was one positive result. They learned from the jeering fans that Bloomers were women's underwear, so the name was shortened to Bloom's. It didn't help their game, but it cut down on the embarrassing insults from the sidelines.

Another plus came out of that season. Sidney discovered that despite his size, 5'6" and 150 lbs., he could hit, catch and throw as good as, and even better, than most of the other kids on the field.

He came through that first season with the best batting average on the team, and baseball became an important part of his life. After the season ended, it was decided to continue having meetings through the winter, and practicing as often as possible with the goal of fielding a better team next year. Over the protests of Mr. & Mrs. Bloom, the name was changed to Sidney and Yussell's favorite subject, The North Stars. Everybody liked it and it had a touch of class that Bloom's lacked.

## 22

Jean and Sylvia Dean, Sidney's cousins who helped look after him at 641 Oxford Street during those early years, prepared some cakes and tea for Itkah, David, Rachel, Edith and Sidney in their apartment on 7th Street, near Berks. Their mother, Rebecca, laid out a clean tablecloth while they moved enough chairs so everybody could sit and talk comfortably at the table.

Their parlor was small, and one wall was dominated by a piano which represented their only luxury. Sylvia, an attractive buxom girl of 30 with upswept black hair and pale skin, took voice lessons whenever she could afford them and possessed a strong operatic soprano. Jean, two years older than her sister and with the same black hair and pale complexion, but taller and more slender, played the piano accompaniment and, when she could be talked into it, Sylvia would entertain her guests with a song or two.

"Things don't look so good in Europe," David remarked as he dipped a cookie into the hot tea. His hair and beard were graying, and he had put on a few pounds around the middle, but otherwise carried his years well.

Itkah, on the other hand, seemed a little tired. The many years spent outdoors in all kinds of weather, raising a large family, the long hours at their store on Girard Avenue, the tragedy of the Depression, all had taken their toll on her. She had survived, but had paid the price. Now, with their small store on Berks Street, and the old age payments recently begun by the government, they tried to live as peacefully as they could. They had earned it.

"It looks like the Germans will roll right over poor Poland," Jean remarked.

"You can't make deals with men like Hitler," David said. "It's like talking to Stalin. You can't trust either one."

"Europe," Itkah snapped. "It never changes there. One country always fighting with another. They never learn. Why can't they leave their neighbors in peace?"

"That's the way with dictators," David said. "They have to show how big they are by picking fights with those around them. Just like a bunch of children. It's disgusting."

"Amen to that," Rebecca said. "But tell me what's going on in the family that I don't already know?" She was a short woman, a little overweight, with gray hair pulled back into a bun.

"With all due respect to my daughter-in-law," Itkah said, "the whole world knows what Nathan is doing."

"Do we have to talk about it now?" Rachel answered, with a nod towards the children.

"Mom," Edith said, "how could we not know?"

"Your father's a smart man," Itkah continued, "and of his business success, I'm sort of proud. I just wish he handled his personal life better."

"Me, too," Rachel said. "But let's talk about other things."

David sipped his tea. "Well, Herman's doing well in his cleaning store at Broad and Girard. Jake's got his tailoring business going, and Ellis opened his little jewelry store at 28th Street. I'm proud of everybody. We all managed to get through the Depression keeping body and soul together."

"I understand Sam is in New York," Rebecca said. "What's he doing there?"

"Wasting his time," David answered. "I wish Jake and Sam both would stop dealing in dreams. It's Communist Party this and Communist Party that. Propaganda and brainwashing. It will never work in America. Those ideas should have been left behind where they belonged, in Mother Russia. Revolution never did any good here except when we broke away from England."

"We?" Itkah said. "To hear you talk, you'd think you spent the winter with Washington at Valley Forge."

Everybody laughed, Sidney louder than anybody.

"That's funny, Grandpa," he said. "I didn't think you knew that much about American history."

"I don't. But I've seen enough to know that we have a good thing here, and that if a person wants to get an education and work hard he can do almost anything."

"You did okay without an education," Sidney said.

"We were lucky. But it just proves what I said. With a lot of effort, and I give most of the credit to my wife, it shows what a person can do here. Trying to make Capitalist America into a communist paradise – they might as well read the Ten Commandments to Hitler. Put that energy to use in a positive way. Communism. The word itself is sickening."

Everybody applauded and Itkah kissed her husband on the cheek. "My husband has become a real Yankee, Depression or no Depression."

"And I'm proud of it," David said. "Supporting revolution in America won't help the world one bit. No country is perfect, but we've got more here than we've ever had before."

"And I'm proud of you, Grandpa," Sidney burst out. "I think you and Grandma are the greatest."

The room was suddenly silent. Nobody ever heard him talk like that before. David and Itkah both came around the table and gave him big hugs and kisses.

"We love you, too," Itkah said, her eyes glistening.

David looked down at his grandson. "It looks like we have another patriot here."

"You bet," Sidney said, not really knowing what he was.

They resumed their seats and Rebecca brought out a pitcher of hot chocolate. David and Itkah each poured themselves a cup.

"What's Joshua doing these days?" Jean asked.

"You probably know that he and his family decided to stay in our old house," Itkah said. "We wanted to give it to him, but he threatened to move out if we didn't let him pay for it. So we asked half what it's worth and put it into the bank for a rainy day. They have two boys and a girl, and I think that's all they want. He says he's getting too old to raise any more children."

"What about the coal business?" Sylvia Dean asked.

David put his cup down. "He's not using horses and wagons any more. He operates three trucks and has his eye on the coal yard at Front and Berks. The owner's talking about retiring and Joshua would like to buy him out."

"He's a wonderful person," Itkah said proudly. "They don't come any better."

"Hannah got herself a good man," Rachel said.

"She surely did," agreed David. "Sid, I hear you're playing baseball in some kind of league. Is that true?"

"Sure is, Grandpa," Sidney said quickly. "It's the Fairmount Park League at 33rd and Dauphin."

"Do they pay you?" Itkah asked.

"'Course not, Grandma. We're only amateurs. It's not the big leagues."

"Do people come out to watch you?"

"Sure. We usually get a couple hundred people sitting on benches and folding chairs."

"Then you should be paid," she insisted.

"We pass the hat around at the end of each game and the teams split the take"

"How much do you collect?"

"Usually a few dollars. One Sunday, a man put a ten dollar bill into the hat."

"Ten dollars," Itkah exclaimed. "My goodness! I'm going to look into this baseball business."

Sidney smiled. "I'd like to see you in a baseball uniform, Grandma."

"So would I." David chuckled.

"Sylvia," Edie said, "how about a song for a change of pace? I see some Yiddish songs on the piano."


On a Sunday in mid-September, after hanging out at Bloom's Candy Store most of the afternoon, Sidney crossed over the trolley tracks and walked up 7th Street to his house. The block was a conglomeration of stores and residences. There was a pharmacy on the corner, followed by two brick row homes, then a dairy store, a shoemaker and a dry goods store, more row homes; Wasserman's grocery, more row homes, a bakery, Steiner's Beauty Parlor, the local butcher and then the fruit store on the southwest corner of 7th and Berks Street. When Sidney crossed the trolley tracks on Berks Street, he was home.

It was late afternoon by now and the store was blessedly quiet. He looked forward to having dinner and then sitting down next to the humpbacked radio in the far corner of the store to listen to his favorite Sunday night programs.

His father wasn't home, nothing unusual for a Sunday afternoon, so it was just his mother, Edith and himself at the dinner table. The chicken soup, another favorite of his, was always a welcome sight any time of the year. It was followed by stuffed cabbage, with string beans and mashed potatoes, and a bowl of strawberry jello that Edith made. He left the table and was about to go into the store when he noticed some clothes on the sofa with a face mask on top.

"What's this?" he asked, picking up the mask.

"What's it look like?"

Sid examined it again. "Looks like a mask."

"Quite perceptive," Edith said. "You passed the first test. Now, how about the rest?"

"Looks like a costume."

"Very good. You're pretty sharp today."

"And you're not so funny today. Who's the costume for?"

Edith looked at her brother and smiled, "It's for Mom."

"You're kidding."

"I'm not!" Edith snapped. "Mom's going to wear that outfit tonight."

Sidney looked first at the costume and then at his sister.

"You're kidding."

"And you're in a rut. What makes you think I'm joking?"

"Well," he hesitated, "I can't see Mom in a costume, that's all."

"That's the trouble," she said. "We can't see her in anything but the stuff she wears cleaning and cooking, with an apron tied around her waist. While you're out playing, Mom's busy making the meals, shopping and keeping the house clean. Tonight's going to be different. We're going to dress her up so she can have a good time at the party."

"What party?"

"The Halloween costume party at the Cat & Fiddle Cafe."

Sid put the radio programs aside for the time being. "The Cat & Fiddle Cafe? That's where Pop hangs out all the time."

"That's right," Edie said. "And if I know Pop, he's going to want to know who this woman with the beautiful figure is."

Sidney thought for a minute.

"You talking about Mom?"

"You catch on fast, brother of mine. Your Mom's going to knock their socks off tonight."

Sid was perplexed. "Mom's gonna do this?"

"In case you haven't noticed, our mother is put together very nicely, but we never see it because to us she's just our housekeeper and maid. Tonight Cinderella's going to the ball loaded for bear."

Sidney forgot all about his Sunday night programs.

"Did Mom say it's okay?"

"Not at first, but I talked her into it. Mom," she yelled, "are you ready yet?"

Rachel came in from the kitchen, her face red with embarrassment. "I still don't think it's a good idea. Your father's going to be awful mad."

"So what?" Edie said. "Can things be worse? It'll help make up for all the times you've been mad at him. Sid, get out while I dress Mom."

She pushed him into the store, but not before he took a close look at his mother. She wasn't fat and he didn't notice any excess weight around her hips and middle. Her legs were not heavy, nor were they thin, and there was a healthy bulge under her blouse which he hadn't seen before. With her pink cheeks and eyes sparkling with anticipation, there appeared before Sidney a person he had never seen before, an attractive woman wanting only acceptance and recognition.

If this revelation weren't enough, when Edith called him back into the room, he was stunned at the sight. His mother looked like a Hollywood glamour girl, with high heels, tight fitting white pants, a tight blouse that accentuated her breasts, a golden mask that covered her face except for her eyes, nose and a heavily lip-sticked mouth, and a white, silky scarf tied attractively around her head to hide her hair. She was sleek, sexy and desirable.

"Well?" Edith asked. "What do you think?"

Sidney was in shock. "I can't believe it. Is that Mom?"

Rachel threw back her head and laughed. "It's me, Sidney. I can't believe it either. Do you think your father will recognize me?"

"Only if you talk," Edie said, "so it's no talking once you're inside. Promise?"

"Yes, yes, I promise. Goodness gracious. I better get going before I lose my nerve."

"I still can't believe it's you," Sidney said. "It's like looking at a stranger."

"That's how I felt when I looked in the mirror. What time is it?"

"Eight-thirty."

"Good," Edie said. "The party started at eight so it should be crowded by the time you get there. Wear my thin coat to cover up until you're inside. Come on, Mom, it's getting late. Remember, no talking."

They pushed her out of the front door.


The Cat & Fiddle Cafe had been a furniture store before being converted to a liquor and food establishment by three men. One of them, unbeknownst to his family, was Nathan Kurtz. They had installed a circular bar, a modest stage for entertainment, and small round tables and chairs, some of which were put aside to make room for nightly dancing. Music was mostly supplied by a nickelodeon, except on weekends when a piano player or a three-piece band performed. Aspiring stand-up comedians and singers willing to brave the noise and smoke, hoping to draw attention to their hidden talents, took their turns at the microphone with limited success.

It was a noisy place, but popular with people looking for drink, food and escape from their everyday problems. The business was conducted legally to draw the least attention from the authorities, except for crapshooting and card games in the back room.

It was this raucous world that Rachel Kurtz was about to enter.

Standing outside on the steps, with the noise and music resounding from within, she hesitated as she reached for the door. This was crazy, she thought. What can be gained by it? Better to go home and forget about this foolishness. But she had promised. And Edie had gone to the trouble of preparing the costume and dressing her. She couldn't turn back now.

Pushing open the door, she stepped inside, closed the door behind her, hung her coat on the rack, and stood there waiting for whatever might come. She didn't have long to wait.

Balloons hung from the ceiling. The bar off to the right was packed with men and women, and men looking for women. There wasn't an empty table in the place and several couples were attempting to dance in the restricted space allotted them. Few people wore costumes, those that did being women. Nobody was wearing a mask. The band finished their song and Rachel was astonished to see her husband get up on stage and take hold of the microphone. He started to introduce the next singer but never finished the sentence.

He stared at the delicious looking creature that had just entered the cafe. She was standing apparently alone and unattended. Other eyes, curious as to what interrupted the introduction, followed his gaze, until, one by one, nearly everybody was looking at her.

She appeared, through the haze and smoke, like a mannequin, silent, sultry, inviting and remote. Nathan finished his introduction and dashed towards her. She started to panic, thinking he recognized her. She was afraid they were going to have a big argument in front of everybody.

"Hello," came his familiar voice. "I'm Nathan, one of the owners of this place. Are you here by yourself?"

Rachel was both relieved and shocked. Relieved to realize that he had no idea who she was, and shocked to discover that he was an owner. So this is where the money's been going, she thought. She struggled to remain silent. Nice of you to talk it over with your wife, you skunk.

"You alone?" Nathan repeated.

Rachel nodded her head.

"Well, never let it be said that Nathan Kurtz let a woman remain unescorted in the Cat & Fiddle. Would you like to dance?"

She was about to shake her head, but stopped. It had been so long since she danced, especially with her husband.

He took her hand and led her to the dance floor. Nathan was dressed in a dark blue suit, white shirt and bow tie, as befitted the owner and master of ceremonies of the Cat & Fiddle.

He's really not a bad looking man, Rachel thought, as he put his right arm around her and pulled her close. The band was playing "East of the Sun", and Nathan danced gracefully around the small floor, pulling her tightly against his body. Rachel found herself enjoying the dancing, but didn't appreciate the way he kept moving his leg between hers and suggestively rubbing his hardness against her. You are a skunk, she thought. The desire to tear off her mask and shout out her contempt for him in front of everybody was overpowering, but the thought of facing the consequences when he came home put an end to that idea. So she danced as she hadn't danced before, with men looking at her hungrily and the women envious of the attention she received. But she never spoke.

When Nathan was needed elsewhere, he left her, saying, "Don't dance with anybody else."

Then other men approached her to dance, hold her close, pressing her with their bodies, offering her drinks and promises.

It was a dizzy whirl, dancing with every available man, and promising via nod of her head to go to bed with all of them, including her own husband, who always managed to muscle his way to the front of the line.

Their hands, as well as his, roamed over her body while they pleaded with her to speak or to remove her mask. As the hour grew late and liquor was making her lovers more aggressive, she was afraid that in their drunken condition one of them would pull off the mask. She pointed to the ladies room, circled around, picked up her coat and left by a rear door, grateful for the fresh air that greeted her.

She quickly slipped into her coat, removed her mask and scarf, shoving them into a pocket, and hurried down Columbia Avenue to 7th Street and then home. She laughed all the way. It had been a night she would never forget. She could picture them looking all over the place for her. As mysteriously as she had arrived, so had she disappeared. It had been marvelous.

Edith and Sidney were waiting up for her when she came in breathless.

"Well?" Edie asked. "How did it go?"

Rachel sat down on the sofa and removed her high heels.

"Wonderful," she answered. "Too wonderful. I had more propositions from your father than in all the years we've been married. Nobody knew who I was, but everybody wanted to. I danced with every man who asked me, and promised to sleep with most of them. But I did have the time of my life, even if it showed up Nathan for what he is." She wiped a sudden tear from her eye. "I saw things tonight that a wife shouldn't have to see, that her children shouldn't have to hear."

She rushed up the steps leaving Edie and her brother standing awkwardly in the living room.

## 23

Sidney was playing touch football on 7th Street when he noticed that he was losing control of his left leg. It didn't react as quickly as he wanted, and after falling down twice, he told his friends he wasn't feeling good and went home.

It was an effort, dragging his unwilling leg behind him. He limped up 7th Street, into the store, climbed the steps one at a time, dropped into bed and fell asleep. When Edie knocked on his door for dinner, he said he wasn't hungry. She reported back to her mother, who came upstairs to see for herself what was wrong.

"I don't feel good, Mom, and I'm having trouble walking. My left leg feels weak."

Although the target of many childhood ailments, Sidney never complained about his health and was not prone to passing up a good meal. Rachel called Dr. Berk whose office was halfway up the block and he came to the house after his afternoon visiting hours were finished. Sidney had a slight temperature and when Dr. Berk asked him to walk, he managed a few steps, barely able to put any weight on his left leg.

"Before I make any definite statements," Dr. Berk said, "I'd like to call in an orthopedic doctor to look him over. I'm reluctant to make a diagnosis that I'm not positive about. I'm going to ask Dr. John from St. Christopher's to come down and take a look. I think he may be more familiar with these symptoms."

Two hours later, Dr. Rutherford L. John was shown into Sidney's small bedroom. Dr. John, a large husky man standing 6'4", dominated the room. Sidney's temperature had risen to 103 degrees and when he was asked to walk, he only managed to take two steps and collapsed. He struggled back into bed, frustrated and embarrassed. Dr. John examined his left leg, asking him to raise and lower it against the pressure of his hand.

When he was finished, Rachel asked him, "Do you think he might have hurt it playing ball?"

Dr. John looked down at her. "We mustn't fool ourselves, Mrs. Kurtz. As much as I don't like to say it, your son has Infantile Paralysis."

She put her hand to her mouth. "Polio?"

"That's it. I'm calling for an ambulance. He'll have to go to the Municipal Hospital for Contagious Diseases for a three week isolation stay. That's when it's the most contagious."

Within an hour the ambulance arrived and a husky attendant carried him downstairs. The neighbors had crowded around at the first sight of the ambulance and there was a murmur of voices as he was carried out of the house. He managed a smile and a tired wave to those standing around. The doors were closed and the ambulance drove away, taking Sidney from his home for three weeks with no visitors except doctors and nurses.


The Philadelphia Municipal Hospital for Contagious Diseases, with its grey stone walls and few windows seemed more like a prison than a hospital. Dreary and gloomy, especially to children not allowed any visitors at all, the prospect of a three-week stay was not very pleasant.

With only one other boy in the room, time dragged by slowly. Sidney marked the days off, one at a time on the wall beside his bed. A daily visit from a doctor or nurse to check on his condition helped break the monotony, and during the third week, he was told the good news. It wasn't the paralytic form of polio, but many muscles up and down his left leg and body were affected. In time, with exercise and treatment, he should be able to walk, if not normally, then without crutches or a cane.

The isolation period dragged to a close and he left the hospital on crutches, accompanied by his mother who was waiting happily with a taxi.


The year that followed was one of recuperation, therapy and confinement to the house. At first, meals were brought up to his room, but soon, with the doctor's permission, he was allowed to carefully come down stairs. This saved his mother and sister the inconvenience of having to carry a tray of food up to his room, and it improved his muscles and provided him with some exercise.

Therapy consisted of bedrest, certain leg exercises to help restore muscle strength, and leg massages administered by a nurse who apparently got her kicks by running her hands a little higher up than necessary to rub a muscle that was not affected and needed no therapy whatsoever. It was a new experience for Sidney and like any red-blooded American boy would do, he suffered through it in silence. He found himself looking forward to her twice weekly visits, when she applied a lotion to her hands, and slid them slowly up his leg, massaging his erection as she asked him how much he liked it. He would climax into her hands as she moved them up and down. She never sought intercourse, but seemed to get pleasure from his sounds of enjoyment.

After four months of therapy, her visits ended, the doctor having decided massages were no longer needed. She had been a pleasant interlude, and an introduction for him into the shadowy world of sensuality and desire.

As he settled into the routine of a recovering invalid confined to his house, certain times of the day became more significant. He shared the breakfast table with his mother, occasionally his father, and Edie who now had a permanent job with the Philadelphia Board of Education. Lunch he ate alone or with his mother, and dinner was a repeat of breakfast, with Edie talking about her work and Sidney relating how he spent his time, which didn't vary much from one day to the next.

Before breakfast, he sat at his 2nd floor bay window overlooking 7th Street watching people go to work, chatting and waving to his friends on their way to school and answering their questions about his illness.

He gave considerable thought to baseball. He really didn't care much about school. It didn't hold his interest and there was nothing in the curriculum to motivate him. He would much rather cut his classes and go see a good movie, which he had begun to do on a regular basis before being struck down.

He knew he wasn't paralyzed, but his left leg was so weak he seriously doubted if he would ever run the bases again. That bothered him. He loved baseball. From the first day that his team played on a regulation ballfield in Fairmount Park, he had felt that this was his sport. Swinging a bat, running the bases, or chasing down a fly ball came as naturally to him as breathing. Stepping onto the diamond became the most pleasurable experience that he could think of, although the nurse came in a close second. When the pitcher threw the first ball, nothing else mattered until the last out was made in the 9th inning.

As with everything else in life, too much of anything could become tiresome, and it soon became apparent that if his recovery necessitated his being confined to the house, he would have to find some activity to help him get through each day. His English teacher at Northeast High, Mr. Connors, who had urged him to think about a career in education, sent him a gift of the Complete Sherlock Holmes Mysteries. It was a timely stroke of luck. As with baseball, one step inside the first story, "A Study in Scarlet", and he was hooked.

The twists and turns of the plot and the proficiency of Holmes to observe and find solutions from the tiniest clues enthralled him. Sidney was drawn into the fog and mist of 18th century London and followed Holmes, magnifying glass in hand, into its shadowy corners.

What a gift to be able to write like that, he thought. He knew Doyle had conceived the idea of mystery writing when, as a young doctor, he waited in his office for patients who never came. Why couldn't I do the same? Sidney thought.

He had no pretensions of being another Conan Doyle, but he liked to write and Mr. Connors always said he had a flair for composition.

He asked Edie to get him a large tablet and he wrote. Every day, for two to three hours, he wrote stories of murder, of sports, whatever came into his mind, but all fiction. He never drew from real life. Being a youngster, he couldn't appreciate the drama of his life around him, his parents and grandparents, his own illness, the problems of the average, everyday Joe who was out there scratching and pawing to survive in society's wilderness.

He didn't have the perception to see that which was closest to him, so he fashioned fictional lives and inserted them into artificially created stories. If nothing else, it gave him something to do through the long days of his recuperation.

Sidney, though still not allowed outside, was getting stronger and the doctor gave him permission to roam the house as he pleased, alternating between crutches and a cane. The glass-enclosed porch in the rear, his prized daytime retreat, had been equipped with a small electric heater, while the little humpback radio was his after store hours favorite. He would occasionally sit unobtrusively in the corner when the store wasn't busy, and listen to the daily serials – The Lone Ranger, The Green Hornet and The Shadow.

Late on a cold January day, snow began falling after lunch and Sidney took his latest story, "The Airliner That Never Landed", and made himself comfortable on the porch sofa which had seen much better days. It was chilly up there, even with the heater operating, but he liked snow. If he couldn't be out in it, at least he could watch it. The outside temperature was well below freezing and the snow lay where it fell, placing a white coating over the street and sidewalks. Everything looked so much cleaner when it snowed, even the backyard and the trash cans became part of the picturesque winter scene.

Across 7th Street was the only house on the block with a garden. It was a large three story building with the garden alongside, fronting on both 7th Street and Berks Street. During the summer, it was green with shrubbery and trees, reminding him of the family's infrequent trips to Krekstein's Farm in Collegeville when he was younger. Now with the snow falling, it looked like the pictures of rural New England that he had seen in a National Geographic magazine that Edie had given to him.

He was wearing a warm sweater and had his Sherlock Holmes Mysteries beside him when he tired of writing. He heard his mother washing the dishes directly below him while his father and his barbers attended several customers who decided to come in before the storm got worse. Even the trolley car looked different as it passed by with the snow blowing off its roof and the usual rattling noise somewhat muffled by the snowfall.

He had written for about a half hour, but his hands were getting cold so he opened up Sherlock Holmes, put his hands in his pockets and started to read.

As he glanced out at the snow, which was now coming down heavier and blowing against the porch window by an increasing northeast wind, he was surprised to see a brown paper bag fly over the fence and land in the yard. Apparently somebody walking down 7th Street had tossed it into the yard and continued on his way. Why would anybody throw a paper bag into their yard?, he thought.

Then the light blinked on and everything was clear. Many of his father's friends were shady characters and greasy looking, cigar smoking local politicians who came into the store on Sunday to play cards, smell up the store with cigar smoke, and prevent him from enjoying a quiet day next to the radio. Some of these characters were numbers writers who took bets on the horse races.

He had heard the phrase "drop zone" mentioned to his father at these Sunday card games. His father had answered, "how about the back yard?" each time. The bags were filled with numbers to be turned over to whoever distributed the winners to the writers, who in turn passed them back to their lucky customers. It was all illegal, and the local police knew about it, as well as the identity of the offenders, but if the right amount of money was placed in the right hands, they looked the other way. An occasional arrest was made for appearance's sake, but for the most part these people tended their trade undisturbed.

Ordinarily, Sidney would have gone back to his reading and not thought anymore about it, but two things were steering him to take action. One, he hated those slobs who filled up the store on Sundays and prevented him from enjoying some of his favorite radio programs, and the thought of getting back at them was tempting. And two, what would Sherlock Holmes do in this situation? Would he turn his back on this case, as slight as it was? No, regardless of how unimportant, he would pursue it to the end and teach these men that nobody is above the law.

He put down his book, grabbed his cane, and hobbled, one step at a time, downstairs and poked his head into the kitchen. Good, he thought, his mother was out. He opened the door to the yard, breathed in the strange odor of fresh, cold air, reached out with his cane and pulled the bag closer to the door. Extending his arm, he picked up the bag, shoved it into his pocket, struggled back up the stairs onto the porch, sat down on the old sofa, and waited with throbbing temples for something to happen.

He didn't have long to wait. He heard a door open and saw his father looking around the yard, first in one corner, then another. He moved the trash cans and looked in the shed and returned to the house red-faced. His excited voice began resounding through the house. Rachel came up from the cellar.

"Did you see a brown paper bag?" he shouted.

"Of course I didn't," she answered. "Do you think I wouldn't give it to you if I did?"

"It should be in the yard and it's not there," he shouted angrily.

"If it's not there, it's not there," she said. "Maybe they didn't deliver it."

"It's been delivered," Nathan replied. "He knocked on the window a minute ago."

"Did you look all over the yard?"

"That's a stupid question. How can you ask such a stupid question? Would I ask you for it if I found it?" He was screaming now and Sidney could hear every word.

"That's what you get for fooling with those goonies. They're a bunch of crooks."

"I'll get a lot more if I don't come up with that bag. Do you know what they do to somebody who doesn't turn in the day's numbers? They could burn the house down."

Sidney didn't like the direction the conversation was taking.

"Where's Sid?" he yelled.

"I think he's up on the porch."

He ran up the steps and burst onto the porch.

"Sonny," his voice shook and his eyes had a strange, glassy stare. "How long have you been up here?"

"About an hour," he answered.

"Did you see somebody throw a bag into the yard?"

"No."

"Think hard," his father said. "It's very important."

Sidney was conscious of the bulge in his pocket. "I didn't see anything," he insisted.

His father ran back downstairs and he resumed shouting at Rachel.

Sidney only wanted to hurt those guys who messed up his Sundays, not his mother. Holmes didn't have any mothers to worry about. Minutes later, she came onto the porch. Her face was wet with tears, her composure gone.

"Sidney," she said, her voice breaking, "tell your father if you saw anything. He'll get killed if he doesn't find that bag."

This was too much. His mother was crying because of him. He

couldn't tell her he had it. He'd have to tell why he took it and he'd be branded a traitor to the family.

"I'll help you look for it," he said and he followed his mother down the steps.

He was right behind her when she went into the yard. He could hear his father outside kicking the snow aside. While she had her back turned, he pulled the bag out of his pocket, reached up and put it on top of the shed.

"Here it is," he shouted, reaching up and retrieving the bag, hoping nobody would notice the lack of snow on it.

His mother screamed with joy. "Where was it?"

"On the roof of the shed. I guess that guy threw it too hard."

"Thank God," she shouted, not realizing he was outside for the first time in four months. She rushed inside to find her husband.

Sidney closed the door and went upstairs as his mother's voice echoed from the store. "Nathan, Nathan, here's the bag!"

Sidney climbed into his bed and lay down, sighing heavily. Too much excitement for one day. From then on, when he saw a brown paper bag arch gracefully over the fence, he went back to his reading. They were better left to professional numbers writers, not young amateur detectives sensitive to their mother's tears.

## 24

As the rain and wind of April passed into a more tranquil and warmer May, Sidney was given permission to go outside as often as he wished, but was cautioned against overtiring himself. With the help of a cane, he was able to walk down to Bloom's Candy Store to see his friends. They cheered and clapped as he slowly approached, greeting him with handshakes, back slapping and friendly insults.

It was good to be out among the living, and the noise of their voices was music to his ears. Questions flew, and soon it was so noisy that Mr. Bloom asked them to get away from the front of the store. They all crossed the street to the church where Sidney sat down to rest.

"How lazy can a guy be?" Al Berman said. He was the team's smooth-fielding 1st baseman. "One whole year lying around the house and pretending to be sick."

"Yeah," Mendy Bush chimed in. "You should be ashamed. While we were eating dust out in Fairmount Park, you were sitting around in your upstairs window watching the girls walking up and down 7th Street."

"It was tough," Sid said. "But there was this therapist who came twice a week."

There was an excited silence as he related her massage technique, starting with his lower leg, moving up to his thigh and beyond.

"Boy, what luck," some remarked. "That was worth getting sick for. I bet if ya didn't have a fever when she started, ya sure as hell had one by the time she finished!"

"Did she sit on you or lay on you?"

"Nope," Sid answered. "She just used her hands and whispered different things while she was rubbing me."

"What did she say?" Mendy Bush asked eagerly.

Sidney hesitated, milking the situation for all it was worth. "Different things. – Oh, it's so nice and big, does it feel good? I love holding it in my hands."

"I can't stand it," Sol Klein said. "I have to lock myself in my room, and you had this woman doing it for you twice a week. There's no justice in this world."

"Depends on your point of view," Sidney answered. "But you have to get polio first."

"Never mind," Al Berman said. "I'll do it myself."

Everybody laughed.

"So what's doing with the North Stars?" Sid asked. "Are ya entered in the Fairmount Park League again?"

"Sure," Mendy said. "Season starts in June and we practice out at the park on Sundays. How about coming out with us this Sunday?"

"That'd be great. I'll have to ask if it's okay first."


His mother was against it, but after seeing how important it was to him, she relented after he promised to take it easy. Thus, on a warm May Sunday, he climbed onto the #3 trolley car for the ride out to the fields at 33rd and Dauphin. It was good to smell the grass and trees, and the dirt on the infield had its own odor too. They loosened up by stretching, then threw the ball around before batting practice.

Sidney put down his cane and picked up a bat, trying a few light swings, finding that if he kept most of his weight on his right leg and just a little on his left, he was able to take a pretty hefty swing. They let him hit practice balls to the infield and fly balls to the outfield. If he put too much weight on his left leg while bending it, it wasn't able to support him, so he soon learned how to balance his weight just right to allow him to catch as well as bat. He could bend with his right leg only. Running was out of the question, and he could only walk without the cane if he kept his weak leg straight.

He knew that it would be a long time, if ever, before he could resume his favorite position in the outfield, but catching was another matter. It was the least sought after position on every team, hot and uncomfortable, but was preferable to not playing at all. If he could get up and down from a crouch position, it might be possible to play baseball this year. But he couldn't run – that was a seemingly insurmountable problem.

Then the light bulb went on again. If somebody was allowed to run for him, the problem would be solved. After last season, the team needed all the hitting it could get, and if he could take his turn at bat it would be a big help.

He suggested it to the team and they said they would ask the park commissioner for approval. The following week, the commissioner said that under these unusual circumstances, it was okay with him if the other teams approved the idea. The rest of the teams in the league raised little objection, stipulating that this should be a one-time exception for an unusual case, and not to be allowed again. They also stated that the runner must stand alongside the batting cage and not to run until the ball was hit.

It was in this manner that Sidney was converted from an outfielder to a catcher.

He played four innings of the opening game, felt comfortable behind the plate, hit a double and struck out, and didn't feel excessively tired afterwards. By the end of the season, he was catching nine innings and batting 312, a respectable figure for somebody just out of a polio sick bed.

He swore the team to secrecy, lest his mother and doctor should hear about it and ship him back into the house. When he came home covered with dust, he blamed it on the wind blowing the dust off the infield and onto the sidelines.

By September, nearly one year after contracting polio, he was walking on his own and secretly practicing how to run with a weak left leg. It wasn't easy, but he found that he could manage a sort of limping trot if he didn't bend his bad leg too far. It just wasn't strong enough to hold the weight. He hoped by the following spring, when the Fairmount Park League started a new season, he might be able to play without a designated runner.

To assist his dormant muscles to recover some of their former strength, and to Sid's delight, Dr. John suggested bicycle riding as good exercise. It was his first bike and it gave him mobility and range he didn't have before. Girard Avenue was now three minutes away and when he re-entered Northeast High, he biked there and back every day, locking the bike to the parking rack before going into classes.

To earn his own spending money, he acquired a paper route that distributed Yiddish language newspapers throughout the Jewish Rectangle. One customer lived outside this area, Mr. Cohen, the coal yard owner at Front and Berks Streets, who Joshua was negotiating with for the sale of his business. This trip to Front Street eventually brought an end to his paper route. The area east of Fifth Street was mostly Irish, and not conducive to young Jewish boys on bicycles delivering Yiddish newspapers.

Five days a week he biked six blocks to Cohen's coal yard and six blocks back, enduring a barrage of small stones thrown at him from passing groups of boys, accompanied by their singing of "Listen to the Mocky Bird." As the stones became larger and their aim better, Sidney decided to make a career change.

He borrowed his mother's small shopping basket and paid a visit to Silver's Bakery at 1820 N. 7th Street, halfway up the block between Bloom's and his home. Mr. Silver had lost the use of his legs in a bad fall down some steps, and now spent his days in a wheelchair tending to the store, while his wife and son arose long before dawn each day except Saturday, and began baking challahs and other goodies that were shipped upstairs and put on display for the morning customers.

But Sidney wasn't interested in challah. The Silvers also sold soft pretzels.

Mr. Silver rolled his wheelchair in from the back room when he heard the jingling of the front doorbell.

"Sidney Kurtz," he said smiling. "It's good to see you back on your feet." Despite his accident, he retained a friendly manner and enjoyed talking small talk with teenagers whenever they came into the store. Sidney was uneasy with Mr. Silver's statement, knowing that he would never be in a position to say the same to him, but he seemed sincere so he took it on face value.

"Thanks, Mr. Silver. How're you doing?" He felt uncomfortable after asking that question, but he was only trying to be polite.

"I'm doing just fine, son. When I heard about you getting polio, I said a prayer for you every Friday night. It's terrible that these things should happen. Me? I'm getting old, but you've still got your whole life ahead of you. I see you go past on your bicycle. That's good. Keep exercising and make yourself strong for the next crisis."

Sidney's face reflected his confusion. "What crisis?"

Mr. Silver laughed. "There's always a crisis, my boy. You can't get too cocky in this world. Just when you think everything's going good, then kaboom! the next crisis hits you. There's one hiding behind every corner just waiting for you to relax your grip, so keep up your guard.

"I promise I will," Sidney said uncertainly.

"If anybody told me five years ago that I would spend the rest of my life in a wheelchair, I would have said he's crazy. Yet, here I am."

Sidney again shuffled uncomfortably. "I'm sorry about that, Mr. Silver."

"Don't be. I'm just spouting off. We older folks think we know everything and that we have to pass on all of our knowledge to every kid that comes along. Sorry."

Sidney shifted his weight. His left leg was getting tired of standing in the same place. "You don't have to apologize, Mr. Silver."

"That's what I like about you, Sidney. You've got nice manners. You're polite to your elders. That's important. Tell me, do you have much pain from that rotten sickness?"

"No pain at all, just a weak left leg."

"You're very lucky. If it hit you in the chest, you might have to spend the rest of your life in a iron lung."

"Yeah," Sidney said. He had never heard of an iron lung.

"I see you have a basket with you. Your mom not feeling well?"

"She's okay. I want to buy some pretzels to make some spending money."

Mr. Silver smiled. "Another businessman. Just what this neighborhood needs. Your father doesn't give you an allowance?"

"Not yet," he answered, embarrassed.

"You're father's a nice guy," Mr. Silver said. "He should spend more time with his family."

Sidney didn't answer.

"He's got a good business going there," Silver continued. "Growing hair on hard boiled eggs. He'll be a rich man someday if he holds onto his money. How's your sister?"

"She's okay, too."

"Is she seeing anybody yet?"

"What?"

"Is she dating somebody, like a boyfriend?"

"No, I don't think so." When is he going to stop, Sid thought. He held up the basket. "Would you sell me some pretzels?"

"Of course, why didn't you say so? Go downstairs from the sidewalk. That's the wholesale department. My wife's probably down there. She'll be glad to sell you as many as you want."

"Thanks, Mr. Silver."

Sidney turned and left the store, relieved of answering any more questions, and went down the outside steps into the basement. In addition to the coal heater, a pile of coal, and the hot water heater, their baking oven and table took up the rest of the space in an already hot, cramped area. Mrs. Silver, a short, heavy woman with a pug nose, drooping dark eyes, and graying brown hair tied into a braided ponytail, looked more Oriental than Yiddish. She squinted at Sidney as he carefully negotiated the steep stairs into the basement.

"Sidney Kurtz," she said, surprised. "It's so good to see you back on your feet."

Sidney hesitated, foreseeing another long discussion. He hunted for something different to say. "Thanks, Mrs. Silver. I want to buy some pretzels."

"Good! To eat or to sell?"

"To sell for spending money."

"Your father doesn't give you an allowance yet?"

Here we go again, he thought. "Not yet."

"Oh, that tightwad. And with all the money he makes growing hair on bald heads. He could be a wealthy man someday if he watches his dollars and stays away from those nogoodniks who hang around the store and the Cat & Fiddle."

He thought of his mother at the costume party and smiled. "I want to buy twenty pretzels," he said, trying to cut it short.

"Ten cents," she answered. "It's none of my business, but your father should stay at home with his family."

"I know," he answered. "Mr. Silver said that too."

"He did? My husband's always sticking his big nose where it doesn't belong. How's your sister?"

"She's okay, too, Mrs. Silver."

She counted out 21 pretzels and put them in his basket.

"One for good luck," she said, patting him on the hand. "You're a polite boy. That's what I like about you."

"Thanks, Mrs. Silver." He started up the stairs with his basket of 21 pretzels, a jar of mustard and a knife. He wondered which way he should go, toward Girard Avenue or just keep in the neighborhood.

"Fresh Pretzels!" he shouted as he walked towards Montgomery Avenue. A large group of men were waiting outside Bloom's for a #65 trolley, apparently just finishing their shift at the Stetson Hat Factory at 5th and Montgomery. One of them motioned to him and he walked across the street.

"One pretzel with mustard and one without," he said.

"Two cents," Sidney replied. Nine other people thought that was a good idea - eat one now, take one home. In five minutes, he was sold out. He rushed back to the Silver's basement.

"Twenty more pretzels, Mrs. Silver."

"My gracious," she exclaimed. "What did you do, throw them down the sewer?"

"I caught people coming home from work. Maybe I'll go over to Stetson's and just stand outside."

"That's a good idea, but if you sell out again, don't come back. We'll be closed. If you're working Sunday, I'm down here at five in the morning, if you want to get an early start."

"Not that early. What about Saturday?"

"Are you crazy? On Shabbus? If you want to sell on Shabbus, you'll have to buy from that Goyisha Bakery up at 4th and Girard. But his pretzels? Tooey, not worth the room they take up."

"Then I won't work on Saturday. Take care, Mrs. Silver."

He climbed up the steps, caught another crowd waiting for the trolley, sold out, except for one which he kept for himself, and went home feeling satisfied with himself. Twenty cents invested, twenty cents clear profit. He had become what his Uncle Jake considered a filthy capitalist.

When he got home, he entered through the side door that the 3rd floor tenants used, not wanting to walk through the store with the basket, climbed the steps to the second floor and came down the back stairs into the living room. His mother and grandmother were sitting at the table with a man who he recognized as a neighbor who lived a few doors away on Berks Street.

"Well, the businessman returns," Itkah said. "How did you make out?"

"Great," he answered. "Sold 40 pretzels and made 20 cents clear profit."

"Twenty cents," she exclaimed. "I think I'll get a basket myself."

"How does your leg feel?" Rachel asked.

"Tired, but today was a long day."

"The doctor said not to overdo it."

"I know." He thought of the baseball games that he had played this past summer. If she knew, he'd probably be confined to the house for who knows how long. "I'll be more careful, Mom."

"This is Mr. Lessy. He lives down the street."

"I know Mr. Lessy."

Mickey Lessy was a good looking man of about 25-30 years old with thick black hair and a ruddy complexion. They had occasionally passed each other in the street and Sidney remembered him being in the store waiting for a haircut.

"I was talking to Doctor John," his mother continued, "and he doubts if your left leg will ever be normal again, so I thought it might be a good idea for you to learn a trade where you don't have to be on your feet all the time. Mr. Lessy is a watchmaker. He said if you come over to his house a couple of times a week, he'd be glad to teach you the trade."

Sidney had no opinion on this one way or another. He knew absolutely nothing about watch repairing, except that it required sitting all the time, which he didn't like to do. He had never considered his future. but he enjoyed reading and writing short stories. They had become a favorite hobby during his recuperation. The advice of his English teacher to pursue a career in education still remained in his mind. Books on foreign lands and ocean sailing were his preferred reading, except for Sherlock Holmes, and before his illness, he dreamed of one day playing professional baseball. His interests included geography, astronomy and of course, sports, but when it came to zeroing in on what would be his life's work, he had no idea. Watchmaking had never entered his mind.

"Mr. Lessy does watch repairing at home and right after dinner would be the best time for him."

"If you think so, Mom," he said.

"Try it," Mr. Lessy said. "If it's not for you, you'll soon know."

So twice a week when he finished dinner, he limped over to Mr. Lessy's house, climbed the steps to the second floor and became an apprentice watchmaker. Mr. Lessy had two benches set up in an empty room where he worked. He cleared some space on one that he wasn't using, allowing Sidney to sit and practice taking apart and putting together old pocket watch movements. He learned how to use an eye loupe and handle jewelers screwdrivers and tweezers.

Mickey had him working on those big old watches until he could assemble them blindfolded. He was unexpectedly nimble with his hands and progressed rapidly from those large, easy to handle movements to smaller wrist watch movements.

It was a nice world of hands, dials, hour wheels, balance wheels and ratchet wheels. He would take it all apart, then put it together again. This process was repeated over and over. He learned how to use a cleaning machine, how to replace a balance staff and how to insert a mainspring. He mastered the art of hairspring straightening and roller jewel replacing and after several months, Mickey occasionally gave him a customer's watch to repair on his own.

It was absorbing for a while, but the stronger and more active he became, the less interesting it was to sit at the bench two evenings a week. He would much rather be watching a good movie or sitting on his back porch writing one of his stories. Mickey sensed his restlessness and told him to take a break whenever he wanted to, which he did quite often.

He had returned to school after missing a year of classes and found it more boring than ever. He started cutting school entirely, heading north on 7th Street, making a hard left at Norris Street, hoping his sister didn't look out of her office window at the Ferguson School and wonder why he was going in that direction. From there he walked into center city to wait for the 11:00 a.m. show to begin at any number of movie houses on Market or Chestnut Streets. His leg was now strong enough for him to discard his cane, and after almost a year in the house, he was happy to roam at will.

During one of his rare days in school, when he didn't have the price of admission to a movie house, he was called down to the principal's office and confronted with his attendance record.

The principal, Mr. Morrison, a slightly built man with heavy eyebrows and receding hairline, looked across his desk at him. "Sidney," he began, holding a card in front of him. "Except for three days, you haven't been to school once in six weeks. Before I send a letter to your parents, maybe you can tell me what the trouble is."

Sidney fished around for an excuse. "I had a relapse. I was sick again and couldn't leave the house."

Mr. Morrison smiled. "That's not good enough, Sidney. You've been seen walking down Broad Street and in center city during school hours. I can't put you in prison for not attending school, but you're making a big mistake. Can't you tell me what it's all about?"

"I'm just bored with school, Mr. Morrison. I don't like it."

"Well, you're not alone. Other students find it boring too, but they realize that to get anywhere in this world, you need an education, so they stick to it. There are many things in life that aren't pleasant, but you'll have to deal with them the best that you can. Mr. Donaldson says you're one of his best students and that you'd make a good teacher."

"I know, he told me."

"Think about it, please. Your whole life might depend on this decision."

## 25

"Nathan," Rachel pleaded. "If you ever talk to your son, now's the time to do it. He wants to leave school. I get nowhere with him. He says he hates it and doesn't want to go anymore. What're we going to do with him?"

"If he doesn't want to go, what can I tell him? He'll just have to go out and find a job."

"But he should at least finish high school. A diploma is important to have."

Nathan spoke to Sidney for five minutes, the longest conversation they ever had together, but didn't do any good. He was 16 years old and this was the extent of their personal relationship, a five minute talk. He left school and applied for a job down on Sansom Street. Mickey Lessy recommended him to Bass & Mantz, a small center city jewelry manufacturer and repair shop. They hired him to polish jewelry, do general work and run errands.

He worked from 9:00 until 5:00 and was paid five dollars a week of which he kept two dollars and gave three to his mother. His mornings were spent polishing the work of the day before, rings and bracelets, special orders and repairs sent in from retail stores. During the afternoons he ran errands, kept the place as clean as possible and watched Mr. Mantz and his elderly father work on the jewelry while Mr. Bass set precious stones and diamonds.

He ate lunch, which was usually a sandwich and a drink brought from home, in the back room with Mr. Mantz's father, an old Jewish gentleman with a full white beard and gray hair. He couldn't speak a word of English and they spent the half hour reading and writing, Mr. Mantz his Yiddish language newspaper and Sidney his latest fiction story. Occasionally their eyes met and a half-hearted smile passed between them.

The shop, one of many that existed on the street, was on the 2nd floor at 720 Sansom, and its windows faced the street. The buildings were old, the floors were wood, bare for the most part, and on a windy day one match would have destroyed the entire block. It was store after store on the first floor, with shops in the rear taking up the entire 2nd and 3rd floors.

During his errands, Sidney wondered how so many jewelry stores and shops so close together survived. They seemed to flourish, with hardly a vacant store or an empty shop. Cars filled both sides of the street and trucks making deliveries were forced to block the middle of the street while horns blared and drivers fumed.

It was the oldest jewelry district in the United States, and the close quarters, congestion, crowded sidewalks, dust and noise, gave it a decided New York atmosphere.

Mr. Mantz, like his father, was a quiet man, hardly ever raising his voice, and issued instructions in a moderate tone. Mr. Bass, on the other hand, nervous, excitable, and unpredictable, talked in a brusque and rude manner. Sidney frequently was the target of his unforeseen outbursts, as he vented whatever frustrations he harbored on his youngest employee. Sidney realized that unless Mr. Bass's attitude changed, which seemed unlikely, he would soon be looking for another job.

On a hot summer day in July, Sidney was at the polishing machine while the four men sat in a row at their benches, facing the open windows. It was quiet for the most part, except for the traffic noise coming up from the street and the hum of the polishing machine motor. Everybody's face was moist with perspiration from the extreme humidity. The heat was oppressive and there was little conversation as the men concentrated on their work.

Sidney's eyelids grew heavy while he relaxed his grip on the heavy gent's signet ring that he was polishing. Half asleep, he was unaware that his hands moved slowly forward. The buffing wheel tore the ring from his grasp, shot it with lightning speed against the dust shield and ricocheted it back past Sidney's ear, passing close behind the head of Mr. Bass, who looked up in time to watch it exit out the window. The silence lasted about one second longer.

"Sidney!" Mr. Bass screamed. "What the hell's the matter with you? What kind of ring was that?"

"A gent's initial ring," Sidney answered quietly.

"Did it have any diamonds in it?"

"No – no diamonds – just a gold signet ring."

"Just a gold signet ring," Bass shouted. "Is that all? Just a gold signet ring! How'd you like to pay for that gold signet ring with your next five weeks wages?"

Sid had no excuse that would stand up under Mr. Bass's anger, but he felt obliged to defend himself. "It's hot in here, Mr. Bass. Polishing is a boring job and I couldn't keep my eyes open."

"If you can't stay awake, then you shouldn't be working here."

Sidney thought the same thing.

"Sam," Jack Mantz said calmly. "It was an accident. It can happen to anybody. I've done the same thing."

Sam Bass gave no indication of hearing what his partner said. He was still concentrating his venom on Sidney. "Get your ass downstairs and don't come back without that ring. Now get going, stupid!"

Relieved to escape this onslaught, Sidney rushed downstairs and out onto the sidewalk. Fortunately, he didn't have to search very far. The ring had bounced off a cardboard box and came to rest beside a trash can by the curb. Snatching it up, he was ecstatic to see the ring was undamaged, not even scratched.

As he rose to return to the shop, he felt something small land on his head. He reached up, dug his fingers through his thick, red hair and pulled out what to him looked like a one carat diamond.

He couldn't believe it. Sidney was no diamond expert, but he had seen the difference between fakes and a real diamond, and this one didn't look like a fake. Looking around and not seeing anybody that appeared to have just lost anything, he rushed back upstairs to display what he had found. He was astonished to see everybody, including the elder Mr. Mantz, on their hands and knees poking around the dusty, wooden floor.

"What happened?" he asked.

Dave Kalewski, a Polish repairman who worked for Jack, came over and whispered in his ear. "Sam lost a diamond. It's better not to talk now. Did you find the ring?"

"Yep, and not a scratch on it." He was about to show Dave the diamond, but he held back. Mr. Bass probably wouldn't show any gratitude for his finding the diamond or retrieving the signet ring. Let him stew for awhile, he thought. Let him sweat. He gave the signet ring to Dave and joined the rest on the floor, pretending to be absorbed in the hunt. While nobody was looking, he pushed the diamond against the inside of the rear wheel of the large safe which stood against one wall, making it practically invisible. Maybe an hour on his knees will do Sam some good, he thought.

Mr. Bass was strangely silent. Very red-faced, but silent. The diamond had popped out of his tweezers, bounced on the bench and disappeared.

Mr. Mantz was the first to suggest that it might have gone out the window. "Sam," he said, "I'll go down and sweep the sidewalk. It doesn't look like it's on the floor. There's nothing to lose."

"Never mind," Sam answered. "I'll do it. Everybody keep looking," he gave a shoebox stuffed with receipts and old invoices to Sidney. "Here, look through this box if you can stay awake long enough. This is all your fault. If you hadn't let go of that fucking ring, this never would have happened."

Go to hell, Sidney thought, mentally adding fifteen minutes more of suffering onto Mr. Bass. He made himself comfortable, sitting on the floor with his back against the wall, and the box in his lap, watching everybody crawling around while Mr. Bass went downstairs, broom, brush and dustpan in hand.

He was halfway through the box, pretending to examine every piece of paper when Mr. Bass trudged back upstairs, his face a deep red and dripping with perspiration. It was obvious to everyone that he had been unsuccessful.

Sidney held a faded card in his hand. "Mr. Bass," he said, "I'm down to your 1926 driver's license. You want me to keep looking?" Everyone held their breath. Sam Bass appeared on the verge of a stroke. A tinge of purple blended with his red, reminding Sidney of a beautiful sunset. He looked like a bomb, ready to explode. He opened his mouth, but nothing came out. He plopped down into a chair and stared straight ahead.

Mr. Mantz brought him a glass of water while Dave extended a dry towel to wipe his face. The elder Mr. Mantz struggled up from the floor, and again the only sound was the traffic drifting up from the street.

"Sam," Mr. Mantz said, "go lie down on the cot in the spare room for a few minutes. You're going to blow a fuse."

Sam didn't move for a minute, then rose slowly and went into the back room.

"Now," Jack Mantz said, "let's be systematic about this. Sidney, you cover the floor around where you're sitting. Everybody else look on top of their benches. I'll look all over Sam's bench, then we go back to the floor. Take your time and be thorough. Remember, if we don't find it, we'll be out about $500.00."

Sidney gulped. Five hundred dollars! I'd have to work two years to collect that much money, he thought. It would come out of Mr. Mantz's pockets, too. That changed things. He had nothing against Mr. Mantz. He'd always treated him civilly, no shouting or swearing. He had no desire to hurt him. Five more minutes, that would be enough, then he would go from goat to hero.

It was a long five minutes. He just wanted to bring it to a close, satisfied that he had milked it for all it was worth. He reached under the safe and pulled out the diamond.

"I found it," he yelled excitedly, holding it up for all to see. "It was behind the wheel of the safe!"

There was general rejoicing and backslapping. Everybody smiled and laughed, while Jack Mantz hurried into the back room to tell Sam the good news. Sid was congratulated by everybody, except Mr. Bass, who came back into the shop and sat down to resume his work at the bench.

Sidney had no way of knowing whether or not Mr. Bass appreciated his retrieving the diamond, but two weeks later his pay jumped up to $8.00 a week. He had begun his climb up the corporate ladder.


A month before Christmas, 1940, Sidney left Bass & Mantz and went to work for his Uncle Ellis who recently opened a new jewelry store at the corner of 28th and Girard. It was a large store, about 60 feet long and 25 feet wide. The stock ranged from jewelry to silverware to small appliances, with credit extended to those customers who had no financial marks against them. He had one outside collector salesman, two inside salespeople, a female bookkeeper and Sidney, errand boy, apprentice watchmaker, window trimmer and fly-speck remover, a job Ellis had raised to the highest art form.

Whenever he finished cleaning and trimming the windows, Ellis would scan every inch, pointing out fingerprints, smears and worst of all, fly-specks. He took it as a personal affront to have a fly dirty his window, and he would have Sidney set out on a search and destroy mission, finding and eliminating every last fly-speck that marred his otherwise beautiful windows.

Ellis did most of the watch repairing. When he was too busy with the store, Meyer Haltman, the other inside man, would sit at the bench. When both were occupied, Sidney was permitted to do small jobs, mainsprings, stems and crowns and crystals. Three times a week on Mondays, Wednesdays and Fridays, he was sent down to Jewelers Row in center city to leave jewelry repairs and to pick-up previously left work or wait for rush jobs. This usually gave him about two hours free time, and more than once he ducked into the nearest movie house, rushing out at the end of the show, picking up the work as quickly as possible and jumping onto the trolley. More often than not Ellis would ask why it took him so long, and he was forced to dream up a crazy excuse that nobody believed.

Meyer was afraid that a family member had been brought into the business to supplant him, and screaming Sam Bass was replaced by jealous Meyer Haltman.

Sidney lay awake nights thinking, is this how it's going to be throughout my entire life, giving up one problem only to inherit another? I'm not after anybody's job. I just want to put in my time and be left alone.

# 26

Sidney and his mother were visiting Sylvia and Jean Dean and their mother Rebecca on a Sunday in early December. The Deans had put together a small lunch of noodle soup, gefilte fish and cold sliced chicken. Conversation was light. He was asked how his job was going, the women engaged in small talk about clothes, the rising prices of food, and family.

It was a mild day for December and Sidney wanted to see if any street games were in progress. He stayed for an acceptable amount of time, then excused himself and left after giving everybody a hug and kiss.

As he closed the front door and started down the steps, a man ran down the street, eyes wild, his arms outstretched.

"The Japs attacked Pearl Harbor," he screamed. "We're at war!" The man ran crazily by, his arms flailing, his voice echoing down 7th Street. People were coming out of their houses and collecting in groups on the sidewalks. One word came from their lips – war. Sidney stopped on the steps, turned around and ran back upstairs and burst into the living room. Everybody stared at him. His eyes were wide, his body trembling.

"What in the world?" Aunt Rebecca said.

His mother came over to him. "Sidney, what's the matter?"

He looked into her eyes. "The Japs attacked Pearl Harbor, Mom. We're at war!"

The women sat quite still. Nobody spoke. His mother was the first. "Pearl Harbor? Where is it? Why would anybody attack it?"

His mother, aunt and cousins, unversed in geography, knowing nothing of international politics and uncomfortable outside their little North Philadelphia world, didn't have the slightest inkling of what he was talking about.


The next day, he stood in the doorway between the store and the living room, waiting for President Roosevelt to speak to the nation. All three barbers were busy and several customers were waiting their turn, devouring the newspapers, reading every word about the attack. The

Pacific Fleet was destroyed, over 3,000 sailors killed. The details were grim. Conversation was subdued, adding to the air of tragedy hanging over the country. Newspapers were lowered as a voice came from the corner.

"Ladies and gentlemen, a radio broadcast by the President of the United States."

It was a familiar voice, warm, comforting, determined. Sidney had heard his voice many times while recuperating from polio. Sitting in the dark store, listening to his "Fireside Chats," he felt a special attachment for this man, also stricken with polio at the height of his youth, paralyzed in both legs, but going on to the biggest job in the world – President of the United States.

"My fellow Americans," he began. His voice was soothing, reassuring, flowing over the listeners with a medicinal balm.

"Yesterday, December 7th, 1941," the store was silent except for some light clicking of scissors. Sidney felt a prickling sensation over his entire body. He clenched his fists. He never swore, rarely used obscenities even amongst his friends, but this was different. "Those dirty bastards," he said under his breath. Sidney was not politically inclined, nor familiar with world conditions, but he had an innate love for his country.

Now they were at war. It was a shaken America that tried to sleep that night.

## 27

Sidney marked his 18th birthday by walking into the draft board and volunteering for the Army. He now walked with only a slight limp, and he naively expected to be given a warm welcome despite his left leg having only half the strength of his right. This past summer of 1942 was the first time since his illness that he ran for himself playing baseball in the Fairmount Park League. It was a slow, limping run, but he was on his own and no longer had to ask permission for a designated runner.

The draft board sent him to the local armory for a physical examination and he was promptly labeled 4F – medically unfit. The sergeant was kind, but unmoved by his pleas. "Man, you wouldn't get through a week of basic training with that leg," he told Sidney. "A forced march in bad weather, carrying a full load would put you in the hospital. Consider yourself lucky."

But Sidney was persistent. Some of his older friends were already away, enlisted or inducted. He didn't want to be left behind. "Aren't there jobs I could do that don't require marching, like ambulance driving or doing some kind of support work behind the lines?"

"Probably," the sergeant said. "But everybody's subject to the same physical requirements. Maybe if things get worse, the Army might lower its standards, but for now it applies to everybody, without exception."

So, that was that, thought a dejected 18 year old as he limped home. The war would be over and he would be deprived of the opportunity to serve his country. What good was he doing in a jewelry store? That was no job when his country was at war.

Wherever he went, he was assailed by patriotic posters showing men in uniform. Even women were able to do their bit by joining the WAC – Women's Army Corps. Billboards screamed for citizens to back up their armed forces, buy bonds, work in defense plants, and he was working in a jewelry store. In future years, when someone asked, "What did you do during the War?" he would say, "Why, I sold jewelry." Very important. The most dangerous part of his job was his uncle finding a missed fly-speck. While men were training and fighting, he was searching for fly-specks. He couldn't stand it any longer. He had to do something meaningful.

Months passed with Sidney frustrated by his inability to resolve his crisis. His country had been at war over a year and here he was, still working in his uncle's store. While on a trip to center city for the store, he had an hour to kill, so he rushed into the Palace to see Across the Pacific, with Humphrey Bogart. But first, he was forced to endure the Movietone News, filled with dramatic footage just back from both the European and Pacific theaters of war.

Troops were sailing every day in both directions. Merchant ships loaded with war supplies travelling in large convoys headed towards England and the South Pacific. Guns, tanks and airplanes coming off American production lines by the thousands crowded the docks on both the east and west coasts, waiting to be loaded on ships. He closed his eyes. It was too much. The whole world was fighting for survival and here he was, in a movie house, waiting for some jewelry to be repaired. It was humiliating.

The announcer's voice droned on. "No sooner do ships tie up at the docks than the waiting war material is hoisted aboard and lowered into the hold by the civilian members of the Merchant Marine, unsung heroes who brave German torpedoes and the stormy Atlantic on every trip."

Sidney opened his eyes in time to see a large convoy of ships heading eastward from America. He saw the men on the bridge, in the engine room, on the deck struggling to keep their footing in rough seas. Then he noticed something, They weren't wearing uniforms, just ordinary work clothes as if they were in a factory. He recalled what the announcer had said. "Civilian members of the Merchant Marines." Civilian. They weren't part of the Army or Navy. They were just civilians, and probably didn't have to pass the rigid physical examinations imposed by the regular services.

Here was the answer, he thought. They were civilians, he was a civilian. He rushed into the lobby, found the phone book and rifled through the pages. Then he picked up his jewelry repairs, walked as quickly as he could to Broad and Walnut Streets, noted the office number listed on the directory, took the elevator to the proper floor, and found himself standing in front of a smartly unformed officer with the letters U.S.M.S. on his sleeve.

He sat behind his desk, broad shouldered, handsome in his blue uniform with gold trim. "What can I do for you, son?"

"I want to join up."

"How old are you?"

"I was 18 last month, October 12."

"Why aren't you in the Army?"

Sidney hesitated. How he answered would determine whether he would fight the war on a ship, or hunting for fly-specks on a store window. The truth might keep him out. On the other hand, if he lied and they found out, he might wind up where he is now, at home, plus it would be on his record forever that he lied to an officer. He decided he might as well tell the truth.

"The Army classified me 4F," he said dejectedly.

"Why?"

"I had polio a few years ago, but I'm better now."

"Polio, huh? Where did it hit you?"

"My left leg. It wasn't paralyzed, but some of the muscles are shot. It's a lot better now. I'm playing baseball and everything."

The officer looked at him with a half-smile. "You know, you have a chance to stay safe at home. You could get killed out there."

"My friends are going. I want to do my share."

"Very noble," the officer said. He took his pencil and threw it on the floor at his feet. "Pick it up."

Sidney bent down and picked it up, handing it back to him.

"Walk back and forth a few times."

He did, trying to conceal his limp as much as possible.

The officer pushed an application in front of him. "Roosevelt did okay with polio. I guess you can, too."

Sidney was overjoyed, but puzzled. "Don't I get a physical?"

"You just got it."

"That's all there is to it?"

"Oh, I forgot one thing. Take a deep breath in and out."

Sidney followed his instructions.

"You'll do. Sign here."


"But, Sidney," Itkah said. "You don't know what war is. It's not like playing baseball."

"And you're too young to die," David said. "You've got your whole life in front of you."

"Listen to your elders," Rachel said. "They know better than you."

"If you don't have to go, why should you?" Lena asked.

They sat around the table in the living room after the store had closed. Nathan was out and Edith was visiting a friend. Rachel had called them together, relating Sidney's decision in the hope that wiser heads would prevail. There was tea and hot chocolate, and cookies were on the table.

"I appreciate how you feel," David said, "Your friends are going and you want to also."

"It's more than that, Grandpop," Sidney said. "I mean, that's part of it, but it's our country. What would you do if somebody attacked you?"

David sipped his chocolate. "I'd probably fight back."

Itkah looked sideways at her husband. "But suppose you could defend yourself without fighting?" she said. "Wouldn't that be better?"

"How?" Sidney asked.

"Well." Itkah hesitated. "You try to talk your attacker out of it." She knew it was a weak argument, but she had to counter David's answer. "Or you have somebody help you."

"But suppose you're alone? What then?"

Itkah was on firmer ground now. "That's a good point. If you're alone, you don't have a choice. But you do. You have plenty of help. Thousands of other boys, healthier than you, are out there. They can fight for you. You just got out of a sick bed. Nobody would fault you for staying home."

"That's right," Lena added. "It's nothing to be ashamed of. If you were 100% healthy and you were trying to finagle your way out of the draft, it would be different. But you're far from 100% healthy."

"If I'm healthy enough to play baseball, I'm healthy enough to sail on a ship. It's not like marching miles in bad weather with 40 pounds on your back. It's probably a lot safer on a merchant ship than in the Army or Navy."

"You've been playing baseball?" Itkah asked.

Sidney hesitated. "Yes, I have," he admitted. "My leg's okay. I didn't say anything. I knew Mom would make me stop."

"You're right," Rachel said.

"It didn't do you any harm," David observed. "But the war. That's different. It's a matter of life or death. Ships are being sunk every day. Why look for trouble?"

"I'm not looking for trouble. All I know is that if I don't try to do as much as I can, I'll regret it for the rest of my life."

Everybody looked at him. "Patriotic fool," Itkah muttered.

David was proud of his grandson, but kept this judgement to himself lest he unleash a storm of rebuke from his wife.

"I know you all want the best for me and don't want anything to happen to me, but there are a lot of guys out there who had to leave home. I can't do any less." Then he aimed below the belt. "This country gave you freedom and a chance to rebuild your lives when you needed it. If we lose the war, that chance won't be available to other people. We can't just take from this country. We have to give something back, too."

There was no answer for that. One by one, they gave him a hug and kiss and wished him well.

"Take care of yourself, Sidney," Itkah said, her eyes glistening. "Don't forget your family."

"I won't," he answered.

"It's the most valuble thing in life – family. And you're a part of it. An important part. More than you know."

Sidney didn't know what to say.

"Before you go away, let me tell you a little story. Did you know that when I married your grandfather back in Lutzin, he already had five children?"

"I didn't know that," he said. "Why did you marry a man with five children?"

"Because I desperately wanted a family. Without family, I was nothing."

Sidney pondered this for a moment. "So all of my uncles and aunts are really your stepchildren?"

"All but Ellis. He alone has my blood running through his veins. But I loved them all as if they were my own."

Sidney tried to think of an intelligent comment. "I bet that took a lot of courage,Grandmom."

"When you want something badly enough, courage comes easy. Just like you wanting to fight for your country. I'm so proud of you."

Sidney's face reddened.

"But what I'm talking about requires a different kind of courage. The courage to look after your family, to keep them together."

"I guess I'll get married some day."

"Yes, but remember you have a mother and sister. Yes, even a father. Aunts, uncles, cousins. They're also family." She leaned closer and held his hand.

"Family must be your bible. Live for them. Hold them close. I've done my best, but I'm getting tired. I don't expect you to understand everything. You're young. But as you get older, it'll become clearer. Don't forget what I've told you. Remember, family is everything. "Here, put this on." She took a chain from around her neck and slipped it over his head.

"What is it?"

"It's the symbol of our people. The Star of David. I put it on the day I swore myself to this family. It's served me well. I hope it'll do the same for you."

Sidney looked down at it, sincerely moved. "But, Grandmom, you've worn it all these years. I shouldn't take it from you."

"You're not taking it. I'm giving it to you. It's time to pass it on."

Sidney held it in his hand. "I really don't know what to say." He ran his fingers over the smooth, well worn metal.

"Is it silver?" he asked.

"No. A blacksmith in Riga made it for me from an old horseshoe. He was a craftsman. The chain was my mother's." She closed his hand around it, then slipped it inside his shirt. "Don't let anything – damage it," she said.

"I won't, Grandmom," he answered.

Now give this old lady a hug." She held him close, feeling his warmth, his vibrancy. Her strength surprised him. His arms went around her. He felt secure, wanted, loved. He rested his face next to hers. Her tears were warm, soon joined by his own. They sobbed quietly, the old and the young.

"It's your last night home," Yussel said as they walked up 7th Street towards Bloom's Candy Store. "The milk shakes are on me, but not at Bloom's. This is a special occasion. No two-bit candy store for you. We're stepping out to Brook's luncheonette at 8th and Montgomery. They have a nickelodeon. We're going to do it right tonight. Music and milkshakes."

Sidney laughed. "If you insist. One milk shake is as good as another."

"Ah, Rusty boy, that's where you're wrong. Like many other people, you take your food for granted. Did you ever watch Sid Bloom make you a milk shake?"

"Some ice cream, milk, chocolate syrup and put it on the blender."

"You're so naive. That might be suitable for the average peasant who doesn't know any better, the casual drinker who simply gulps it down to quench his thirst. But it's not good enough for my friend, Rusty, who's going off to the war to fight for our country. The thought of you lying dead in a strange land without tasting a real milk shake is more than I can bear."

"Thanks a lot."

"We take too many things for granted," Yussel continued. "Little everyday things like walking and talking. Did you ever stop and think about how many muscles we use when taking a step? When we smile? When we frown?"

Sidney opened his mouth to speak, but Yussel didn't give him a chance. "Of course, you don't. It's the same thing with milk shakes. There's always somebody that makes a better mouse trap. Here we are. In you go."

The store was brightly lit with a soda fountain and six stools facing the door, and seven booths to the left. The nickelodeon was against the wall beside the end booth. Several of the booths were filled with teen-agers sipping slowly on sodas, making them last as long as possible and listening to Glen Miller's band playing "Chattanooga Choo-Choo."

A man about 21, wearing an apron, was sweeping the floor, while behind the soda fountain a young girl was filling an order for two ice cream sundaes.

"Now, isn't this classier than Bloom's?" Yussel asked. "Come on, we'll sit in a booth."

"Hold it," Sidney said. His attention was drawn to the young girl topping off the sundaes with whipped cream. Her brown hair was swept back and tied with ribbon behind her head. Her brown eyes were warm and her smile was natural and friendly. A very pretty girl, he thought, and she had seemed to notice him when he came in.

"Let's sit at the counter," Sidney said.

"At the counter?" Yussel spluttered. "No counters for you tonight, my friend. Would you ask General Sherman or Robert E. Lee to sit at the counter? Would you ask President Roosevelt to sit at the counter? Of course not, it would be a booth for them, and it's a booth for you. Nothing less than a booth is satisfactory for a war hero."

"I'm not a war hero yet," Sidney said. "I'll be just as honored to sit on a stool. After the war, I'll take a booth." He sat down and Yussel reluctantly joined him.

"You're making a big mistake," Yussel said. "Years later, when you think back, will you remember sitting on a stool? No. But being served in a booth, that's special."

Sidney looked at the girl opposite him. "I'll remember the stool," he said.

"You're Rusty Kurtz, aren't you?" Her voice was soft, easy on the ears.

"How did you know?" he asked.

"I watched you playing baseball out in Fairmount Park. You're a good hitter."

He felt his face getting warm. "Thanks."

"But you're a slow runner."

"I had polio a few years ago. It left me with a weak left leg."

She lowered her eyes. "I'm sorry," she said earnestly.

"That's okay," he answered. "You had no way of knowing."

She pushed the sundaes aside. "Mike," she called, "your sundaes are ready."

Mike strolled behind the fountain and picked up his order. He was husky but not muscular, and his resemblance to her marked him as her brother. He gave them both a quick glance and returned to his customers.

"My name's Sylvia," she said.

"Nice to meet you, Sylvia."

"Nice to meet you, too, Rusty."

"Anybody care about meeting me?" Yussel asked.

Sylvia laughed, a giggly infectious laugh.

"This is Yussel Estrin, a friend of mine," Sidney said.

"Pleased to meet you, Yussel."

"Pleased to meet you, Sylvia," he said. "How about you and me sitting in a booth and leave this uninteresting clod alone here at the counter?"

"You're funny," she remarked. "Are you two ordering anything or are you heat customers?"

"We're cash customers," Yussel answered. "I'm treating this future war hero to a night on the town and I brought him in here for one of Brook's legendary milk shakes, not the bland variety simpletons like him can get anywhere in the city. Tell this uneducated slob what you put into your creation."

"Three large scoops of ice cream, a large glass of milk, your favorite flavored syrup, an egg, and some malt if you like."

"Now that's a milk shake. Mix up two, Sylvia, and wish this guy good luck in his travels."

"Going into the Army?" she asked.

"No. The Army wouldn't take me. I'm going into the Merchant Marines."

"What's that?"

"Ships. They carry the supplies to the armed services all over the world."

"Sounds adventurous," she said. "You men have all the luck. You go all over while I'm stuck behind this fountain." She put the metal containers onto the double mixer, then poured the contents into large glasses and set them on the counter.

"Now the ultimate test," Yussell said. "See this straw? You plunk it into the glass and bravo - does it lean helplessly against the side of the glass? No. Does it float over the edge? No, it's stuck right in the middle. It stands straight and true all by itself. It takes a healthy pair of lungs to pull that stuff up the straw."

Rusty tried it and Yussel was right. He was barely able to draw the shake up into his mouth. "I'll need a spoon for this," he said.

Yussell clapped his hands approvingly.

"Two spoons, young lady. Straws are not good enough. Congratulations! You've made me a man of my word."

"Sylvia," Rusty said, "this shake is delicious. It's the best I ever had."

"Don't forget me when you come back. I'll make you another one."

"It's worth coming back for."

"Me, too?" Sylvia asked, looking directly into his eyes.

His face was getting warm again. "You, too," he finally said.

"I'll be right here waiting for you."

"You'll probably be married by the time I get back. How old are you?"

"Almost seventeen."

"You'll be married."

"You wanna bet?"

"Okay. What are the stakes?"

"If you come back and I'm married, I'll make you a free shake."

"And if you're not?"

She thought for a moment. "I'll make you a free shake anyway."

They all laughed. Yussel leaned closer to his friend. "Ask her when she gets off, you idiot. She likes you."

"Lay off, Yussel, you're embarrassing me."

"A fine war hero you are. Afraid to ask a girl for a date."

"What are you two whispering about?" Sylvia asked.

"Rusty wants to know what time you get off," Yussell said.

Sylvia smiled. "If he asks me, I'll tell him."

This time, Rusty was on the receiving end of a kick. He gave Yussel a menacing stare, then turned his attention to Sylvia who was fussing unnecessarily with some dishes.

"What time do you get off?" he asked.

"About 12 o'clock," she answered. "I'll meet you outside."

Yussel smiled triumphantly and went over to feed the nickelodeon. Presently, the smooth voice of Vaughan Monroe was heard. "Racing with the Moon, High up in the Starry Sky."

"The final touch," Yussel said. "I told you you'd have music tonight."

Rusty bent over his milkshake and wondered what to talk about at 12 o'clock.


At a quarter to twelve, Sylvia stepped outside as promised. She had changed her clothes and put on lipstick. She looked very pretty.

"Where do you want to go?" he asked.

"Let's just take a walk. It's a nice night."

It was warm but not uncomfortable, and they walked up 8th Street, which was deserted at this hour.

"Thanks for not charging us for those shakes," he said. "Won't you get in trouble?"

"Not as long as my father doesn't find out."

"The secret's safe with me."

"I've never given anybody a free milk shake before."

"Then I'm honored," Rusty said.

They walked several blocks up to Diamond Street, turned right and returned via 7th Street, passing the firehouse and Ferguson Grade School on the way. He wanted to continue the conversation, but was hard pressed to find something to talk about. Sylvia saved him the trouble, filling in the gaps with her bits of small talk.

"Did you graduate high school?"

"No, I left in the 10th grade. I lost a year when I was sick and after that I just couldn't get interested. How about you?"

"My father pulled me out of school to work in the store. My three brothers, my sister, and I are slave labor. None of us finished school and nobody gets paid."

"You mean you work for nothing?"

"Just about. We have a place to sleep and eat – that's it."

"There ought to be a law against that," he said.

He felt more at ease by the time they reached the store, and he was grateful when she asked him to sit with her on the bench outside.

The store was dark, the only light coming from the street lamp. A #47 trolley, nearly empty, rumbled past and the neighborhood was again quiet. An occasional meow from a late night cat echoed between the row homes.

"I'm not much of a talker," he confessed.

"I don't like people that talk too much. I don't mind if you're quiet."

"I could do better on a breadbox."

Sylvia looked questioningly at him.

Rusty laughed. "Yussel and I used to sit on his uncle's breadbox and talk about all sorts of things."

"What sorts of things?"

"Oh, baseball, the stars, the earth. Do you know the stars are like our sun, but they're so far away they look like little sparkling dots in the sky?"

"I didn't know that," Sylvia said, looking up at the sky.

"That's right," he continued, suddenly feeling superior. "The starlight we see started travelling towards us years ago."

"Is that a fact?" Sylvia asked.

"Some scientists think that we're the only life in the whole universe."

She thought about this for a moment. Her life revolved around her father's luncheonette. She worked in the store, ate and slept upstairs and didn't think much about anything beyond 8th and Montgomery. "Then I suppose we shouldn't waste too much time," she said.

"I suppose not."

"And you're going away tomorrow? Why did you sign up?"

"Our country's at war. Do you want Germany and Japan to take over?"

"Of course not."

Another trolley crossed over Montgomery Avenue and rattled on up 8th Street.

"It's getting late," she said. "I better go in. It was nice walking with you. Maybe we can do it again when you get back home."

"I'd like that," he answered.

She leaned over and kissed him on the cheek. "I'll be waiting," she said, and unlocked the door and went inside.

Rusty walked up 8th Street, touching his cheek. It was warm.

Nice girl, he thought, and pretty too.

## 28

"New London!"

Rusty pulled down his duffle bag from the overhead rack. He exited onto the station platform with hundreds of servicemen headed for different objectives. He and about 15 other boys in dungarees, pea jackets and sailor caps stood around eyeing each other. A voice called out to them from the street. "Over here! The bus!" They clambered aboard and in 15 minutes were passing a large sign – U.S. Maritime Officers Training School.

It was a strange place for them to be. They certainly weren't officer material. The bus, its brakes screeching, stopped before a long, low barracks-like building, where they alighted to the tune of "You'll Be Sorry," sung by groups of men standing along the route. The recruits smiled at each other. This was it. They were in the war at last.

After a brief physical they received work clothes and a uniform to be worn while on base grounds. It was the same as a Navy uniform, but with U.S.M.S. on the sleeve. They were given sleeping quarters and were separated into daily work details in groups of five. Rusty noted that one of the recruits had a much more pronounced limp than he did, and another man wore glasses with thick lenses. We're not the cream of the crop, he thought. As they got to know each other, he learned that most were classified 4F, rejected by the military for physical reasons, and like himself, had joined the U.S.M.S. to contribute to the war effort.

After a week in New London, it became obvious they were signed up to do nothing more dangerous than washing and waxing floors, scrubbing out the heads, maintaining the grounds, and keeping the base clean for the hundreds of merchant seamen studying to be officers.

In three weeks, most were grumbling about being sent to New London instead of out to sea as they had hoped. Rumor had it that the Army Transport Service, in charge of all military cargo shipping, was in need of seamen to man vessels carrying supplies to England and Russia. A phone call to their office in New York affirmed these rumors.

Their spirits lifted, about a dozen men applied for discharges, but were told they must serve three months before they were eligible. This was disappointing, but they had no choice except to work out the time as best they could. It wasn't all bad. Once the officer candidates got to know you, certain entertaining diversions became available.

One Sunday when Sidney was sitting on the dock watching some of the men preparing to go out on lifeboat drill, he was invited to go out with them. He jumped into the lifeboat joining nine officer candidates in their working blues. They shoved off, allowing him to handle one of the eight oars until they reached that part of the river where some breeze was blowing. They shipped their oars and raised a sail, preparatory to simulating a lifeboat at sea.

It was a Sunday he would never forget, sailing down the Thames River, tacking first toward one shoreline and then to the other. For three hours they practiced raising and lowering sail, as they would if they were forced to abandon ship in the middle of the ocean. On one tack they crossed in front of a submarine headed for its berth at Groton, Connecticut. Rusty never realized how big subs were until this one passed them on the starboard side. One of the sailors on the sub was shouting something.

Rusty asked the man closest to him what he was shouting about.

"I don't think he likes our passing so close across his bow. We probably shouldn't have."

He looked back at the sub.

"Look, it's diving," Rusty said excitedly.

"They do that all the time out here. Just like we practice lifeboat drills, they practice diving and learning to handle a sub. Ever been on a sub?"

"No."

"Then don't. You'll get claustrophobia before ten minutes are up. It's no picnic. I don't see how they do it, confined to those cramped quarters for months at a time. I couldn't wait to get off. It's not for everybody."

Rusty looked back again, hoping to catch it rising to the surface, but it was nowhere to be seen.

"You expect to spend the whole war up here in New London?"

"Hell, no," He answered defiantly. "After three months, I'll be signing up with the Army Transport Service."

"You like ships?"

"This lifeboat is the first one I've ever been on, except the ferry that runs between Philly and Camden. When I cut school I used to go back and forth across the river all day long on a nickel. Sometimes they'd chase me off, but mostly they would look the other way."

"It's a good career if you love the sea. After a couple years with the A.T.S. you could apply here for officer's training."

Rusty's eyes lit up. "I never thought of that." Maybe I'll do that, he thought. It would be better than selling jewelry or repairing watches. And I'll see the whole world, too. Places that people spend thousands of dollars to see would be his for the asking. He visualized himself in a smart uniform, standing on the bridge, giving orders to the man at the wheel as the ship pulled into a romantic harbor on the other side of the world.

Suddenly, the lifeboat bumped, lurched upward and listed to the port side. He had the sensation of being in an elevator and carried upward. The men were yelling while he grasped the side of the boat in a vain attempt to keep from being thrown into the river. The boat went upward several more feet, then slid sideways back into the water.

Rusty was underwater for what seemed minutes before coming to the surface, splashing and kicking. The other crew members were swimming toward the lifeboat, now upside down only a few feet away. He struggled towards it and soon they were all holding on to the overturned craft. He found himself next to the man he was talking to before.

"What happened?" Rusty spluttered.

"Look behind you," he answered.

There, 50 yards away and continuing its journey upriver was the submarine whose path they had crossed earlier.

"We could have been killed," Rusty exclaimed. "Did this ever happen before?"

His companion laughed as they slowly paddled toward shore.

"Only when you cross their bow too closely," he said.

"You mean they did it on purpose?"

"You got it," he said. "It's their way of telling us not to let it happen again. It's just a game."

Some game, Rusty thought.

Three days later, he was awakened in his upper bunk bed by a hand gripping his arm. It was John Szabo, the dark-haired New Yorker who occupied the lower bunk.

"Let's go, Rusty," he said. "They want us over at the mess hall on the double."

"What's up?"

"Don't know. They want 25 men over there as soon as possible."

They scrambled into their work clothes and hurried outside where a strong breeze blew a light rain against their faces.

An officer, the same one who had answered his questions while in the water, was standing beside a pile of storm coats and foul weather gear.

"There's a big storm coming up the coast," he said. "A bad northeaster was supposed to go out to sea, but now it's headed right at us. We've got ten lifeboats tied up on Thames Creek Tributary. A report just came in telling us that they broke loose and are floating all over the place. Normally, we'd let them be until after the storm. The cove is protected on all sides but one. It's open to a northeast gale and that's where the wind will be blowing from. We've got to round them up before they get wrecked. We'll be travelling in two trucks. Put on one of these storm coats and let's load up. We have to finish before the wind gets too strong." He handed a coat to Rusty. "Nice to see you again, Reds. You must be a glutton for punishment."

"Just another volunteer." He smiled, trying to sound as matter of fact as possible.

"Good. My name's McCallister."

"Mine's Kurtz."

"Okay. You and nine other guys come with me and the rest get in the other truck. Let's go. We don't have any time to spare."

They rushed outside. The rain was heavier and the wind increasing.

McCallister motioned Rusty into the cab with him while the others scrambled into the back.

"How far is it?" he asked.

"About ten miles. These boats were loaned to us by the Navy and we don't want them ruined, or we'll never be able to borrow anything from them again."

"How're we gonna do this?"

"I'm not sure. We have an old Coast Guard cutter that I requested for assistance, but we can't count on it. We've had trouble with the engine, but with every Navy unit screaming for spare parts, we haven't really been able to bring it up to par. If they can't get it to us in time, we'll have to work with what we have. That's why I wanted so many men. With the cutter, we could do the job with five or six guys. Always prepare for the worst, Reds."

"Yes, sir."

"The sir isn't necessary tonight. First names will do."

"My name's Sidney, but everybody calls me Rusty."

"Rusty it is. My name's Charles. Guess what everybody calls me?"

"Chuck."

"You've got it."

They drove on down the deserted highway with the rain splashing against the windshield and battering the truck's canvas top, making conversation difficult. The dashboard clock read 3:10 a.m. The road was dark except for the truck's headlights, which were attempting to provide adequate visibility on the slick road.

They soon turned onto an even darker back road.

"This will take us to the inlet," Chuck shouted. "We should be there in about five minutes."

They fell silent as McCallister guided his truck through large puddles and around broken branches. Another turn in the road and the truck's headlights illuminated a wild scene. The inlet was a mass of white foam as gale force winds whipped the surface into two and three foot waves. Pulling their hoods down and buttoning up their coats, they jumped out of the truck and were almost blown over by the fierce wind.

"I don't see the cutter," McCallister called out. He cupped his hands to his mouth. "We'll have to do it the hard way. Twenty of us, ten in a lifeboat. We'll try to corral the missing boats. The guys left on shore will secure them as we bring them in. Rusty, bring 18 men with you and tell the others to stand by near the piers while we round up the strays."

"I only see one boat that we can use," Rusty shouted.

"There's another one hung up on a low lying tree branch," McCallister pointed up the beach. "You ten men! Get aboard that boat with one lookout in the bow and one at the tiller and follow us out into the inlet. Stay in hailing distance, but try to avoid collisions."

McCallister, followed by Rusty and eight men, waded out to intercept the lifeboat heading their way. A wave caught it and sent it racing down towards them, but luckily the stern caught in a small sand bar and halted momentarily, giving everybody a chance to climb aboard.

"I want one man at the bow as lookout. I'll handle the tiller. The rest of you pick up an oar and row like hell. We've got to get her off the sand!"

Szabo took the lookout position while Rusty sat next to oar #1. Eight oars, four on each side, were placed in the oar locks and dropped into the water. The oarsmen tugged haphazardly at the oars, all striking the water at different times.

"All together, god damn it," McCallister yelled. "When I say row, drop your oars together and pull this thing out of the sand. Now! – Now pull. That's it! Again! Don't you guys have any muscle? Try again! – Pull – again!" It was no use. The boat was stuck. If eight oars couldn't free it, they were in trouble.

McCallister was beside himself. He looked down the beach. The other men had managed to free the boat from the tree and were just now beginning to row.

"Here, you four nearest me. Get out and help me lift this mother out of the sand. Quick!" They reluctantly jumped back into the cold water and positioned themselves on either side of McCallister.

"Now heave, you landlubbers. Heave! You men in the boat, keep rowing! That's it – once more," he screamed. There was a lurch. "She's free!" Everybody back in – lively now! Okay, we're on our way, now keep rowing." He waved toward the other boat to pull up behind them and both boats moved slowly out into the inlet, rocking crazily in the choppy two to three foot waves.

It was all they could do to maintain headway against gale force winds and short, choppy seas. Unlike the open ocean where the troughs were wider and the waves farther apart, here in the relatively shallow inlet there was no respite. The waves were continuous, constantly battering the lifeboats until it was impossible to distinguish flying spray from wind-whipped rain. The rowers at least had their backs to the wind and water. McCallister and John Szabo were at the tillers looking straight ahead, and were subjected to the stinging combination of wind and water.

Rusty, his muscles already aching, looked past McCallister. He could barely make out the other lifeboat. He wondered to himself how they could possibly retrieve any boats under these conditions, and if they did, how they would manage to turn around without capsizing, and how the maritime service would react to the loss of 20 men trying to rescue a dozen lifeboats.

McCallister guided his lifeboat towards a small island about 100 feet long by 50 feet wide. There were some trees growing there and overgrown shrubbery. So far no lifeboats were spotted. After 15 minutes of back-breaking labor, they approached the lee shore of the island where the water was fairly calm and the trees and shrubbery provided some protection.

McCallister aimed his boat right at the beach and shouted back for the second boat to do the same. With quieter water and lessening wind on this side of the island, the boats, with eight rowers each, picked up some speed and rammed into the narrow sandy beach.

"You in the bow," McCallister yelled at John. "Jump out and make the line fast around that tree. Now, everybody get out and pull the boat up a little higher, then help the other boat do the same thing."

The men were now thoroughly soaked. After both boats were pulled up on the beach, McCallister gathered them together. "You men, rest here. I'm going across to the other side to see if I can spot anything."

They sat down as close to the trees as possible and watched the rain blowing almost horizontally over their heads. Rusty looked across that part of the inlet they had just crossed. The far shore was invisible. Although they were in a relatively secluded spot, it was obvious that the storm was still going full blast. His hands were blistered and his arms hung at his sides. He had never worked so hard in his life.

Suddenly a sound not related to the storm reached his ears. It wasn't the wind or the noise of the water thrashing around them. He stood up and turned around. It was a voice, a familiar voice. It was McCallister, and he didn't like the sound of it.

"You men stay here," Rusty said loudly. "I'll be right back."

He started across the small island as the wind and rain assaulted him once again. As he broke out into the open to receive the full fury of the storm, he heard McCallister's voice off to the right, and turning in that direction saw him lying on his right side, holding his left leg. It was bent at a peculiar angle.

"Chuck!" he shouted above the wind. "What happened?"

"I broke my fucking leg," he said. "There's a hole behind me and I stepped right in it. How dumb can a guy be? I was busy looking ahead. I heard a noise out on the water, and down I went."

"God!" Rusty said. "What do we do now?"

McCallister pushed himself onto his elbows. "First, take a look out on the water and tell me what you see. The noise sounded like wooden boats banging together."

Rusty walked through the remaining brush and peered out onto the inlet. From what he could see, it appeared that the inlet widened out at this point. Maneuvering lifeboats here would be tougher than on the side they just came from. Then he heard the noise McCallister was talking about – bump-bump-bump – wood against wood. It was coming from the right. He turned and put his hand up to his eyes to protect them from the relentless rain. There were large rocks running for about 50 feet along the beach. The lifeboats were being blown against these rocks. Two boats looked wrecked and the others were banging so hard it was only a matter of time before they too would be rendered useless.

He hustled back to tell Chuck what he saw. "And the water's worse on this side. The waves look like five feet. How did the boats get out here when the wind's blowing in the opposite direction?"

"They've probably been loose for days, winding up wherever the wind took them. Now listen to me, Rusty. Send two of your strongest men to carry me back. The rest of you get into the water and try to pull the undamaged boats around the rocks and drag them as far up the beach as you can. Is there enough beach for that?"

"I think so."

"Good. We'll leave them there for the time being and go back for them another day. Now get going!"

"Yes, sir," he answered. "I mean, Chuck."

After making certain McCallister was moved to shelter and made as comfortable as possible, he joined the rest of the men in trying to salvage the remaining lifeboats. The water was waist deep with waves occasionally breaking over their heads. The two wrecked boats were hung up on the rocks in a "v" fashion, forming a barrier between the rocks and the ten other boats, and they were all locked together in such a way, like a jigsaw puzzle, so that despite the high wind, they were not free to be thrown against the rocks.

John Szabo was beside him. "We'll never get those son-of-a-bitches apart," he shouted. "They're wedged in too god-damned tight. It's only a matter of time before they break each other up."

He's right, Rusty thought. Unless the storm dies down, which it gave no indication of doing, they're finished. He looked at the boats locked in a tight grip. We can't just let them break up, he thought. He studied their positions from the innermost boat to the one farthest out.

"John, I have an idea. We'd drown trying to wade out there. But if we climb over the rocks, we could get at them fairly easy."

"So, what then?" Szabo asked. "You going to push them suckers all away from the rocks?"

"Of course not. Get the rest of the men and line half of them up on the rocks, starting at the boats and ending where the rocks meet the beach. Have the others stand by on the beach. There's a coil of rope in each of our boats. They'll go with you and me."

John and Rusty scrambled carefully over the wet rocks, a coil of rope around their necks. Rusty reached the first boat and carefully jumped in, waving John to do the same.

He grabbed the bow rope and then jumped over to the second boat. He tied the rope to the tiller post. John followed, doing the same.

It took about 20 minutes to tie them all bow to stern, then Rusty took one end of his coil of rope and attached it to the bow of No. 10, the one farthest out. He shouted to John to tie the end of one coil to the end of the other, then toss the remainder to the nearest man on the rocks.

"Tell him to pass the rope down to the men on the beach and when I raise my arm, have them start pulling from as far away down the beach as the rope will reach. The other guys will have to do their best to keep the boats from piling up."

Rusty clambered back into boat No. 8 and called to John to join him.

"Okay, here's where we try to take apart this puzzle. Let's push together. We've got to get the bow of this last boat facing out so the guys on the beach can pull it in."

The wind was blowing as strong as before and the rain was blinding. Water poured down their faces.

"Okay, now together. Let's push!"

The lifeboat gave a little but the wind was too strong.

"Let's try again, push!"

It gave a little more this time, but again wedged itself back into position.

John tapped him on the shoulder and shouted in his ear. "If we push the bow out and to the right at the same time, the wind might swing the stern to the left."

"Good idea. Let's try it."

As lifeboat No. 10 retreated a few inches, they shifted their strength to the right. The bow scraped the boat on the right, the wind caught the stern and in one motion, the boat was free. Rusty raised his hand and the long rope to the beach tightened. The lifeboat moved away slowly, rubbing its starboard side against the starboard side of boat No. 9.

They leaped into No. 7 boat and started pushing the bow of

No. 8 which soon followed the other toward the beach.

"You men on the rocks. Don't let those boats get hung up! Push them off toward the beach!"

One by one they untangled, and as each boat reached the beach, several of the men pulled their bows onto the sand. In the end, ten boats were lined up side by side. Rusty reported back to McCallister.

"All the boats are beached in good condition except the two that were messed up at the start."

"Great job, Rusty,"

He beamed at the compliment.

"Now take a piece of wood, tie it around my leg and get me into a lifeboat. We've done our job."


Officer Candidate McCallister, off to one side and on crutches, watched his team take batting practice before their game with the U.S.

Navy Sub Base. Alongside the batting cage, Rusty swung a bat, waiting his turn.

The previous day, Rusty saw a notice on the bulletin board asking for a volunteer batboy and had hurried over to the athletic office hoping somebody didn't beat him to it. He was surprised to see McCallister behind the desk.

"Well, look who it is," McCallister exclaimed. "You all recovered from the other night?"

"I'm just fine. How's your leg?"

"The same. I'll be on crutches for a while."

"Too bad."

"Could have been worse. What's up?"

"I saw that request on the bulletin board for a batboy. Is it taken yet?"

"Nope, you're the first. We start practice next week. We meet right here on weekends at 8:00 a.m."

"Great. You think I could get to practice with you, too?"

"Hell, man, you're the local hero around here. Every officer candidate knows who you are. You can take any kind of practice you want. You play much baseball?"

"That's my game."

"Ever do any catching?"

"That's my position, until I can run faster. I had polio a few years ago and that slowed me down to a crawl."

"That's my position, too. But my playing days are over for this year. Tell you what. The guy that's taking my place is really an outfielder and he's not happy behind the plate. Can you hit? Maybe you two can share the duty."

"I hit pretty good in the Fairmount Park League."

"This isn't the Fairmount Park League. You'll be batting against pitchers who were in the majors last year."

"No kidding?"

"No kidding. That Navy base across the river has an ex-Cincinnati Reds pitcher who throws bullets."

"I'll do my best."

McCallister smiled. "Good man. I'm sure you will."

The practice pitcher threw some slow pitches to Rusty to get him started and he lined them through the infield. The pitches started coming in faster and were sent back through the infield faster. Rusty wasn't a homerun hitter, consistent line drives were his specialty, singles and doubles, and McCallister liked what he saw.

When practice was over, he took Rusty aside.

"Our first game is in two weeks over at the submarine base in Groton. You and Parker can split up at catching."

"Thanks, Mr. McCallister."

He received a menacing look.

"Sorry. Thanks, Chuck."


As McCallister had predicted, the Sub Base had their ace, the ex-major leaguer pitching the opening game. Rusty watched him warming up, and he was fast. He studied his motion and delivery. When it was his turn to bat, he would have to start his swing before the ball left his hand. A fit of doubt overtook him. McCallister was just being kind to him after the incident on the island, he thought. After this game, he'd be back waxing floors and cleaning latrines. He was certainly a long way from 33rd and Dauphin Streets.

After two innings, his left hand was hurting. His own pitcher was no major leaguer, but he was no slouch either. His pitches smoked into Rusty's glove with a loud smack. The game was scoreless when he came up to bat in the 3rd inning. That guy out there was tough, striking out five of the first six batters he faced.

Rusty used the lightest bat he could find and planted himself squarely in the back of the batters box, as close to the catcher as possible, giving him an extra fraction of a second to swing. It didn't help. The first two pitches were past him before his bat came around. The third pitch was a fast curve that made him back up but cut back over the inside corner. Three strikes and he hadn't gotten his bat around once. His only consolation was that his teammates weren't doing much better.

But his pitcher was doing a workmanlike job, too. Not as fast as his opponent, he nevertheless had great control. He consistently kept his pitches over the outside corner and he had a wide sweeping curve ball that mixed in with an occasional knuckleball, kept the hitters off balance.

It was still scoreless when Rusty came up to bat in the sixth inning. The maritime team had not put a man on base yet, and a no-hitter was a distinct possibility. Their only hope lay in the other team bringing in another pitcher, which they didn't seem to have any intention of doing. The Sub Base had a few hits, but were unable to bring them around.

Rusty looked out at the opposing pitcher. Tall, lean, he was a picture of confidence, a professional whose presence dominated the mound.

The first pitch was a wicked curve ball – strike one. Rusty stepped out of the box. That guy's probably figuring that I'm expecting a fast ball this time, he thought, so he'll throw me another curve. He stepped back in. Rusty had watched him closely to see if there was a change in his motion when throwing a curve as opposed to his fast ball. It seemed that he didn't kick his left leg as high and his arm came around more from the side when throwing his curve. Watch his leg, then his arm, he thought.

Sure enough, his leg didn't come up as high. He leaned a bit more to the side. Sidney was ready for the curve. There was a loud crack as bat met ball – a clean single to right center – a double for a faster runner. His teammates were cheering. There wouldn't be a no-hitter today.

The pitcher smiled approval from the mound.

Rusty took a short lead off the base. With a lightning move, the ball was thrown to first for the pick-off, but the first baseman, just as surprised as Rusty, froze as the ball zipped past him into right field. Rusty took off for second and headed for third when he saw the ball still bouncing around in the foul area in right field.

The next batter managed a bloop single to right field and it was the Maritime Base 1, Sub Base 0. The players on the sidelines were ecstatic. It wasn't often that they scored against this team.

Rusty returned to the dugout, glorying in the back-slapping and handshaking of his team mates. McCallister came over to him.

"You think you can catch the whole game?"

He was getting tired, but wouldn't admit it. "I thought I was supposed to split the game with Parker?"

"Parker ripped off a fingernail warming up."

"That's too bad," Rusty said. "I can go all the way."

The next inning, his pitcher walked the first batter, hung a curve a little too high and the score was 2-1, Sub Base ahead.

And so it went into the top of the ninth as his team came up to bat. The clean-up hitter slammed a double down the left field line, an error put men on first and third, and the next two men struck out. Rusty looked over at McCallister for any sign of a pinch-hitter, but seeing none, stepped up to the batters box. The opposing pitcher hadn't changed his style, high kick for a fast ball, a lower kick and a slight lean to the right for a curve. Rusty stepped as far back as the rules allowed.

It was a high kick. He was ready, but the blistering fast ball whooshed past his bat. Doesn't he ever get tired? he thought. He got set for the next pitch. The kick was lower, his body leaned a little to the side – the curve came over the outside of the plate. It never reached the catcher. There was a resounding crack and the ball sailed high and far toward right center field. With two outs, both runners were going. When the ball bounced off the top of the fence, Rusty was on second with a long double. Score, 3-2.

The Sub Base went out in order in their half of the ninth and Rusty joined his team celebrating their win over a pitcher that had beaten them every time.

He fell into his bunk that night very tired and very happy. He had gotten two hits off a major league pitcher, batted in the winning runs, and caught a complete game. It was the best day of his life.


Two days later he was called to the administrative office along with his bunk mate, John Szabo. They were given their discharges and were free to go down to the U.S. Army Transport Service in New York. Sidney suspected that McCallister had something to do with expediting his discharge. He and Szabo packed their duffle bags, said goodbye to their friends and went to the train station.

"Take care of yourself, Rusty," McCallister had said sincerely. "Maybe we'll meet on the same ship someday."

"Maybe. Thanks for everything. You've been great."

## 29

Wearing newly purchased pea jackets and sailor caps, with duffel bags on their shoulders and newly grown beards, Rusty Kurtz and John Szabo got off the train in Charleston, South Carolina, after a long, slow trip down from New York. Upon signing contracts verifying they were civilians working for the U.S. Army Transport Corps, they took the first train south out of Pennsylvania Station. As the ride north had been several months earlier, the train was crowded with uniformed men and women from various services and representing many allied countries. Men stood in the aisles or sat on the floor, playing cards, shooting craps, swapping stories or just trying to sleep. There was little room to walk and once they found a niche, they didn't stray too far. The air was heavy with humidity and clouded with cigarette smoke. The train stopped at nearly every town and city along the way, constantly forced onto sidings to allow 100-car freight trains loaded with war materials to rumble by.

Rusty and John exited the station at Charleston, S.C. and asked a policeman for directions to Pier 14 South. After a bus ride of several miles, they found themselves on the waterfront looking at every type of vessel imaginable tied up at the piers. There were sleek destroyers and cruisers, military transports and cargo vessels, floating cranes and dredges.

At the Pier, they looked for a ship with LT 677 on its bow, as noted in their orders.

Only one ship was tied up at Pier 14 South, a large, converted passenger vessel, painted white with a giant red cross on its side, a hospital ship. They were elated, having heard that duty on a hospital ship was the best kind, with good food, comfortable quarters and little chance of being attacked. Only one thing was wrong, there was no sign of LT 677 anywhere. Instead, S.S. Theodore Roosevelt was printed in dark letters on the bow.

They looked at their orders again.

"Let's go aboard anyway," Szabo said. "Maybe LT 677 is its coded name for security reasons."

"That's it," Rusty said. "Everything is coded today. LT is probably code for hospital ship."

They walked up the gangway to the open port. Inside were gleaming decks and bulkheads painted white with nurses walking back and forth. It was beautiful. A Marine guard stopped them inside the port.

"Where're you guys going?"

Szabo showed him the orders. "This is the only ship at Pier 14 South," he said. "We figured that LT 677 was the code name for this hospital ship."

"You figured wrong," the tall Marine answered. "You're on the wrong side of the pier."

"What do you mean?" Rusty asked.

The Marine pointed. "Your little bucket is over there."

They looked across the pier. There, lying close to the water was the gray shape of a tug – a large tug. On its bow was LT 677 – Large Tug 677. They were dumbfounded. Three months at New London, wrangling discharges to join the Army Transport Service, a long, uncomfortable train trip. All this to be assigned to a tug. It was unbelievable.

"This can't be," Rusty said.

The Marine smiled. "It not only can be. It is! Don't feel bad. I joined the Marines to fight and here I am an armed guard. We all have our cross to bear."

"Shit," Szabo said. "What's a tug got to do with fighting the war? We signed up with the Army Transport Service."

"That's an Army tug," the Marine replied. "The biggest that they make. It's used for ocean towing."

They shook their heads.

"Good hunting," the Marine shouted with a laugh as they walked disconsolately down the gangway to the opposite side of the pier.

The tug was large, about 100 feet long, and painted battleship gray. The bow was high out of the water, the stern low down. She was ugly.

Rusty looked at Szabo. "The guy that signed us up in New York must be laughing his head off."

"You two Kurtz and Szabo?" a voice called from the open bridge.

Rusty looked up. "Yes, Sir," he said to the uniformed officer with a couple stripes on his shoulder.

"Well, get aboard. We're taking her out on shakedown. See Mr. Anderson for instructions."

They had barely stepped down into the stern when lines were cast off and the tug moved slowly away from the pier.

Another officer approached them.

"Kurtz and Szabo? Follow me. I'll show you to your bunks and clothes closets. Then we'll go back on deck and see how this baby operates."

They looked around. The paint was fresh, no rust spots, no odor of the sea. A brand new tug.

Rusty had a lower bunk on the port side and Szabo would occupy the upper. There were 24 bunks, 12 on each side with a large table between them.

Rusty looked at Mr. Anderson's uniform. "I thought we were all civilians working for the Army."

"Technically, we are," he answered. "There are four U.S. Maritime Service officers aboard. We're the only ones in uniform, except for the radio man, he's Navy. Even the captain wears civvies. We're all paid by the Army. The galley's just out here. The ship's small but comfortable. You'll get to know everybody in no time. There are only 28 men on board. Come on, let's go on deck."

The LT 677 was already out into the channel and was moving right along. A steep wake, higher than the stern, was left behind them as the captain kept her at high speed.

"This isn't so bad after all," Rusty said to Szabo. "It's like being on a large speed boat." The crew not on duty stood around watching the stern wake rise higher and higher.

"She really digs down deep," one of them said.

"You can feel the power."

Rusty wondered to himself why all this power was necessary. Over the next few days, he became acquainted with shipboard routing. The watches were Navy. Four hours on, 8 hours off. Every deckhand took a turn at the wheel and the ordinary seaman was considered low man on the totem pole. Discipline was lax. This was the Merchant Service, not the Navy, but everybody was expected to know his job and do it to the best of his ability.

The deck hands were responsible for the care of everything on the tug except the engine room and the radio room where "Sparks," the Navy radio operator, reigned supreme. He monitored radio messages, received weather forecasts and passed on all information, important or otherwise, to the captain.

Rusty and Szabo, not having any training whatsoever, spent two days becoming familiar with the workings of the tug and practicing knots, from figure eights to squares.

They hosed down the decks, inspected the cramped quarters of the engine room, were shown the bridge and how to box a compass, learned how to get out the metal towing cable and roll it in again, and to their consternation, how to operate an acetylene torch. "You'll find out why," they were told.

The day before sailing, they watched apprehensively as a 50 caliber machine gun was hoisted on board and secured to the outside top of the overhead behind the bridge. Rusty glanced at Szabo. The war was getting closer.

## 30

The next morning LT 677 left Pier 14 South, and headed down river, passing bustling piers, busy dock yards and smaller tugs pushing barges upriver against the outgoing tide.

Rusty and Szabo, the newest and lowliest additions to the crew, were both assigned to the 4 – 8 watch with each scheduled to put in one hour per watch at the wheel.

Before reaching the mouth of the river, LT 677 pulled alongside a huge floating crane tied up at a dock south of Charleston. Rusty went up on the top deck to get a better look at this floating monster. The crane, as high as a ten-story building, was sitting atop a huge barge whose deck was on the same level as the tug's bridge. As long as a football field and just as wide, it was built to clear harbors of wreckage and obstacles to shipping. It had no power of its own, having to be towed to wherever it was needed.

Second Officer Anderson called up to him. "Come on down, Kurtz, and lend a hand at the towing cable."

I'm supposed to be off watch, he thought as he hurried down, but he was certain Anderson was aware of it. Szabo was there, too, as well as the men on watch. Part of the stern was enclosed on three sides, housing a motor and a roll of 4" thick metal cable. The remainder of the stern was open to the weather and low in the water. The tug moved ahead of the crane then backed into it, stern to bow, the crane's bow being high and wide, not pointed.

A motor on the tug began paying out its load of heavy cable to hook up to the crane's eye.

"Everybody line up and guide the cable as it comes out," Anderson shouted.

On the bridge the captain kept a critical watch over the activity below. "Keep that cable off the deck," he shouted. "No need to scratch up a new paint job!"

The cable paid out. The hook and eye were joined, led back through the hawser opening and dropped into the water.

"Okay!" Anderson shouted. "Pay out 100 feet of cable once we're away from the dock, and 100 yards when we reach the open ocean, but not until you're told!"

"Yes, sir," the man operating the motor shouted back.

"Now everybody stay away from the cable. It can knock you over the side if you're not careful."

The LT 677 moved slowly to mid-stream, pulling the ponderous crane behind it, then turned toward the mouth of the river in the direction of the open Atlantic to join a convoy of other tugs and slow freighters.

Rusty walked over to Szabo. "Big sucker, isn't it?"

Szabo nodded. "I wonder where we're taking it?"

"Probably up or down the coast somewhere to another port."

"I don't think so," Szabo answered. "I heard some of the crew talking. We have enough fuel for 14 days, then we refuel at sea."

"At sea," Rusty said in a surprised tone. "We're not taking this thing out on the ocean?"

"Why else would we have to refuel at sea?"

He didn't answer, but looked back at the floating crane towering high above the water. Fourteen days of fuel, then refueling meant at least two weeks out on the open ocean with that beast towering behind them. This was not how he had expected to fight World War II, pulling a barge with a crane attached to it. Just wait until I see that guy in New York, he thought. If he was laughing before, he must be splitting his sides by now.

As they passed from the confinement of the channel out into the Atlantic, 100 yards of thick cable were paid out behind them. The tug hesitated as the cable took hold, momentarily rising out of the sea. The tug strained its engines maintaining speed and gradually LT 677 and the floating crane moved forward together.

LT 677 rose easily with the first rollers moving in from the open sea, but the tow behind them did not take kindly to a frontal assault by the ocean. Waves slammed against her flat bow, causing sudden tension on the cable and sending a shudder through the tug. Rusty grabbed the rail for support. It's going to be a comfortable trip, he thought.

"Kurtz!" It was Anderson again. "I know you're not on watch now, but we need some hands below in the bow hold to balance out the cargo. We loaded fast and too much weight was put on the port side. Go down and help them."

The hold wasn't large, and the cargo consisted mostly of cartons of canned goods, crates of tools, spare engine parts and extra clothing. Szabo was there with other men, passing cargo from port to starboard. The hold was warm, stuffy and beginning to smell like a locker room. Added to this was a more pronounced dip and roll as the tug encountered larger waves.

Sid found himself gulping frequently and yawning as the motion of the vessel disturbed his normal equilibrium. He was getting sea-sick. The seaman next to him, slender, with thick, dark hair combed straight back looked at him.

"My name's George Cole."

"Rusty Kurtz."

They shook hands. "I guess I feel as bad as you look," he said.

"I think I'm getting seasick," Rusty admitted.

"Me too."

"What do we do?"

"Throw up, I guess, but not down here."

"I'm not that bad, yet," Rusty said. "But it won't be long. God, it's close down here."

"Isn't it? We'll be finished here soon. Try to hold out."

"You an ordinary, too?" Sid asked.

"Yeah, the crumb of the crop. They told me in Norfolk I was signing up for the Merchant Marines. I never expected this."

"Me neither. Kind of a dirty trick," Rusty said.

"I suppose so. Still, it's a job that has to be done. And we are merchant seamen, just working for the Army."

"I didn't know ships were part of the Army."

"We have a lot to learn," Cole said. "How old are you?"

"Nineteen."

"I'm 25. My grandmother told me that we never stop learning until we die. She said just to consider this a learning experience and it won't seem so bad."

"Sounds like good advice." Rusty thought of his conversation with Grandma Itkah. "Has your grandmother ever been seasick?"

Cole laughed. "When I get back, I'll ask her."

Anderson's voice shouted down from the deck, ten feet above them. "You guys can come up now, she's all balanced out."

Rusty staggered up to the lee rail and threw his breakfast into the ocean. Cole wasn't far behind him. They both ran their sleeves across their mouths.

"Whew," Rusty gasped. "That was awful. I'm going to lie in my bunk until my next watch. Maybe I'll feel better by then."

"If you're lucky," Cole said. "I hear some people are sick all the time."

"God, I hope not. I'll never last that long."

It was a horrible three days as the LT 677 refused to give up its violent motion. Rusty haunted the vessel, searching for a comfortable spot to rest his wretched body, but there was none. Dragging himself through his watches, he ate nothing, and after the first day, threw up nothing. Dry gut, he was told. He went through the motions of his duties on deck and at the wheel. The veteran crew members smiled knowingly at his discomfort, having lived through that agony a long time ago.

The captain alone was sympathetic. He was sick, too. Not as bad as Rusty, but suffering nevertheless. On the fourth day, as the aching subsided, Rusty learned that it was the captain's first sea assignment. He was a tug master at various ports for 25 years, never having gone to sea before this trip.

After his first meal in three days, Rusty stood at the wheel watching the compass and admiring the size of the waves coming from the port bow. Third Officer James Walford, a husky, sandy-haired southerner with slightly crossed eyes that had kept him out of the Navy, stood at the windshield checking their position with other ships in the convoy.

Captain Herman Sugarman, a tall, heavy, balding man in his fifties with a friendly countenance, came in from the open bridge. He glanced at Rusty. "It's good to be alive again, isn't it, Kurtz?"

"Yes, sir. That was the worst three days I ever had."

"As you saw, Captains are not immune. I ate like a horse today."

"Me, too," he answered. "I was really in bad shape."

"You sure were. Remember asking me to lower our lifeboat and let you row back to Norfolk?"

Rusty smiled sheepishly, keeping his eyes on the compass. "Vaguely. I really was in bad shape, wasn't I?"

"You and me, and every guy on his first trip."

"Except Szabo," Rusty said. "He didn't even burp."

"Some guys are lucky. They never get seasick."

"I heard some never stop. How can they stay at sea?"

"People are tough. They can get used to anything. What's your course?"

"105 degrees, just south of east."

"Walford," Captain Sugarman said. "Check out the men on the fantail. Make sure they know how to work that torch. Sparks reports heavy weather ahead. I hope we don't ever have to use it."

"Yes, sir." Walford left the bridge and went below.

"I don't even know what that acetylene torch is for," Rusty said.

"You learn how to use it?", asked the Captain.

"Barely. I've been so sick. I'll ask Cole or Szabo to go over it again. I know we all have to put in one hour of each watch on the fantail with it. Why?"

"In case the tow is torpedoed or capsizes in bad weather, that cable has to be cut damn fast or we get pulled under with it. It's important, so make sure you know how to work it."

"Yes, sir," Rusty answered, feeling new respect for that floating crane 100 yards astern.

The captain looked out at the convoy. Eight slow freighters and three other tugs pulling their tows with two destroyer escorts leaping around, keeping the ships close together for safety. "So far, so good."

"Where are we taking these things?" Rusty asked.

"To England. There'll be plenty of wreckage that'll need clearing out. That tow to our starboard is a floating powerhouse. It can supply enough electricity for a small city."

Rusty thought for a minute, setting himself against a large wave. "We're really pouring a lot of stuff over there," he said.

"More than the Germans and Japanese ever thought we could. America's the greatest industrial power in the world. We're protected by two oceans and we're producing more stuff than the rest of the countries put together. Speaking of Germany, Kurtz is a German name, isn't it?"

"It might be," Rusty answered.

"You Jewish, Kurtz?"

"I am," he answered hesitantly. With his red hair and beard, everybody thought he was Irish.

"I thought so. I saw that silver star of yours flapping in the breeze when you were throwing up. What was your family name before it was shortened?"

"I think it was Kurtzman. How did you know it was changed?"

"Many Jewish families did, so they wouldn't sound so Jewish, self-protection and all that. Not many of us in the Merchant Marine. My father was a proud man, said he wouldn't change the family name for anybody. I'm glad he didn't. Sugar, Sugarman. I can't decide which is worse. But I don't broadcast it. War or no war, there are still a lot of kooks out there who believe we crucified Christ, started the slave trade, and are responsible for the war. Stupid, isn't it?"

"Sure is," Rusty said. "We're all in this together."

They were both quiet as Third Officer Walford returned to the bridge.

"Everything under control, sir, but that cable has me worried. When it tightens up, it starts singing like it's going to break into a million pieces."

"I'll go down and have a look. Take over. We're on course, 105 degrees. Keep an eye on the ships around us." He left the bridge.

"Repeat course," Walford asked.

"105 degrees."

"105 degrees it is. Keep it steady."


Rusty was relieved at the wheel by the 8 – 12 watch and he went below for some breakfast. The small mess room smelled delicious. Eggs, toast, bacon, brown potatoes, coffee – odors that would have sent him rushing to the rail two days ago.

He found Szabo and Cole already eating. Grabbing a tray and helping himself to some eggs, toast and potatoes, he sat down opposite them.

"Welcome back to the living," Szabo said.

"Very funny. Only characters like you didn't get seasick. How come?"

"I'm descended from a long line of sailors. My father rented out rowboats in Central Park and my grandfather worked in a shipyard."

"I should have known better than to ask," Rusty said. "The captain told me we're taking our tow to England.

"That's not news, Szabo said. "I heard that the second day out. You guys have been away for three days."

"Forget it," Rusty said. "I think I'll just eat my breakfast."

"The ocean's calmed down quite a bit today," Cole said.

"Let's go up top after chow and look around. Maybe we'll see a whale or something."

"While you guys were in upchuck land, I met some of the crew," Szabo said. "Do you know we've got one Australian, one Polish refugee and two Norwegians on this tug?"

"No kidding?" Cole said. "A real melting pot."

"The Pole escaped from Poland after the Nazis took over the country and the Norwegians did the same."

"They must've had a rough time," Cole commented. "I guess this is their way of fighting back."

"Who captured Australia?" Rusty asked.

"Nobody, wise guy. He was turned down by his own army so he came to the United States. No luck, he was turned down here, too, just like us. So he joined the Merchant Marines."

Rusty laughed. "This bucket is the floating version of the French Foreign Legion. A haven for misfits. What about you, Cole? Were you 4F too?"

"Not exactly," Cole said. "It's a long story."

"If we don't like it," Szabo said, "we'll just throw you overboard."

"Back home I was threatened with more than that."

"What did you do?" Rusty asked. "Murder somebody? Do you have leprosy?"

"I might just as well have."

"Hell," Szabo said, "we're all fighting the same war. What crime did you commit that was so terrible?"

Cole took a deep breath. "You know what a conscientious objector is?"

"Isn't it somebody that doesn't want to fight for his country?"

"No," Cole answered. "It's somebody that doesn't want to fight, period. There's a big difference."

"Don't you believe in the war?" Rusty asked.

"Sure I do. If we don't beat the Nazis and the Japanese, we're in big trouble."

"So what's the problem?"

"I'm a Quaker. My whole family is. We're related to the Pennsylvania Quakers going back to the 1700s. We don't believe in guns, killing or any kind of violence."

"But you're here in the Merchant Marines."

"That's the deal my lawyer made with the draft board. I didn't want to be part of anything that kills people. In the Army, Navy or Marines, I wouldn't have much choice. Here I feel like I'm saving lives rather than killing them. The faster we deliver the goods, the shorter the war, less people being killed."

"I never thought of it that way," Szabo said.

"It's the next best thing to fighting. I'm supporting my country and still sticking to my beliefs."

"Do all Quakers think like that?" Rusty asked.

"They should. There're always some dissenters, just like in any group, but for the most part, we're all nonviolent."

"This war really put you in a spot," Rusty said. "Have other Quakers done the same as you?"

"Some. Many are in defense work or helping the Red Cross care for poor families left behind. Some have broken ranks and have joined some branch of the service. It's sort of letting your conscience be your guide."

"Tough decisions. I guess Szabo and I had it easy – no fighting with our conscience."

"Speak for yourself, Buddy," Szabo said. "I had to tear myself away from a beautiful girl, and what do I have to show for it? Bunking down with a red-bearded Jew and a peace-loving Quaker. Not much of a bargain."

Everybody laughed.

"War is hell," Rusty said.

"It sure is."

The rough weather forecast by Sparks never materialized, and for several days the ocean was calm and the skies relatively clear. Brilliant sunrises and sunsets were daily attractions and the convoy continued on a southerly track away from the stormy North Atlantic. Schools of porpoise swam alongside, easily surpassing the six knot speed of the convoy, rising out of the water and dipping below the surface in one graceful, curving motion, sometimes bumping purposely against the hull to tell everyone they were there. An occasional flying fish, with fins outstretched, would glide past, then splash back into the sea. Sea birds dipped and swooped hoping for a free meal, but were destined to be disappointed, as dumping waste and garbage was severely restricted for security reasons.

At night, with blackout enforced, the sky in every direction was filled with more stars than Rusty had ever seen. He thought of Yussel. He knew he was a bombardier with the 8th Air Force in Britain, and they had been engaged in high altitude daylight bombing of Hitler's Europe, sustaining many losses. He murmured a silent prayer.

Here on the ocean, away from the haze and glare of populated areas, the starlight cast an eerie glow on the ships and faces of their crews. Rusty could barely make out the Big and Little Dippers amongst the bright clutter of the heavens.

Cole stood unseen beside Rusty for some time before making himself known. "Quite a sight, isn't it?"

"I never saw anything like it."

"Discouraging to think that if something happens to us, we'll never see it again."

"When I was younger, my friend Yussel and I used to sit outside his uncle's grocery store and talk about the stars. He's in the Air Force in England. We could see maybe one-tenth the stars that we're looking at now, and they weren't nearly as bright."

"We're like grains of sand," Cole said. "Here we are scratching and clawing each other, and for what? A little more land? Is it worth it? Will the world be better off for it?"

"Tough questions," Rusty said. "The human race is a strange

breed." He again thought of his grandmother. She would have answers.

They lapsed into meditative silence, each with his own thoughts. The LT 677 moved smoothly on, leaving behind a phosphorescent wake that eventually splashed against the shadowy hulk of their tow.

The following day and evening continued with calm seas and clear nights. They were one week out of Charleston, maintaining six knots an hour, a maddeningly slow pace.


Rusty, Szabo and Cole had finished their evening watch and were lying in their bunks reading. The gentle rolling of the vessel and the occasional jerk as the crane tightened up on the cable were suddenly interrupted by a tremendous hammering noise that resounded through the tug and tumbled them out of their bunks, holding their ears.

"What the hell was that?" Szabo asked.

"You've got me," Rusty said. "What do you think, Cole?"

"I'm in the dark as much as you. Never heard a noise like that in my life."

They went up on deck and stopped the first man they saw. It was the Norwegian, Ericson.

"What was that noise?" Cole asked, excitedly.

"Now don't you boys get all upset," he said calmly. His accent was heavy. "Nothing to worry about. Just a sub poking around. One of the escorts probably dropped a depth charge. You boys will get used to it. It sounds like the devil himself banging against the hull. It ain't so close like it sounds."

"Too close for me," Szabo said. "How do we know if they got anything?"

"We don't, until somebody tell us. We'll find out sure enough."

Too nervous now to go back to their bunks, the three remained on deck staring into the darkness.

"Well, our tow's still there," Szabo said.

"I can only make out one escort," Rusty said. "The other must be on the far side of the convoy."

Another tremendous noise shook the tug, forcing them to instinctively grab the rail for support.

"God, what a racket," Cole said. "It sounds right next to us."

A sudden flash in the distance lit up the sky and briefly silhouetted the convoy as it continued on.

The voice of Third Mate Walford rang out from the deck above them. "Somebody's been hit!"

There was a clatter of feet as the crew rushed out to see what was going on. The initial flash was followed by a flickering light that meant only one thing – a ship on fire.

"Poor bastards," Szabo cried. "I hope they get off on time."

"We could be next," Rusty said, his voice shaking.

"Not likely," Cole answered. "Cargo ships come first. It has to be a cold day in hell when they waste a torpedo on a tug or it's tow."

"I don't know," Szabo said. "If they get desperate for good targets, we'd be better than nothing."

Rusty saw the captain out on the flying bridge looking at the scene through binoculars. Not much we can do, he thought. After an hour on deck with no further explosion they went below to try to get some sleep.

But sleep was not to be that night. Somewhere out on the dark ocean and beneath it, two professional fighters – a destroyer escort and a German submarine were playing cat and mouse. Long periods of silence were followed by three or four successive poundings on the hull, indicating an attack.

Just as sleep claimed the crew, another series of blows resounded throughout the LT 677. Rusty wondered about the engine room gang. A direct hit and they were finished. A torpedo would blow the tug into little pieces. He thought of home, his back porch, his favorite spot near the radio, his grandmother. He wondered what everybody was doing. He could see his father explaining his hair growing system to a customer, his mother cleaning and cooking, Edie working at the school.

While he was waiting for the next explosion, they were going about their daily activities. They were probably wondering where he was. His last letter from New York cautioned them against hearing from him any time soon. He should have brought the Complete Sherlock Holmes with him. It's probably still sitting out there on the porch, he thought. He wondered if the politicians and numbers writers still took over the store on Sundays, playing cards, smoking cigars, spitting into the spittoons. From 500 miles out on the Atlantic, it didn't seem so bad.


For five days and nights it was touch and go with the enemy. Stretches of tense calm were punctuated by sudden slammings against the hull. There were no more sinkings, but Sparks reported sightings of torpedo wakes by several of the ships in the convoy. The nights were too long, the days too short. Three hours sleep was considered good, and the cable watch was doubled in case a U-boat captain decided to release any frustrations with an attack on the tow. On the sixth day the weather turned sour as a front with squalls and fog settled over the area, creating navigation problems, but providing a welcome respite from submarine attacks. The seventh day saw a steady rain with the wind and seas rising dramatically.

Rusty was at the wheel when Sparks came down from the radio room with a weather bulletin. A tropical storm had formed just ahead of the convoy with the possibility of it becoming a hurricane within 24 to 36 hours.

Captain Sugarman looked at Rusty. "Aren't you glad you joined the Merchant Marines?" he asked.

Rusty smiled weakly. "I was just thinking yesterday how nice it used to be sitting on my back porch reading Sherlock Holmes mysteries, and watching brown paper bags sail over our fence." He related the experience to the Captain.

"That's a funny story," he said. "Was your father a numbers writer?"

"No. He has a barber shop, but the house is used as a drop-off point. All the greasy politicians and small time crooks hang out there. I hated their guts. They're noisy, dirty guys with filthy mouths and filthy habits, spitting, filling the store with cigar smoke, and cluttering up the place with trash. It's a wonder customers want to come in there."

"Maybe he's a good barber."

"My mom says he is. She wishes he was as good a husband and father as he is a barber."

Captain Sugarman didn't answer.

"He says he has the only hair growing system in Philadelphia. He's got customers coming from all over for this treatment."

"Does it work?"

"He says it does. He tries it on himself. He doesn't have much hair on top, but he's always showing me fuzz on his head that he claims is new hair."

"Do his customers believe him?"

"I guess so. They just keep coming."

"He sounds like a good salesman."

"He is. He doesn't talk much to us, but in the store he's a different person."

Captain Sugarman was silent again.

"After hours he spends his time at the Cat and Fiddle Cafe. He's part owner."

"He sounds like an interesting character."

"I guess so," Rusty said. He then told him how his mother found out he had a stake in the cafe.

The captain threw back his head and laughed out loud. "That's the funniest thing I ever heard. He didn't know who she was?"

"Nope. She never said a word and didn't take off her mask the whole night."

Captain Sugarman laughed again, then checked himself.

"I'm not laughing at your family, just at the situation."

"I understand," Rusty said. "We laughed, too, when she came home. But I think she was crying when she went upstairs." He was about to continue, but he was startled by the captain's urgent shout.

"Hang on, Kurtz!"

A tremendous wave loomed high above the tug on the port quarter. It lifted the LT 677 at a sickening angle, at the same time breaking over the small vessel. Rusty held tight to the wheel and planted his feet firmly against the flat wooden platform. For a moment the bridge was under water as the tug was nearly rolled over on its side. Above the noise, he heard the men below yelling excitedly. The captain was thrown to the deck and across the wheelhouse, hitting the bulkhead with a nasty thud.

The tug shuddered, leaned momentarily on its side, then

gradually rose up trying to rid itself of its watery load. As the water poured from the tug, it slowly recovered.

If not for his death grip on the wheel, he would have joined the captain on the deck, leaving the tug out of control and in danger of being run down by the tow.

"Where the hell did that come from?" he shouted as the captain breathlessly regained his feet.

"It's one of the seamen's worst nightmares – a rogue wave. It broke over us. We're lucky to be alive." He picked up the intercom and shouted orders. Everybody was accounted for and damage was minimal, although much material was scattered all over the place. The cargo in the hold needed straightening, and a loud pounding on the hull at the bow indicated the anchor had broken loose. With each roll of the tug it threatened to punch a hole in the side.

"We've got work to do," Captain Sugarman stated. "I'm going to see if our cable held. I'll send somebody up to stand watch with you. Keep an eye out for another one. It was probably a loner, but if you see one, turn a little to port. We don't want to get knocked over again."

The next several hours were spent redistributing the cargo in the hold and putting aside perishables that were ruined by the water that had broken open the hatch. The single lifeboat had been swept away and the two-man watch on the fantail had only survived by holding fast to the cable, swallowing much sea water in the process. It took the crew an hour to haul the anchor up onto the deck and lash it fast to the port bulkhead. Seaweed and flapping fish were everywhere and the tug looked like a ship risen from the bottom of the ocean.

After LT 677 was restored to a semblance of order, Rusty looked around. The tow was still afloat, but they were later informed by another vessel that for a few seconds the only thing visible was its tall crane sticking out of the water before its natural buoyancy brought it upright again.

The wave was the prime topic of conversation for the next 24 hours, with everybody relating their individual experiences when it struck. It was a miracle that nobody was lost. Anderson, who was standing near the list counter and hung to it for his life, swore he saw the needle at 68 degrees, twenty five degrees more than the tug was built to withstand. He had thought it was the end and had been about to swim for it when the tug struggled back up.

But the vessel still moved ahead, its inanimate engines oblivious to this near catastrophe.


The tug and its crew had barely returned to normal when the tropical storm forming ahead of them struck with full fury. The wind increased to a steady 60 m.p.h. and the waves, not as large as the rogue, were nevertheless huge and successive, battering the convoy with painful regularity. The ocean was relentless. The escorts and freighters dug their bows deeply into each wave, sending water cascading against their bridges and rushing the length of the deck. After fighting off one wave, they prepared for the next.

The tugs were swept about like corks, They listed sharply first to port then to starboard, riding up each mountain of water, pausing at the peak, then diving into the trough. The tow was not so fortunate. Its high, blunt bow, resisted every wave, forcing the tug to keep engines at full speed merely to keep from going backwards.

On the fantail, Rusty and George Cole stood their acetylene watch, keeping a wary eye on the tow which disappeared as the tug descended the far side of a wave and reappearing when they reached the top. Wearing one-piece storm suits, they hung tightly to the rail surrounding the cable motor housing, sometimes waist deep in water.

The storm raged for two days and nights before moving west. The third day dawned clear and warm as the sea calmed down and the winds gradually lessened. Doors and hatches were opened to help dry out the tug. The sun was warm, and the crew, lounging on the open deck, sat around swapping stories and expressing relief at the passage of the bad weather.

The convoy was approximately in mid-Atlantic, still moving along at six knots per hour, two weeks out of Charleston. During the early afternoon, a Navy tanker joined the convoy and the laborious job of refueling began. Lines were shot by gun to each vessel in turn, and fuel lines were dragged aboard and connected. Some oil spilled onto the deck and men were soon slipping and sliding, reaching for whatever support was available.

By day's end the refueling was finished and the tanker picked up speed and soon disappeared over the horizon. In the evening, Rusty climbed up to the bridge and relieved Szabo at the wheel.

This was his favorite duty, standing at the wheel, maintaining course, and looking about at the ships around him. During wheel watch he was in control, and the tug responded to his slightest move. He could occasionally feel the tow pulling on the cable, but it was a gentle pull, not the terrifying wrenching and rending that occurred during the storm. This was what sailing should be – a bright sun over a sparkling sea, the steady rise and pull of the tug, men comfortably standing at the rail, and Rusty at the wheel watching over everything.

Captain Sugarman relieved Mr. Anderson, checked the compass heading, and looked out at the convoy. "This is more like it, isn't it?"

"Anything would be better than what we had," Rusty said. "I never saw anything like that ocean. I thought we'd never get through it."

"Oh, we'll make it all right. It's this damn six knot speed that bothers me. It makes the trip seem longer than it is."

"How long before we get to England?"

"Normally it's a three week trip, but with the weather and submarines, it looks like another 10 days to two weeks."

"Two weeks," he exclaimed. "That means a month to cross the Atlantic. That's no faster than the old sailing vessels used to take."

"A lot slower. With a good wind, they could do 10-15 knots an hour. Of course, without wind they were helpless. They were at the mercy of the weather."

"So are we."

"To some extent. But we have the advantage of engines. We don't need a breeze to keep moving."

They were both quiet for a while, enjoying the peaceful day.

"What're you planning on doing after the war?" the captain asked.

"I don't know. Go back to watch repairing, I guess."

"Ever think of making a career in the Merchant Marines?"

"Can't say that I have."

"You could put in a few years at sea, then apply for Officers' Training School. There'll still be a need for Maritime officers after the war."

Rusty thought for a minute. "What about all the officers serving now? The government won't need that many once the war ends."

"That's true, but most of them will go back home. There'll always be room for a good career man. You're reasonably intelligent. Stick with it long enough and you might make captain some day. Those guys make good money."

There was another moment of silence.

"From what I've seen of the weather out here," Rusty said, "I'm not sure I want to spend the rest of my life being thrown all over the ocean."

"You don't have to serve on a tug, although there are good points about a small vessel like this. The big ships are more comfortable – the quarters are better and you can't beat the food. It's up to you. Find out where you're best suited and stake out your spot."

"Thanks," Rusty said. "I appreciate your advice." He felt a warm attachment for this man who could have ignored a young ordinary seaman on his first sea voyage.


Three weeks out of Charleston, the convoy turned northeastward toward the British Isles. They were on the homestretch. Rusty, Szabo and George Cole felt like veterans. Tested and battered by the enemy and the Atlantic, and away from home for the first time, they had overcome seasickness, homesickness and the unique danger of life at sea.

Their beards had come off. Not only were they itchy and in need of special care, but it marked them as green landlubbers at sea for the first time. That was the last image they wanted to present. Sven Ericson, the Norwegian in the crew, stared at Rusty.

"I never would have known you. That was a beautiful red beard. The girls in Norway would go crazy over it."

Rusty's face was now as red as his beard had been. "Too bad we're not going to Norway."

"Maybe we will some day. You come home with me. My younger sister would love you."

Five days from England, the tug's boiler broke down. Rusty was off watch and had just dozed off in his bunk when the forward motion of LT 677 slowed to a halt and the steady rise and fall of the ship was replaced by an uneven and disorganized rolling. Unable to meet the waves head on, she was flung about, first facing the convoy, then slowly turning toward the tow.

He hurried up on deck and joined the rest of the crew at the rail, eager to see what was going on.

The sun had set one hour ago and they all looked out over a dark seascape. With all ships blacked out, there wasn't much to see, just some dim shapes in the distance. One of the shapes came closer and soon they recognized one of the escort vessels approaching.

"Hello!" came a voice from its bridge. They were not risking low powered radio contact that could possibly be detected. "What's your trouble?"

Captain Sugarman lifted his bullhorn to his mouth. "We have a broken boiler. We can't continue."

"How long before you can make repairs?"

"Several hours. We're working on it."

"Okay. We'll have to leave you for a while. Good luck."

The captain thanked them as the escort turned to rejoin the convoy, already pulling slowly ahead. He picked up the phone to the engine room. "Chief, you'll have to work fast. We're going to be all alone up here."

"That's great," Szabo said. "A sitting target for whatever comes along."

"And that doesn't help," George Cole said pointing to the eastern horizon. A large, nearly full moon was rising, its light reflecting off the ocean.

"Couldn't be better than if the Germans had planned it," Szabo said. "They may not waste a torpedo on us, but they sure as hell wouldn't mind throwing a couple shells in our direction."

"What next?" Rusty exclaimed. "If it's not one thing, it's another."

Sven Ericson was standing behind them. "You have to get used to these things when you go to sea. It's just like being on land. Nothing goes right all of the time."

Szabo wasn't mollified. "At least on land you don't have to deal with German submarines or waves 50 feet high."

"That's strange," Rusty remarked as the tug rolled from port to starboard in an uncommon fashion that was beginning to bring a familiar feeling to their stomachs. "I don't see the tow back there."

They all looked, trying to see into the darkness. No matter how black the night, the large hulk of the tow could usually be seen bucking up and down in the waves, it's crane rocking high above.

"You're right," Szabo said. "The tow's not there!"

"My God," Cole said aloud. "We've lost our tow!"

They rushed to the stern where two men were hovering over the cable, acetylene torch in hand.

"Cut that goddamn cable," Szabo yelled, "before it drags us under!"

"Wait a minute," shouted Ericson. "Not so fast. Where's that cable?"

"It's hanging straight down," shouted one of the seamen. "The tow must be right under us."

"Then why isn't it pulling us down?" He ran toward the bow and quickly returned. "You guys go take a look. We turn around 180 degrees. The tow's in front of us."

They all ran forward and sure enough, looming high and moving even closer, was the cursed tow.

"Son of a bitch," Szabo exclaimed. They stared at it in silence. "And it's getting closer. If we don't get moving soon, that thing'll run over us."

The Captain approached and leaned over the stern. "Shit! You four men come with me." They followed him down into the engine room where the heat and steam from the defective boiler made it difficult to breathe. Down here, out of sight, flashlights and other emergency lighting could be used.

"How's it going, Chief?" Captain Sugarman asked John Baker, the short, husky, middle-aged man who presided over the engine room.

Baker mopped his perspiring head with his sleeve. "It looks like three hours or more. We have to knock out some parts that have locked together. No lubrication. We may have to custom make something to fit. It'll be a noisy job."

"I don't have to remind you, Chief, how sound travels through water. And those subs have big ears."

"Sorry, sir. But it's that or we sit here until somebody comes for us."

"I don't like that choice," the captain said. "Okay, go to work. Make it as fast and as quiet as you can."

They followed him up on deck to the bow. "Now, if that tow starts hitting us, it'll knock us around pretty good. Each of you get yourselves a fender and keep it between the tug and the tow to soften the blows, but keep your arms out of the way."

For two hours, the tow loomed over the tug. The waves threw them together, first the tug rising up and nearly being thrown onto the deck of the tow, then as they turned about each other in a violent nautical dance, the tow crashed against the defenseless tug. Great dents appeared wherever they came together, and more than once the tow nearly landed atop its little adversary. The crashing impacts echoed across the water. At this point the engine room gang could bang away as much as necessary.

The inside of the tug was again a shambles and Captain Sugarman ordered the life rafts untied. If necessary, they would have to get off fast. The fenders were next to useless. The large bulk of the tow and its weight squashed them with each contact. Just as the captain was considering trying to tie the tug to the tow, a breeze sprang up and slowly pushed the tow away. The crew cheered wildly as their tormentor moved farther off their bow, leaving its victim bruised and bent, but still afloat.

Rusty turned to Szabo, "If the subs didn't hear all that racket, they won't hear anything."

By four in the morning when he relieved the wheel watch, seven hours of loneliness had passed. The engine room gang worked without rest to repair the boiler. The tow was now a dim shape in the distance. All hands nervously paced the deck, watching the bright moon rise overhead in a cloudless sky.

"We're a perfect target," Szabo said. "If we don't get it now, we never will."

George Cole agreed. "I guess the subs are following the convoy. They may not even know we're here."

"Look," Rusty said. "There's the escort coming back!"

It was a beautiful sight, the sleek destroyer cutting through the waves under a bright moon, throwing sparkling water to each side. Captain Sugarman filled in the escort on their progress.

The destroyer's captain had definite orders. "In two hours, a British escort carrier will be in your vicinity. If LT 677 is not under way at that time, transfer crew to the carrier and leave tug and tow behind. Another vessel will attempt to tow both to port at a later date. Good luck, again."

The faint glow of dawn was lightening the eastern sky as the escort disappeared over the horizon and a message came up from the engine room. "Repairs finished – ready to move."

The crew was alerted, all men went to their watch stations, and the captain sent down the signal – Slow ahead. The tug moved ahead, the cable became taut.

Rusty felt the wheel respond to his touch as LT 677 resumed its northeastward course. Men went about their normal duties and the tug was once again a living thing, pulling its former oppressor closer to their destination.


LT 677 sighted the English coast on its 30th day at sea, the last seven days alone, except for occasional patrol planes from escort carriers and bases in England. Everybody was on deck as the tug passed from the wide expanse of the Atlantic, into the narrower confines of the English Channel.

The cliffs of England did indeed look like chalk as they sailed slowly up the busy channel. The constant roar of airplanes flying toward occupied France to attack railyards, military emplacements and industrial areas in Germany, were welcome sounds to the crew. Everybody stared at the shoreline.

"I wonder where we'll wind up?" Rusty asked Cole as the shoreline drifted by.

"I heard London. The tug needs repairing. We may be here a month or more."

"A whole month," Szabo exclaimed. "What a break. And London, too. They say it's just like New York with a British accent."

"What about the tow?" Rusty asked.

"I guess we'll be dropping it off pretty soon," Cole answered. "The captain just ordered the cable brought in 50 yards to cut down on the chances of it getting tangled up in channel shipping."

Sven Ericson joined them at the rail. "You guys feel better now? I told you we make it."

"I had my doubts back there," Rusty said. "When that tow tried to climb on top of us, I thought we were finished."

"That was scary," Ericson admitted. "I never see anything like that in my life. But soon we get rid of it."

"When?" Szabo asked.

"Probably before dark. They don't want this thing trailing behind us all night. Wait a minute! Do you hear that?"

"Hear what?" Cole asked.

"That buzzing noise – shush – listen!"

They followed Ericson's gaze skyward and listened. Sure enough, there it was, a soft buzzing sound from above, like a giant bumble bee. Their eyes searched the sky but nothing was sighted.

"What is it?" Rusty asked, his voice trembling.

"It's a buzz bomb," Ericson answered. "You never see them until they land, then big explosion! Wait – listen."

"I don't hear it anymore," Szabo said.

"Now you worry," Ericson answered. "It's no use hiding. We just have to wait."

They stood silently at the rail, some still looking up, and others looking out across the channel.

"I don't understand – ," Cole never finished. About 2,000 yards to starboard something splashed into the channel. A large geyser of water rose high above the ships. Almost instantly a tremendous muffled explosion threw a mountain of water hundreds of feet into the air, scattering spray over nearby vessels.

Rusty, Szabo and Cole were awestruck.

"God in Heaven!" Cole exclaimed. "What was that?"

"Buzz bomb," Ericson answered. "You don't have to worry about them until they stop buzzing. You never know where they land.

They're unguided flying bombs the Germans send over once in a
while hoping they will hit something. They are terror weapons, scare
tactics."

"They sure accomplished that," Cole said. "My body's still
tingling. Do they ever hit anything?"

"Sometimes, mostly in London, It can't miss hitting something
there."

"London," Szabo shouted. "You mean we'll have to be dodging
those things while we're in London?"

"Every day," Ericson answered. "Hardly 24 hours goes by
without one of those bastards coming over."

"But why doesn't the Air Force destroy them?" Rusty asked.
"They must know where they're coming from."

"They've destroyed some, but they keep moving the launching
sites. It's not so easy. You'll just have to get used to it. V-2s also."

"V-2s?"

"Sure – they're like buzz bombs but without the buzz. Like flying
torpedoes. No sound till the explosion. London gets them every day."

"It might be safer at sea," Rusty said.

Ericson laughed. "There is no safe place here. You're right in the
middle of the war."

"That's just great," Szabo said. "How the hell can people walk
around every day not knowing when or where one of those fucking
things is going to drop?"

"Like I told you – you get used to it. Welcome to England,
boys."


Just before sundown. a British Navy tug tied up to the side of the
tow. The bridle was released, the towing cable was hauled aboard the
LT 677 and the tug was at last free of its burden. It was now the
responsibility of His Majesty's Navy. Every seamen cheered wildly as
they pulled rapidly away, moving faster than six knots an hour for the
first time in four weeks.

"Good riddance," Rusty yelled. "If we never see it again, it'll be
too soon."

LT 677 moved into the Thames estuary, picked up a harbor pilot and headed for the East India docks of London. No sooner did the pilot step aboard than the thickest fog that any of the crew had ever seen swallowed the LT 677 and all shipping around it. Fog horns were soon blaring from everything afloat and the bow of the tug was invisible to those standing on the stern.

Third mate Walford took the wheel as the tug moved slowly up the Thames River. Captain Sugarman posted Rusty as lookout on the open bridge and rejoined Walford and the harbor pilot. Rusty leaned forward into the fog as if the extra few inches would help. The pilot kept LT 677 moving slowly up river despite what seemed like zero visibility. "He must know those waters blindfolded," Rusty murmured softly.

A ceaseless symphony of fog horns and whistles came from all directions in the thick swirling mist. Sven Ericson and Cole joined him on the bridge.

"What do you think of life in the Merchant Marines?" Sven asked.

"You can have it," Rusty answered. "Out of the last four weeks, we had about three or four days of trouble free sailing. It's been one thing after another."

"So what?" Sven answered. "On land, it's the same. You never know what's going to happen. You get hit by truck – murdered by thief – cheated by business people. Here you know you can depend on your shipmates. We all pull together for common good. After the war, the only problem will be the weather. No more submarines – no more bombs."

"It could be a good life," Cole said. "If you don't mind being away from home so much. You going home after the war, Sven?"

"You betcha. I escape from Norway after Germans took over. This is my way of fighting them. I leave mother and three sisters behind. My father is mayor of small town. The Germans take him for questioning and we never see him again. After that, I must do something. I join underground and we sabotage and kill wherever we can. I finally escape to England and sign up on British ship. It is torpedoed in Atlantic and we are picked up by American vessel. I sign up again in Charleston and here I am."

"Boy, what a story," Rusty said. "I hope everybody's okay when you get back."

"Me, too," Sven answered. "My family in Norway and other people in occupied countries live more dangerous life than we do at sea."

"I never looked at it that way," Rusty said. "I signed up because my country was at war and many of my friends were drafted or enlisted. I guess the real heroes are the people living under the gun."

"All of us will be heroes before this thing is over," Sven said. "There's enough war to make a world full of heroes. Out here we're just closer to the action. I hope we all survive to see the end of it."

"Amen to that," Cole said. They were quiet for a while as the tug moved slowly through the fog. Horns and whistles echoed around them.

The pilot knew his stuff. Shortly the shadowy outline of a pier became visible to port as the tug turned out of the main channel. Faint figures appeared as lines were tossed ashore. The LT 677 tied up at a dock of the old East India Company, exactly 31 days after leaving Charleston, South Carolina.

## 32

That night after docking, the tug was quiet. The crew enjoyed their first good night's sleep in a month as those on watch poked about taking inventory of damage and estimating time needed to make repairs. By morning, the physical condition of the tug was assessed and the crew was informed that LT 677 would be in port about one month while repairs were effected, with shore leave being granted as equitably as possible.

The oil pump needed replacing. The emergency repair to the boiler had been adequate to get them to port, but still needed new parts. The lifeboat which had washed overboard would have to be replaced and two wheelhouse windshields, cracked when the rogue wave swamped them also needed replacing.

The two main 1800 HP engines, other than requiring routine maintenance, came through in good condition, but on closer inspection one of the propeller shafts was found to be slightly bent out of shape, possibly when the tug was being thrown high against the tow.

It was a lot of work to be done in a country where shipyard labor was prioritized by larger and more vitally needed vessels, and parts and supplies for LT's were at a premium. A month in London now seemed like a conservative guess.

Five days of scrubbing, painting, and clothes washing returned the 136 foot vessel to something resembling a normal state. The captain granted two days of shore leave to 3/4 of the crew, the remainder to follow when they returned.

Rusty, Szabo and Cole, wearing their cleanest dungarees, pea jackets and sailor's hats, joyfully stepped from LT 677 to the solid ground of the dock.

"Feels funny," Szabo said, "walking on something that's not moving."

"Yeah," Rusty said, "but we'll get used to it."

"I'm used to it already," Cole said.

"Onward and upward," Szabo shouted. "Where do we go first?"

"Picadilly Circus. That's where all the action is."

"How the hell do we find it in this fog?"

"Sven's been here before. He said take the No. 3 bus at the far end of the pier. It goes into the center of the city."

"I've seen fog," Rusty said," but this is ridiculous. This stuff hasn't lifted since we got here."

"England's a big island surrounded by cold water," Cole said. "The North Sea on the East and the Atlantic on the West. No severely cold winters, no hot summers, but lots of rain, wind and fog."

"So what?" Szabo said. "It's solid ground. That's all that matters."

A friendly British bobby directed them to the bus stop and it wasn't long before a double-decker bus, its headlights suddenly materializing out of the fog, slowly pulled to a halt to pick up three American seamen in London for the first time.

As the bus moved away from the river area the fog thinned out and they were able to look at the neighborhoods they were driving through. For the first time, they saw firsthand the destruction caused by the German Air Force. Block after block of rubble, with very few buildings intact. It was mostly factories and warehouses near the river, with little change as they passed through surrounding residential areas.

The headlines back home had not been an exaggeration. Rusty, Szabo and Cole looked out of the fog-stained windows at the endless rows of empty shells of buildings and homes. The destruction was unbelievable. First one, then the other would point out a particularly bad section, but for the most part they were silent except for an occasional gasp or whistle of amazement. The Germans had tried to bomb England to its knees, and had come close to doing it.

The bus driver watched them in his rear view mirror and smiled. "Never seen nothin' like it, have ya, Yanks?" He was an older man, probably in his sixties, too old to be in the military, but still able to do his job on the home front.

"Never," Cole answered. "We heard about it and read about it in the papers, but until you see it – "

"That's what they all say," the driver continued. "If there was a hell on earth, this was bloomin' it. Nothin' but sirens, planes and bombs and fires. Sometimes even the sirens weren't working. There were days when the whole city was lit up."

"How did you all survive?" Rusty asked. They moved to a seat nearer the driver.

"When it all started a lot of us was killed, but then the government shipped most of the women and kids out of the city – too dangerous here. We learned how to get to the bloomin' air raid shelters right quick. Pretty soon there was nothin' left for them blasted Jerrys to hit but wreckage. But that didn't stop them from comin' every blasted night – night after night."

"And you're still here," Szabo said.

"You're blinkin' right we are. Them Jerrys thought we'd give up but we don't give up that easy. And they didn't count on our boys in them Spitfires. The Huns lost so many planes they was the ones that finally give up. Now it's just V-2s and buzz bombs."

"Yeah," Szabo said. "We saw one land in the fuckin' channel on our way up here. It made quite a splash."

"They're the devil's work, they are. But it ain't gonna do them no good. They're as good as finished. The little corporal couldn't beat us so he went after Russia. Every blasted soldier but Hitler knew it was a mistake. He looked good for a time, until he got to Moscow and Stalingrad. Now the shoe's on the other blinkin' foot. Any of ya ever been to Russia? No? It's big. Bigger than the States – and horribly cold in the winter. That Frenchy, Napoleon, found it out and now it's the Fuehrer's turn. He had his chance and he muffed it. Now with you Yanks here and American planes helpin' out, we're gonna give him what he give us – only double."

So this is England, Rusty thought. Bombed out, burned out, determined to survive, determined to win. While Americans back home were going about their business, the British were working amidst the wasteland of war, picking their way through the rubble and attempting to continue living.

As the bus turned into Regent Street, the sun was making a brave attempt to break through the fog and bring some brightness to the morose landscape. It was a losing battle, and the dim light revealed a land of vague shadows that could easily be mistaken for an alien planet. Brick and stone walls framing piles of wood, broken furniture and pieces of plumbing that once were offices and homes – men, women and their families had worked and lived here. The offices and factories were once alive. The homes were lit up with families sitting around the dinner table, talking about work, their hopes, their future.

"Picadilly," the driver called out as he brought the bus to a slow stop. "Good luck to ya, Yanks," he said as they stood at the front door. "Glad to have ya here."

"Thanks," Cole said. "And good luck to you."

"If y're looking for nightlife," the driver added, "y're in the right place. Shows, movies and stores is all around, them's what ain't been bombed out. Soho's off to the left, the Trocadero's right in front and girls is all over."


"Nice guy," Rusty said as the bus crossed into Coventry Street.

"He gave me a different perspective on things."

"Very tough," Cole added. "I think we'll appreciate the U.S. a little better when we get back."

"But in the meantime," Szabo said, "we've got two days to do as we please."

"Right," Rusty agreed. "What's first?"

"Rubbers, rubbers, rubbers," a voice whispered as they stood on the sidewalk. They looked around at a thin, unshaven man, slightly bent over, wearing clothes that were far past their prime. He came toward them our of the shadows.

"Ya gotta have y'r rubbers, mates, or the girls won't touch ya. Buy 'em from me and I got three girls just waitin' for three healthy boys like you."

Cole looked at his friends. "You guys have rubbers with you?"

Rusty and Szabo exchanged embarrassed glances.

"I thought so," Cole said. "You can't travel around London without rubbers, unless you're not interested in girls. How much are they, pal?"

"A pack of 12 cost ye only one pound."

"We're only here for two days my friend, but give me 12 and these two virgins can share them with me. You guys are virgins, aren't you?"

Rusty and Szabo didn't answer.

Cole laughed. "I knew it. Well, you couldn't have your first in a better city. But use them. If you bring anything back to the ship, you'll get thrown overboard. We'll take a dozen, sir, and find our own girls. My treat this time. It's an occasion. If either of you need any assistance, I'll even help you put it on."

Rusty and Szabo looked at the rubbers and put them in their pockets.

"Let's walk into Soho first," Cole said. "They call it the Greenwich Village of London."

They crossed Regent Street and turned into Shaftesbury Avenue, passing jazz and musical instrument shops on the left and the Trocadero, site of shops and varied entertainment, on the right. They strolled up St. Anne Street to Old Compton and then on to Charing Cross Road.

"Wait a minute," Cole said. "There's a British Friends House."

"What's that?" Szabo asked.

"It's run by the Quakers. You guys can keep going if you want, but let's meet back here about six. Maybe we can spend the night here. We'll have chow together. If we get separated, remember, it's the No. #3 bus on Regent Street back to the East India Docks. Okay?"

They all agreed and Rusty and Szabo continued up Charing Cross. A tall, attractive girl, wearing a tight sweater and a skirt a little short for the times approached from the opposite direction, looked at them both and stopped in front of one of the many small clubs on the street.

"Goodbye," Szabo said. "Now's as good a time as any."

"Okay," Rusty answered. "See you around six." Good for Szabo, he thought. She was really put together. He crossed the street to Collet's Book store and looked in the window. He really had nothing decent to read and what books were on the tug had been ruined during the tumultuous four-week trip.

The bell rang as he entered the small store. Inside were narrow aisles with book shelves piled high. The walls were also lined with shelves, each filled from end to end. In the rear was a short flight of steps leading up to another level, also packed with reading material. There wasn't an open space anywhere. Several people were browsing through the aisles and a woman who had been seated at a desk near the door walked over to him.

"Are you looking for anything in particular?" she asked.

Her words were soft, easy on the ears. Sid looked at her. She was not a youngster, about 35-40 he guessed, with shoulder length, wavy brown hair, hazel eyes and a pleasant smile that did not seem forced.

"Thank you," he said. "I'm just looking for something to take back to the ship. It all got ruined on the way over."

"Merchant seaman?"

He nodded.

"You don't talk like one, not as rough as some that come in here. Your first trip?"

He nodded again.

"Well, let me know if you need help. We have a large selection."

"You sure have," Rusty said.

"Almost up to the ceiling and down to the floor. See, look here." She bent down and pointed to the bottom shelf and as she did so her blouse fell away from her body, revealing the whiteness of her breasts. He had the urge to slide his hand inside her blouse, to touch the softness, to press his hand against them, but he didn't. All he could do was blush.

She stood up. She was about two inches shorter than his 5'7" and he felt that she had leaned over intentionally.

"I've never seen a merchant seaman blush before."

"You're embarrassing me," Rusty said.

"I know. It makes you terribly attractive. You're not experienced with girls, are you?"

"Not much."

"That makes you even more attractive." A bell on her desk rang out. "I have a customer. Meet me on the upper level. I'll only be a moment."

He went up the steps and pretended to search for something to read but he couldn't concentrate. Her soft voice had warmed his body and her manner was exciting. He was sure that she had plans for him, unless he was mistaking a friendly approach for something more than it was. She might be nothing more than a British citizen extending a warm welcome to a lonely sailor who's travelled 3,000 miles to help her country.

Presently, she returned and stood close to him in the narrow aisle. The odor of her perfume swept over him. He breathed it in deeply. A shiver ran through his body and he felt dizzy and put a hand on the book shelf for support.

"Don't you feel well, my dear?"

Rusty straightened up and looked at her. Her eyes were inquiring, her voice concerned. Did she really care how he felt or was she making fun of him, he wondered. "I feel fine," he said.

"Do I make you nervous?"

He gave up his attempt to appear indifferent. "Very nervous."

"Would you feel more comfortable if we could have some tea or coffee together?"

"Sounds good."

She reached into her skirt pocket and brought out several keys on a ring. She held up one with a red spot on it. "This is the key to my rooms. When you leave here, turn left, then left on Oxford, then left on Brook. It's the 3rd street. I'm No. 21B, the second floor. I get off the job in an hour. How does that sound to you?"

"It sounds wonderful."

"Okay, then. Make yourself comfortable there and I'll be along in a bit. By the way, what's your name."

"Sidney, but my friends call me Rusty."

"Because of all that curly red hair." She reached up and removed his cap, running her hand through it. "You're a beautiful young man." She moved closer until their faces were inches apart. "Open your mouth just a wee bit," she said, lifting his hand and placing it on her breast. Her lips were on his, full and warm. She held him tight against her.

Rusty couldn't think. He surrendered to the moment. These strange, marvelous emotions he had never known. The feel of her breast against his hand – her warm mouth against his – their bodies close.

She suddenly pulled back. "It wouldn't do to get too worked up here, would it? Let's save some for later."

"I don't want to stop," he said.

"We have to," she answered. "I'll see you in about an hour. Rusty. What a lovely nickname."

"What's your name?"

"Catherine."

"That's a nice name too."


By American standards her apartment was small. The parlor and the tiny kitchen area shared the same room, with a three foot high breakfront separating them. A two-seat sofa was against one wall with a matching chair at right angles to it, both positioned so that anyone sitting there was not forced to look directly into the kitchen. A small, square coffee table with artificial flowers in an old wine bottle was in front of the sofa. On the wall facing the sofa hung a print of a park with trees, walkways and pedestrians strolling on a sunny day. Catherine had framed this picture with white curtains, scalloped at the top, curving down on each side and tied near the bottom. This was her window in this windowless room, a view of Grosvenor Square.

To Rusty, after four weeks at sea, a suite at the Waldorf couldn't have looked better.

Not seeing anything that resembled a closet, he hung his pea jacket and hat on a clothes hook attached to the door. Turning, he saw an open door off to one side of the kitchen. He peered into her bedroom. It was just large enough to accommodate a bed, a bureau and one night table. There was a small mirror over the bureau and the same pseudo-window arrangement. This print showed a tree-lined country lane with shafts of sunlight slanting down through the heavy foliage. It was very effective. A meager closet was filled with clothes and a curtain hid the entrance to the bathroom, consisting of a toilet, sink and stall shower. Rusty returned to the parlor, turned on a small radio sitting on the breakfront and made himself comfortable on the sofa.

He had no sooner sat down when the same buzzing noise they had heard in the channel sounded somewhere over his head. He looked up instinctively, but there was nothing to see but the wallpapered ceiling. The noise grew louder, then suddenly stopped. This was it, he thought. He dove beneath the coffee table and covered his head with his hands as a thunderous explosion rocked the building. He waited for the expected crash of brick and mortar around him, but the apartment remained intact.

He stood up and looked around. Miraculously everything was

still in place. He rushed down the steps and out onto the sidewalk. Fire and smoke poured out of several buildings down at the end of the block, the same corner he had passed barely an hour ago. Fire trucks were already arriving at the scene and air raid volunteers pitched in to help put out the fire and try to rescue anybody still trapped inside. Across the street a wide gap about the width of six apartment buildings filled with bricks and rubble showed where a previous bomb had landed. This was indeed the devil's weapon. He started walking toward the scene when he heard Catherine's voice behind him.

"Rusty!" She was running toward him, gasping to catch her breath. "Thank God you're all right. I ran all the way home. I thought sure it was the end."

"So did I," he said. "But I think you should get a larger coffee table. I barely fit under it."

She looked at him for a moment, then burst out laughing. "You tried to hide under that?" she asked. "In the future, don't bother. Anything above the first floor doesn't have the least bit chance to survive."

"Now you tell me," he said, smiling.

"If you're here long enough, you'll learn when to duck and when not to."

"I'll be here as long as you want me to be here."

Now it was her turn to smile. "After only one kiss? How will you feel after the next one?"

"I can hardly wait."

She took his hand. "Come upstairs and I'll make us a small supper. It's nice to have somebody to fuss over."

She warmed some left-over soup, cooked a pot of noodles with sauce, baked two potatoes and served tea with raisin biscuits.

"It's not much," she said, "probably not as much as you're used to, but meat is severely rationed and everything goes to the military first. We're low on the British totem pole."

They ate at the coffee table and Sid had the opportunity to watch her as she carried the food back and forth between the parlor and the kitchen. Her body moved gracefully, athletically, and although she wore a flowing, ankle length skirt, it was clear that she didn't believe in girdles. Each time she returned to the table, she smiled approvingly at him.

"I like the way you smile," he said.

"I have something to smile about," she said. "Where in the States do you come from?"

"I'm from Philly."

"Where's Philly?"

"Philadelphia, Pennsylvania."

"That's better. Philly I never heard of. Philadelphia we know about. William Penn founded it. He was an English Quaker."

"I know he was English. I didn't know he was a Quaker."

"Stay close to me and I'll teach you a lot."

"I'll bet you're a good teacher."

He helped her carry the dishes back to the sink and dried while she washed.

"And I'll bet that you think I do this all the time," she said.

He hesitated. "Truthfully, I hadn't thought about it. I've been too busy handling my emotions."

"Is that an honest answer?"

"It is."

"Well, just for the record, I don't. I was married, lost two babies in miscarriages and a wonderful husband in this miserable war. I get very lonely, but for the most part I'm celibate. There are times, though, ...."

"What does celibate mean?"

"Don't they teach you anything in America? It means abstaining from sex, no intercourse."

"And now?"

"There's a little more to it than that," she said. "You remind me of him. Same height and build, reddish hair, shy and sensitive. Irish, like you."

Rusty smiled. "What's your last name, Catherine?"

"Bowers. Catherine Bowers."

"Well, Miss Catherine Bowers, I have a surprise for you. The closest I've been to the Irish was when they threw stones at me in Philadelphia when I was delivering Yiddish newspapers."

She stared at him.

"My last name is Kurtz. It used to be Kurtzman, but my family shortened it when they came to the U.S. Kurtz didn't sound so Jewish."

Her eyes filled with tears. "So you have a personal stake in this war."

She put her arms around him and cried softly on his shoulder. He held her close. He didn't know what to make of it. It had been only a few hours. They hardly knew each other. He let her cry and didn't let her go until she finished. Her face was wet when she looked at him.

"Rusty, I have to tell you. I'm a fatalist. Things happen because they're supposed to happen. Like my children and my husband dying. What the reason is I don't know. Maybe I'll find out some day. But I was supposed to meet you too. Something led you to my store. It had to be.

"I've never thought about stuff like that," Rusty said.

She put her hands up to his face. "For the time being, you don't have to believe it. Just accept it."

"I'll try."

"And now, my love, it's time to come to bed with me. It will be a pleasant night for both of us."


And it was – a glorious, wonderful night. One of thrilling sexual discovery for Rusty, emotional and sexual fulfillment for Catherine. She guided his hands as they explored her body. She played with him gently, knowing that in his young eagerness, he would lose control quickly. And when he did, they rested and showered together. Finally, they lay back, her head on his shoulder, his left arm around her.

"What's this star you're wearing?"

"My grandmother gave it to me. She wore it a long time. She figured it would protect me."

"From women like me?" Catherine asked.

Rusty smiled. "I don't think she had that in mind."

"It's a Jewish star, isn't it?"

"The Star of David," he answered. "She told me to remember my heritage – who I am, my family. She said family's the most important thing in the world."

"And she's right," Catherine said. "Without it you're nothing."

"That's exactly what she said," Rusty answered.

Catherine sighed heavily and was quiet for a moment. She moved closer, held him tighter. He could sense her loneliness.

"It's nice having you here," she finally said. "But I'm tired. Are you tired?"

"A little," he said. "But it was great. I'll never forget it."

"You shouldn't. It was your first time. Savor it, treasure it. And in the future, when fate deals you some hard knocks, think back to this night in London with Catherine. Surrounded by death, we shared a special moment together."

"I can come back to London. It doesn't have to end here."

"It's already ended, Rusty,"

He loved to hear her say his name.

"If you want to stay a few days, that's fine," she said.

"I do."

"But we're no good for the long haul. You have your entire life ahead of you, if you survive this war. Mine's behind me. If a buzz bomb or V-2 landed on this house, I'd have no regrets. In fact, I wish for it. I've had my fill of this world with its cruelty and selfishness. Perhaps the next will be better."

He didn't know what to make of this kind of talk. "You shouldn't say things like that. You still have a lot to live for. The war won't last forever. After it's over you could meet someone else you like. You could remarry."

"What for? To see him die in another war? I tell you, I've had enough. I don't want to talk about it anymore. Kiss me goodnight and let's enjoy the blessed peace of sleep."

She pulled herself closer and kissed him warmly.

"Don't try to understand me. I was just in the wrong place at the wrong time." She put her head on his shoulder and rested her arm across his chest. "I'm tired. Very tired. Goodnight, my young lover."

He wanted to say something to ease her hurt, but he could think of nothing. "Goodnight, Catherine."


For three days, one more day of leave than he had been allowed, they were together. He, enjoying the comfort of her rooms and the warmth of her body. A strange woman, he thought. Delightful before they went to bed, gloomy and sad after. And that fatalism stuff. Now that he thought of it, he felt that life was just a series of random happenings, hardly meant to be. Certain situations can be forced or manipulated by planning, like joining the Merchant Marines, but describing a visit to a book store after a month at sea and meeting somebody who allows you to spend three days with her as a happening seemed like too much.

She said goodbye to him at the front door. Halfway down the block, he turned to wave at her. She was gone. Oh, well, he thought, it was nice while it lasted. At least, nobody could call him a virgin anymore. He passed the wrecked building that had been hit by the buzz bomb. It might have been Catherine and he that got it. She was right. Death was as close as the closest explosion.

He felt sorry for her losing her family. There must be many like her in England. Innocent victims of a war not of their making. America was fortunate, protected by two oceans, taking its luxuries for granted. He was a witness to all of it. When he got home, he'd tell everybody how tough they had it here. And Catherine? She would stay special, private, a treasured event in his life. Nobody would believe it anyway.

## 33

The bow and stern lines were cast off and the LT 677 drifted away from the pier and moved slowly out into the ebbing tide of the Thames. There was only a light mist hanging over the river and it gave every indication of burning off by mid-day.

Their month ashore had been reduced to seven days and questions were flying back and forth. Hasty repairs had been made to the boiler. An auxiliary generator and two lubricating oil pumps had been stripped from a tug damaged during an air raid. A lifeboat was salvaged from a half sunken freighter, and after closer inspection, it was decided the LT 677 could operate with a slightly bent propeller shaft.

Rusty joined Szabo and Cole in the messroom for lunch. "Anybody find out yet why we're going out so soon?"

"No idea," Cole said. "Sven doesn't even know and he's usually on top of everything."

Szabo was in no mood for making guesses. "I'm really pissed off," he grumbled. "First we're told we'll be docked for at least a month, now here we go out again in a week. What the fuck's going on?"

"You've got me," Cole said, "but throwing four letter words around won't help any."

"Excuse me," Szabo said, bowing awkwardly. "I forgot we got a Quaker gentleman on board our cruise ship."

Cole ignored the slight. "It must be some kind of emergency if we're leaving so soon."

"I got an emergency, too," Szabo answered. "I promised Judy I'd see her tomorrow. If I don't show up my goose is cooked."

"There are other geese around," Rusty said.

"Not like this one. What a lay job she was. She couldn't get enough. Just because you guys bombed out doesn't mean I gotta suffer."

Rusty didn't answer. He already told them, to satisfy their curiosity, that he'd been to bed with somebody, but that was as far as he went. Cole was engaged to a girl back home, and true to his Quaker upbringing, had no intentions of having physical relations with anybody else.

"We'll find out soon enough," Cole said. He turned to Rusty. "What did the captain say when you came back one day late?"

"He was hot, but I wasn't the only one. Second Mate Anderson was AWOL, too. We were sent to his cabin, separately. I don't know what he told Anderson, but he said since this was the Merchant Marines and my first trip, he'd forget it. He told me no more shore leave for a week. It doesn't matter much now."

Szabo jabbed at his hamburger. "Shit, next time I don't come back at all. If the old man don't like it, tough. He can take this tug and shove it!"

"I know how you feel, John," Cole said. "But don't blame the captain. He didn't even go ashore, except to use his influence to get our food lockers stocked up again. We're just a small dot on a large map. Every ship afloat, and all the military services are probably screaming for supplies. I'm sure they're all complaining, too. Just remember, a lot of sailors, soldiers and civilians have died in the last four years. We have to do our job, whatever it is. The sooner we do it, the sooner we get back home. The sooner people will live in peace again."

Rusty thought of Catherine. When they got back to London, he'd visit her again.

Cole's words seemed to mollify Szabo somewhat. He finished his lunch in silence and went to his bunk.

Rusty liked Cole. He was mature and steady, and had a touch of class. "What're you going to do when we get home?" he asked.

"I'm not sure," Cole said. "I majored in journalism at Swarthmore, but I may go into religion. That way I can utilize both interests. How about you?"

"Nothing so profound. I learned watch repairing before the war. I'll probably go to work in some jewelry store."

"Seems to me you're cut out for something more than that."

"Well, I never finished high school. What else can I do? Captain Sugarman suggested I stay in the Merchant Marines and some day go to Officer's School."

"If you like this sort of life. This is wartime. Many people like us are doing jobs we're not crazy about. When the war's over, they won't need such a large Merchant Marine."

"That's what I said."

"You could go back to school, go to college and get that piece of paper. You're young. Now's the time to get your act together."

A shout from the deck interrupted their conversation, followed by Sven Ericson poking his head into the mess.

"Come up on deck, you guys. I think that you should see this. Where's your friend, Szabo? This'll make his hair stand up."

Rusty and Cole looked at each other and scrambled up the steps. The sun was visible through the mist, and receding off the port side were the last of London's docks and barrage balloons. The Thames was wide here before emptying into the North Sea, and ships had plenty of room to anchor before continuing up river or out to sea. On the starboard side the view was blocked by a hulking mass of metal with a crane rising high above. It looked disturbingly familiar.

"It's our tow," Rusty shouted. "What's going on?"

Sven was at the starboard rail staring up at their old nemesis. "Well?" he asked. "What you think about that?"

Rusty was thinking the unthinkable. Cole put his thoughts into words. "Don't tell me we're getting it back again?" he said.

Before Sven could answer, Szabo burst up on deck.

"Son of a bitch! Son of a bitch! I just saw Chief Bailer. I thought he was conning me. Son of a bitch! We're getting it back again. First it's no more leave in London and now this. Will somebody fuckin' tell me what this is all about?"

"I heard from Third Mate Walford," Sven said, "that the British tug that took over from us, you remember? Well, two nights ago she was hit by a V-2. One minute it was there, then boom! Nothing. Twenty-eight men just like that." He snapped his fingers. "Gone!"

"God, that's terrible," Cole said.

"Just an explosion away," Rusty murmured, more to himself than to his shipmates.

"So now we're stuck with it again?" Szabo shouted shrilly. "Is that it?"

"That's it," Sven said. "I wanted to be the first to tell you. It's going somewhere else."

"Shit," Szabo said. "Of all the stinking luck."

"I think our luck's been pretty good," Cole said. "It could have been us instead of that British tug."

"That's true," Sven said. "Just be glad for every day you wake up."

They stood silently as the LT 677 moved closer to the tow.

"I wonder where we're taking it this time?" Szabo wondered, a little more subdued.

"The Third Mate said Captain Sugarman would let us know once we get underway."

Anderson called down from the bridge. "Back to the fantail, you guys. We're hooking it up."

Half the deck crew guided the tug cable into place. Soon the LT 677 slowly pulled away and allowed the tow to drop back about 100 feet before locking the towing machine. Once again it was lengthened to 100 yards after reaching the open water where the Thames emptied into the North Sea. The tug turned to port, away from the English Channel and headed directly toward the North Sea.

Ericson checked his waist compass. "Well, we sure is not taking it back to South Carolina."

"Where the hell are we going?" Rusty asked.

"Wish I knew," Cole said. "Let's get a map from Sparks in the radio room. That might give us an idea."

They found Sparks sitting at his desk wearing his ever present headset. Even though he was Navy, he dressed like everybody else – dungarees, work shirt and sailor's cap. They pulled a map of England and Northern Europe from the drawer and poured over it.

There was no doubt of it. They were between Southern-on-Sea to port and Margate to starboard, heading up the east coast of England directly into the North Sea. From there it was anybody's guess where they were going. It could be Northern England. Norway and Denmark were still under German control. It didn't make sense.

"Sparks," Cole said, "you know everything that's going on around here. How about it? What gives?"

Sparks uncovered his left ear and held the headset against his right. "I'm not sure," he said. "And even if I knew, I couldn't tell you, not until the captain speaks up. I'm Navy and I have to follow procedure."

"Aw, come on, Sparks," Rusty begged. "We won't say a word to anybody, Cole and I aren't blabbermouths."

Sparks looked around cautiously, "You're not going to like this."

"Why not?" Cole asked. "Can it be worse than crossing the Atlantic?"

"Look here," he laid out the map. "We're here, just leaving the Thames going northeast. If what I heard is right, and I hope it isn't, when we get to 57 degrees North, we head East into the Skaggerrak, south between Denmark and Norway and into the Baltic to Riga in Russia."

"Russia?" Cole asked. "Why Russia?"

"That's all I know. I put it together from bits and pieces that I heard here and there. You'll have to wait for Sugarman to tell you the rest. Now, remember, you promised to keep your lips buttoned. I could get into trouble."

"Don't worry," Rusty said. "You've got our word. But what does Russia want with a lousy floating crane?"

"Not only that," Cole said. "Look at that map again. There can't be more than 10 miles of water between Norway and Denmark. How're we going to get through there?" He looked at Rusty. "It's suicide."

Rusty shivered. This was serious stuff – sailing through German controlled waters with a tow. What was the military thinking? He looked again at the map. If what Sparks said is true, it did look like suicide. He looked for Riga. He ran his finger along the Polish coast, up around the horn of land enclosing the Bay of Riga, and there it was, Riga – in the Soviet Union. About a thousand mile trip. Riga, he thought to himself, there sure is something familiar about that name. Where had he heard it before?

## 34

Rusty was on the port outside bridge with Second Mate Anderson as the LT 677 proceeded slowly through a dense, grey fog that was common in the cold waters along the 57th parallel. At this point, Denmark was a large, irregularly shaped peninsula situated between Norway and Sweden to the north and Germany to the south. It separated the North Sea on the west from the Baltic Sea on the east. The only access in either direction was a narrow 70 mile long channel.

Rusty and Mr. Anderson peered into the darkness, but could see nothing. The binoculars in their gloved hands next to useless. They spoke in whispers. Strict silence was the watch word and all unnecessary noises would face the wrath of the captain. He stood at the windshield of the wheelhouse next to a stranger in civilian clothes who was wearing a heavy overcoat with the collar up. He was a tall, thin man with a hawk-like nose and prominent chin and a pipe jammed between his teeth. He wore a fur hat with flaps extending around his ears, his overall physical appearance reminding Rusty of the descriptions of his favorite detective from the Complete Sherlock Holmes.

"Who is he?" Rusty asked in a low voice.

"He's a Danish fishing boat captain," Anderson answered. "He escaped to England when the Germans took over and he's one of the many unofficial advisors to the British on these waters. He's on loan to us."

"We'll sure need him," Rusty said softly. "I can't see anything but fog." This seemed like a good time to pump for some information. "What's so urgent about getting this crane to the Russians that we risk a tug with 28 men?"

"Riga is a port," Anderson said. "The Russians need as many supplies as we can send them. A lot of stuff has been getting through to Murmansk in the last month, but at a terrible price. Some convoys are losing 50 percent of their vessels. The Allies believe that Germany will soon leave Norway to fight on the Russian front. This crane will help the Russians clear the harbor to get ready for the time when we'll have free access to these waters. The powers that be figure it's well worth the effort. The worst that can happen is one tug and 28 men won't return."

Rusty thought about this. "One tug and 28 men doesn't sound like much when you say it fast and when somebody in a comfortable chair in a warm office far away is making the decision. We're the ones that have to live with it."

"Easy does it, Kurtz. You haven't been in this war very long. You'll work under less stress if you just do your best to carry out decisions made by the higher-ups, rather than worrying about the right or wrong of it. Many men and women are making the ultimate sacrifice right now. We can't do any less."

"Sorry, sir, I was just speaking my piece."

"And you have a right to. But remember, it's easy to do the things that you enjoy doing. It takes a lot more effort to do the those things that you detest. Nobody likes this war, and I doubt if anybody on this tug thinks that this trip to Russia is worth it, myself included. Don't use up your energy fighting two wars. One is enough."

They remained quiet for a while. Rusty looked at his watch. It was almost 1600 – 4:00 p.m. –– time for him to take his turn at the wheel. He entered the wheelhouse and handed his binoculars to the seaman he was relieving.

"Eighty-five degrees east is our course."

"Eighty-five degrees east," Rusty repeated as he stepped onto the six inch raised wooden platform which gave the man at the wheel better traction during rough weather.

Captain Sugarman turned toward him. "Kurtz, this is Mr. Herning. He's here to help guide us through the channel to the Baltic. You'll take orders from him just as if he was the captain. What he says goes, understand?"

"Of course."

"Please to meet you," Herning said. His manner was authoritative, his english perfect.

Rusty looked at the engine speed – slow ahead. He looked out of the starboard window and saw Cole standing lookout, his scarf around his neck, his seaman's cap pulled down around his ears. Herning was talking to Captain Sugarman in a subdued voice.

"We'll stay in mid-channel through the Skaggerak. It's about 65 miles wide here and if this fog holds up, we shouldn't have any trouble."

"The Germans have any E-Boats in these waters?"

"Most of them hang about near England where the traffic is heavier, but they've gotten very cautious lately since they no longer have aerial superiority. The party is over for them, but they'll come out for a good kill."

"Would they consider us a good kill?"

"Normally, no. Hardly worth a torpedo, but lacking a better target, they might go after us."

Rusty had heard some wild stories about the German E-Boats, their reputation for daring and resourcefulness. Their ability to come from nowhere, attack, and disappear into the North Sea.

"In any event," Herning continued, "they wouldn't sink us before finding out who we are. You're flying no flags, I take it."

"All identification has been removed but the LT 677 on the bow."

"Good. How about the tow?"

"Nothing on that but some numbers."

"Excellent. If they do stop us, let me do the talking. It's not unusual to see a tug in this area now and then."

"What about lookouts on the coasts? They're certainly not unguarded."

Herning relit his pipe and sent two large clouds of smoke toward the ceiling. "A year ago this trip would have been impossible. Today the garrisons have been sent to the Russian front, leaving only a handful of soldiers to patrol hundreds of miles of coastline. The Danish and Norwegian underground have been asked to divert their attention elsewhere. They're very good at that. I have high hopes of getting through without incident." He checked his watch. "We should be abeam of Hjorring on the Danish coast. "Mr. Kurtz, bring the wheel up to 90 degrees, if you please."

"Yes, sir," Rusty replied, turning the wheel slowly to the right.

"In an hour we should be opposite Grenen, that's the northern tip of Denmark. We'll turn into the Kattegat and stay close to the Swedish coast down to Angelhorn, that's about 12 hours. If it's still foggy in the morning we'll anchor behind a small uninhabited island off Angelhorn. The channel to the Baltic is too narrow to trust to dead reckoning in a heavy fog, even in daylight. Tomorrow night we'll hug the Swedish coast again. We should be able to see the village lights on the shore, plus the neutral Swedes maintain navigation lights and buoys in their waters. In 10 hours, with a bit of luck, we will be into the Baltic. From there, it's 4 or 5 days to Riga."

"That sounds good," the captain said.

It doesn't sound so good to me, Rusty thought. At least in the Atlantic we had escorts to protect us. Here we're on our own.

Cole came in from the outer bridge, allowing the fog to come swirling in and joining with Herning's pipe smoke.

"Not much to see out there, Rusty. What's our course?"

"Ninety degrees east," he replied as he gave up the wheel.

"Ninety degrees east it is," Cole answered.

"I'll go down and relieve Szabo at the cable."

Rusty found Szabo sitting next to the cable motor housing with the acetylene torch in his lap. He related what he had heard up in the wheelhouse. Szabo didn't answer.

"What's the matter?" Rusty asked.

"Tell me the God's-honest truth. When we signed up, what kind of ship did you expect to sail on?"

"The truth?"

"The god-damned truth."

"A cargo vessel or a troop ship. That hospital ship in Charleston would have been nice."

"I was thinkin' the same thing. So where do we wind up? Towing a fuckin' floating can opener across the ocean at the record breaking speed of six knots an hour. That's not what I thought the merchant marines were all about."

Rusty could only smile at his friend's frustration. Three weeks ago, he would have joined him wholeheartedly. He might even have been tempted to cut the crane free, as Szabo had once urged. He had come to accept duty on the LT 677 as his part in fighting World War II. Sven was right. Somebody had to do it.

"Come on, John, all this resentment won't help. We're here so let's make the best of it. Remember what Ericson said. A lot of guys are putting up with much worse."

"Yeah, I know, but still..."

"I heard those Russian girls are hot stuff, and we should be in Riga at least a couple of days."

Szabo perked up. "Ya think so?"

"I don't see why not. Sven says they're built like block houses."

"It might not turn out so bad after all," Szabo said.

"It's your turn for lookout on the bridge. You better get going." Rusty put the torch in its rack, then went to the stern and looked in the direction of the tow. It wasn't visible, but the distant splashing of waves and the rise and fall of the cable showed it was still there. He sat down by the motor housing and marvelled at how the war had transformed his life. The streets of Philadelphia seemed far away.

As Rusty sat there thinking of home, his grandparents, his parents and sister, Bloom's Candy Store and baseball, his eyes began to close. Two hours of peering into the fog had made them tired and the soft sound of water splashing as the tug moved slowly forward was putting him to sleep. He was back in Catherine's apartment and she was crying in his arms. He held her tightly to him, her warm body trembling. They were in bed. There was a buzzing noise, then an explosion. He woke with a start. Chief Engineer Baker was looking down at him. He got up awkwardly, embarrassed to be caught asleep on watch.

"Sorry, Chief. I couldn't keep my eyes open."

"Don't apologize," Baker said. "We've all done it. I've fallen asleep in the engine room. I walked in on Sparks once. He was asleep with the earphones in his lap. We all get tired. That's why I came on deck, to get some air."

Baker was a short, middle aged, career man. He had a slight beer belly, a round face with alert blue eyes and a full head of dark blonde hair. When he smiled, the creases around his eyes and mouth seemed to spread over half his face, making him look older than his years. His shirt was smeared with dirty oil.

"Where are we?" he asked. They stood by the starboard rail examining the bleak, grey fog all about them.

"We just passed the northern tip of Denmark and headed down the Kattegat, the bay that separates Sweden from Denmark. We're going to sneak around the coast, then run through the channel into the

Baltic."

"Good trick, if we can do it."

"Our Danish pilot thinks we can."

"Good for him. How the hell does he know where we are? You can't see a thing out there."

"Dead reckoning," Rusty said, remembering what Herning had mentioned. "He must know these waters pretty good."

"I hope so," Baker said. "Anyway, it looks like the fog is lifting a bit and – "

"Quiet," Rusty hissed. "Don't make a sound."

Baker tightened his grip on the rail. "What is it?"

"I thought I saw something through that little opening in the fog. Did you see anything?"

Baker shook his head. "No, but I think you've been staring into the fog too long. You start seeing things that ain't there."

"I could swear I saw something. Wait. Can you hear that?"

They listened closely, turning their heads to better pick up any sounds.

"You're right, by God," Baker whispered. "It sounds like an engine revving at low speed."

"Something's out there," Rusty said, his voice shaking. "I'm going up to the wheelhouse. Don't move and don't make any noise. I'll be right back." He rushed to the ladder and climbed up to the outer bridge. Szabo was there looking through the binoculars. Before he could speak, Rusty put his finger to his lips and whispered in Szabo's ear. "There's some kind of vessel off our starboard side, a bit aft. Don't make any noise."

He opened the door and closed it softly behind him.

"Captain, there's a vessel off our starboard side, a little bit aft. I only caught a momentary glimpse of it. It wasn't big. Baker and I heard it. He says it sounds like an engine at low speed."

The captain and Herning looked at each other. "It must be an E-Boat," Herning said softly. "Swedish vessels blow their horns. Keep our speed low and tell the crew not to make a sound. The least noise will give us away. Do you have any weapons on board?"

"A machine gun is on deck above us, but nobody's been trained to use it."

"Then what good is it?"

"I think it was installed for aesthetic reasons, to make everybody feel better."

Herning swore in Danish under his breath. "You Americans, sometimes I wonder. Kurtz, get back on duty and keep us informed."

"Yes, sir." He rushed back to the stern. "Have you seen it yet, Chief?"

"No, but I can still hear it. It seems to be keeping up with us, like it's going in the same direction."

Just then Cole joined them. "Szabo's at the wheel. That guy Herning is on the outer bridge, still holding his pipe in his mouth. What's doing here?"

"It's still out there, whatever it is."

"Herning thinks it's an E-Boat."

"Shush. There it is again." They all listened as the unmistakable sound of engines reached their ears.

"If they see us, we're finished," Cole whispered.

Standing at the rail, the three figures were motionless, barely breathing. Then a voice sounded from the direction of the engines. The words were German and were quickly followed by another voice, more authoritative. Then all was quiet again. Rusty looked up at the starboard bridge. There was Herning, both hands on the rail, his head thrust forward, the pipe still in his mouth.

"He may know these waters," Cole whispered, "but I wish he'd put that pipe out. I can smell the smoke from here."

"That's right," Rusty answered. "Damn, if we can smell it, the Germans might, too. Somebody should tell him."

Baker looked at them with a half-smile. "Who's going to be the lucky man?"

"I'll go," Rusty answered. "I don't want to get killed because of a lousy pipe." He ran forward and up the ladder to the bridge. Herning looked at him. "What are you doing here, Mr. Kurtz? I want you on lookout on the stern."

Rusty almost turned and left, but at the last second stood his ground. "Beg your pardon, Mr. Herning, but..."

"But what? Out with it."

"Well... down on the fantail, we can smell tobacco smoke."

"So you think it might be coming from that boat? The Germans aren't that careless."

Rusty breathed deeply. "It's not the Germans, sir. It's your pipe. If you don't mind my saying so. If we can smell it, we thought that the Germans could, too."

Herning removed his pipe from his mouth, looked at it, and tapped it silently against his hand, allowing the tobacco to fall in the water. He put the pipe in his pocket.

"You're quite right. I forget it's there sometimes. Thank you, Kurtz."

"You're welcome, sir."

"Now get back to your station."

"Yes, sir!" He climbed quietly down the ladder and rejoined Cole.

"What did he say?"

"He thanked me and put it out."

"Good man," Cole said.

"The fog seems to be lifting," Rusty said. "Shit, now that we need it – "

"There it is." Cole whispered, pointing toward a break in the fog."

It was visible for seconds, then was swallowed up again.

"It seems to be dropping back," Rusty said.

There was suddenly the sound of a sputtering engine.

"They're having trouble," Baker said. "Their engine's conked out."

"Good. Let's get the hell out of here." He ran back up to the bridge. Before he opened his mouth, Herning had his hand up. "I heard it," he said. "They don't usually operate so close to the Swedish coast. They've probably had engine trouble for several hours and drifted over here. We were lucky this time."

Rusty rejoined Cole and Baker at the stern and repeated what Herning had told him.

"I guess I'll get back down below," Baker said. "It's too dangerous up here."

As he turned, the sound of an engine again came through the fog. They all froze in their positions. This time the engines weren't sputtering. They were going full blast and rapidly coming closer. There was no need to inform the bridge, everybody could hear it. Baker, Cole and Rusty stood motionless. The Germans had apparently corrected the problem and were hurriedly racing back up the channel toward the Kattegat. The noise of their engines didn't concern them. The fog was still thick enough to conceal both the E-Boat as well as the tug and its tow. The E-Boat roared invisibly past them and quickly receded up the channel, its wake rocking the tug as it went by.

"I'll never say a bad word about fog again," Cole said. "It saved our skin."

"You're not kidding," Rusty said. "One man's hazard is another man's salvation."

Cole laughed. "Getting philosophical in your old age."

"Old age is right. I feel like I've aged ten years in the last couple months. By the time the war is over, I'll have a beard down to here and you'll be calling me Whitey."

"That's about the color of your face right now," Cole remarked.

"Your's isn't exactly too healthy looking either. How about you, Mr. Baker?"

Baker had already returned below decks to the engine room where he was more comfortable. Sometimes it's better not to see what you're up against. Catherine was right, Rusty thought. If fate has your number, there's not much you can do about it.

## 35

At 1:00 a.m., Rusty, Cole and Szabo dropped into their bunks, exhausted. The strain had taken its toll. Normally off duty at 8, they were kept on watch five extra hours until the tug had cleared the channel and turned northeastward into the Baltic Sea.

It seemed that only ten minutes had elapsed when they were shaken awake by Third Mate Walford.

"Come on, sleepyheads," he shouted, "you're late. You guys expect to sleep all day? Szabo, get to the fantail. Cole, you're on bridge watch. Kurtz, it's the wheelhouse for you – get going!"

They staggered to the head, grumbling and swearing, threw cold water on their faces, then scattered to their stations. Cole relieved the seaman on the open bridge and Rusty took over at the wheel. The course was 45 degrees northeast along the Swedish coast. It was still dark, but the fog had thinned to a light mist with visibility about five miles. Lights on the Swedish coast were plainly visible and with a neutral country to port and the Baltic Sea to starboard, the tension of the night before had eased somewhat. Enemy ships and planes stayed clear of Swedish waters, and with a Russian offensive keeping the Germans busy on the mainland, it was unlikely that the incident of last night would be repeated.

James Walford, the Third Mate, was in the wheelhouse, and Captain Sugarman and the Danish pilot, Herning, were nowhere to be seen. Walford and Rusty had not crossed paths very often, their watches and duties barely bringing them together. Whatever he knew about Walford he had learned at the mess table. He was about 5'10" with sloping shoulders that accentuated his hollow chest cavity. While the other officers might stand around with their hands in their pockets, Walford preferred his hands behind his back. With his prematurely thinning brown hair, alert hazel eyes, and a pair of round, metal-framed eyeglasses that rested on the lower part of his nose, he looked more like an accountant than a third mate.

"Good morning, Kurtz. How are you this morning?" His voice also didn't fit in with his physical appearance. It was strong but friendly, with each word enunciated clearly.

"A little tired after last night," Rusty replied. "We only got about three hours sleep."

"Par for the course," Walford said. "I don't mind admitting that last night completely unnerved me. There's nothing as frightening as an unseen enemy close by."

"It's some comfort to know that officers get scared, too," Rusty said.

"Anyone that goes to war and never admits to fear is either a liar or a complete fool."

Rusty warmed to him. "Where's Captain Sugarman and our Danish pilot?"

"Taking a well-deserved sleep. They're to be called only in case of an emergency. With visibility lifting and the coast always in sight, they shouldn't have to be disturbed." He looked at the chart laid out on the desk to the left of the wheel station.

"Those lights must be the town of Simnishann. Some of these Swedish names are real tongue twisters. We're going to cross Hano Bukten, a small bay about 50 miles across, then we'll be in Kalmarsund Channel between the coast and Oland Island, that's about another 80 miles. By this time the day after tomorrow, I expect we'll be heading east to Riga. I imagine before the war, being in this part of the world never entered your mind."

"I might as well have thought of walking on the surface of the moon," Rusty replied.

"That's what war does. It puts farmers on ships and makes men out of boys, prematurely I might add. It takes ordinary people and makes them heroes. Unfortunately, many get killed." He gazed at the disappearing shoreline as the tug started across Hano Bukten Bay. He placed his hands behind his back and paced back and forth as he talked. "The world never learns from history. There's always some maniac who wants what the other fellow has. They stir up the great mass of people and drown them in nationalist propaganda."

"How much longer do you think this thing will last?"

"Everybody's been asking me that lately. Just because I teach history I'm expected to know what's going on behind the scenes. Judging from the news reports Sparks has been picking up, maybe another year. The Germans are on the defensive everywhere."

"Still another year," Rusty moaned. He decided to change the subject. "What brought a history teacher into the Merchant Marines?"

Walford unfolded his hands and raised the binoculars to his eyes. "The same as you, probably. I wanted to be part of it. Instead of teaching disinterested students dry book history, I wanted to see first hand what it was really like. The Army and Navy rejected me because of my eyesight and a bad back. The Merchant Service was accepting anybody that could walk."

"I guess everybody on this tug is a reject for some reason or other."

"More to their credit. They could have ridden out the war as 4F and nobody would say anything against them. I'm proud to call myself a member of this crew."

The radio room door opened and Sparks stuck his head out. "The weather's like this almost all the way. Fierce fighting around Riga and up and down the Russian front. Germans moving top tank division to French coast for the invasion. A message to the troops manning Fortress Europe – 'The Allies must be stopped on the beaches.' I'll type up a news flash for the bulletin board." He pulled his head in and closed the door.

"I thought Riga was already liberated," Rusty said.

"I was under that assumption too."

"That'll be great, pulling into the middle of a battle with the tow behind us," Rusty said.

The starboard bridge door opened and Szabo came in to relieve him.

"Good morning, Szabo," Walford said. "How are you feeling today?"

"A little tired," he said, taking the wheel.

"Forty-five degrees northeast," Rusty told him.

"Forty-five degrees northeast. Where are we?"

"We're moving northeast along the Swedish coast," Walford said. "In about 36 hours we should turn toward Riga."

"It's about time," Szabo said irritably. "I ain't had a good night's sleep since London."

"You're not alone," Walford said. "Mind your compass."

"See you later, Szabo," Rusty said as he went out onto the bridge.

Thirteen hours later, just after 5:00 p.m., Rusty was sitting near the cable motor housing looking at the tow. The tug was halfway up the Kalmansund Channel with Oland Island to starboard and Sweden to port. The channel was only four miles wide at this point and villages and towns were clearly visible in the fading daylight. People could be seen walking in the streets and on the beaches, going about their daily activities, and small fishing boats came out to look at the passing visitor. Here and there lights flickered on. Sven Ericson joined him on the fantail.

"Anderson says to bring in the tow to 50 yards. He don't want any accidents in this narrow channel."

Rusty threw the release handle and pressed the recover button. The motor rumbled to life and the cable was slowly rolled into its housing.

"The tow looks bigger than ever," Rusty said. "Do you think when we drop it off at Riga, that'll be the last of it?"

"We can't drag it around forever. Did you see the news on the board?"

"About the fighting at Riga?"

"If they're still at it when we get there, we may have to stay out in the gulf for a while."

"And if the Germans retake the city? Then what?"

"That's why we have a captain, to make decisions like that."

"What would you do?"

"I would do what the captain will probably do, stay off shore and see what happens."

"How long can we stay out there?" Rusty said.

"As long as we have to. Hallo. What's that?"

Coming toward their starboard side was a boat about the size of the tug but higher out of the water. As it came closer, they could see armed, uniformed men standing at the rail.

"A Swedish patrol boat," Sven said.

"Can they stop us?"

"Sure thing. We are inside the three mile limit here. The captain took a calculated risk by coming up this way instead of the underside of the island. It's safer this way. I don't think the Swedes will hold us."

"Why not?"

"They've probably been tracking us since we entered the Kattegat, but we never went inside the three mile limit. Besides, even though they are officially neutral, unofficially they are anti-German. Let's go over to the rail."

The patrol boat circled round and came along the starboard side. An officer on the bridge raised a bullhorn to his mouth. "We know who you are," he said in english. "We have been advised of your destination. Control of the city is in doubt."

Captain Sugarman was on the starboard bridge with Third Mate Walford and Cole.

"We are aware of that," the captain said.

"If you wish to anchor here for several days, it is approved by us so long as you stay outside the three mile limit. We cannot permit you to land."

"I understand," the captain said. "Thank you for your kind offer, but we will continue on and hope the situation clarifies itself by the time we get there."

"As you wish. Goodbye and God be with you."

The crews waved to each other as the patrol boat dropped back.

"They were nice enough," Rusty said.

"If we were German they could have held us for the duration. For Allied ships, they look the other way."

"Convenient. And they knew all about us."

"They are neutral up to a point. I'm sure they're in daily contact with the Allied forces to help however they can without stepping on the toes of the Germans."

Rusty looked up toward the bow. "The channel's widening."

"Yes, get ready to pay out cable to 100 yards again."

## 36

The Gulf of Riga is shaped like a large, irregular horseshoe, approximately 100 miles across with its open end facing northwest into the Baltic Sea. The entrance is protected from storms by Paarmah Island, a rocky piece of land that stretches almost from one tip of the horseshoe to the other.LT 677 passed between the southern end of the island and the lower tip of the horseshoe. Unlike the Swedish coast, no lights were visible anywhere.

Another ten hours of sailing brought them within sight of the Soviet Union.

In the wheelhouse, Captain Sugarman, Linus Herning and Third Mate Hank Anderson stood at the windshield, trying to get their first view of the Russian coast. George Cole was at the wheel, Szabo and Sven Ericson on lookout on the open bridges. It was a cloudy night, but a light offshore breeze was keeping the air clear.

"We're about 20 miles west of the coast," the captain said. "I think it's time to turn south to Riga." It was a suggestion, not an order. He was deferring to Herning who, as their pilot, had technical command of the tug.

"My knowledge of these waters is not any better than yours," Herning said to the captain.

"Cole," the captain said, "bring her around to 180 degrees due south."

"Yes, sir, 180 degrees due south." He turned the wheel slowly, looking out of the starboard window as he did so. The tow was coming around easily.

Cole watched the compass as the LT 677 moved parallel to the coast. "180 degrees due south, sir."

"Okay," the captain said. "Mr. Anderson, ask Sparks for any news about what's going on ashore. We've got to have some idea of what we're getting into. I don't have scouts to send out."

Anderson was back in several minutes. "The city's under control of the Russians. The Germans have pulled back to a river about 40 miles south of Riga. Sparks has gotten a message from London through Sweden. They want us to turn the tow over to any military authorities on the scene and get back to London by the same route we came."

"That's okay by me," Captain Sugarman said.

Chief Baker came up from the engine room, his hands and face covered by the usual grime. The odor of fuel oil filled the wheelhouse. "Excuse me, sir. We have a problem below." ·

Sugarman twisted his mouth. "What's the trouble now, Chief?"

"Those oil pumps and the engine cooler we salvaged in London are acting up, and the engines are overheating."

"We're only six or seven hours from our destination, Chief. Can you give us the time?"

"We can, sir, but once we stop we have a lot of work to do. There's also a faulty bearing in one engine. We're talking about five days work."

"Shit! In five days the Germans might have the city back. We'll be sitting ducks again."

"Can't be helped, sir. We can't continue on like this. The engines will lock up tighter than a drum."

Captain Sugarman punched the bulkhead in frustration. "I guess we don't have a choice. But the minute we stop, get working on it. We can't afford to hang around here very long."

"Right, sir. We'll do the best we can."

"I know you will, Chief."

Sparks came down out of the radio room. "Swedish meteorologists are forecasting northeast winds of 30 mph with heavy rain within 24 hours."

Sugarman groaned. "Any more good news?"

"The Russians are expecting a German counterattack before bad weather sets in." Sparks said, oblivious to the Captain's remarks. "They've been fighting back and forth here for two weeks."

"If that's good news, I don't want to hear the bad."

Szabo came in from the starboard bridge and relieved Cole.

"180 degrees due south."

"180 degrees due south," Szabo repeated.

Cole went aft to the fantail where he found Rusty standing at the stern rail and peering into the darkness. The water here in the gulf was fairly calm with only slight ripples caused by the offshore wind. The irridescence of the open sea was gone and the tug cutting smoothly through the water left a black and white wake trailing behind. There was no thunderous crashing of waves against the high flat bow of the floating crane, only the soft splashing as water was pushed aside. All else was quiet, and if the news from the Chief and Sparks was set aside, along with the ever present danger of being in a war zone, the night could be called peaceful.

"What's doing?" Rusty asked.

Cole repeated all that he had heard in the wheelhouse.

"Sorry I asked. Take a look at the tow. Anything strange about it?"

Cole raised his binoculars. "It's pretty dark but it seems okay to me."

"Doesn't it look a little lower in the water?"

Cole looked again. "Now that you mention it, yes, it does."

"I think it's taking on water," Rusty said.

"We'll keep an eye on it." Cole lowered his binoculars. "We'll be better able to confirm it when it's daylight. The captain has enough on his mind right now."

"But somebody should know. What if it starts going down?"

Cole thought this over. "Anderson's on duty in the wheelhouse. I'll see if I can get his attention."

Several minutes later he was back with the Third Mate. Anderson studied the tow through his binoculars. "You might be right," he said. "But I agree with you. I think it can wait until daylight. If there's any change for the worse we have no choice but to let him know. After your watch get some sleep. You may be needed early."

True to Anderson's words, they were roused out at 2:00 a.m. and sent up to the wheelhouse. It was crowded. The 12 seamen who constituted the entire deck watch were there along with Chief Baker and the officers. Everybody was looking at each other, waiting.

"We're approaching Riga," Captain Sugarman said quietly. "And I want you to know why we're going to be here for a while. Our engines are in danger of seizing up and repairs have to be made. We have to unload the tow where it can do the most good. From then on it's in the Russian's lap, but nobody's going to say we didn't do our job. I've instructed Mr. Walford to photograph the whole operation so the Russians won't have any complaints. I don't trust them, but we're on the same side for the time being, so we'll do the right thing. We saw gun flashes in the distance indicating that fighting must be going on right now. There may not be anybody on the docks to help us, in which case, we'll need every hand, so be ready to do whatever's needed in a moment's notice. By daylight we should be in position to get started. Pay attention to orders and no dilly dallying. I don't want to be here any longer than you. Any questions?"

"Sir," Walford said, "do we have anybody on board that speaks Russian?"

"Yes, Mr. Herning speaks some and so does Ericson. Between the two, we should be able to tell what the Russians are saying about us." This brought some laughter from the crew. "We've been married to this tow for 4,500 miles and six weeks, and I think we've been lucky to get it this far and in one piece. Anything else?"

Anderson looked at Cole and Rusty. "Sir, I have to tell you that there's a suspicion that the tow's taking on water."

Captain Sugarman gripped the desk until his knuckles turned white. "When did this happen?"

"Seaman Kurtz noticed it about five hours ago, but I decided not to bother you about it until daylight when we could get a better look. I just came from the stern and the tow seems to be holding its own. But it's so dark."

The captain looked at the ceiling and then around the wheelhouse. "Walford, lower the lifeboat and take four men with you. Climb aboard the tow and ascertain the extent of the leak, if there is one. Fix it if you can. Next time, Anderson, don't be so considerate of my feelings. We've wasted five hours that could have been put to good use. We'll slow down to allow you to get on board. Remember to take flashlights with you. Now, get going."

The lifeboat was lowered and the five men leaped in. Rusty looked at Szabo as they pulled on the oars of the lifeboat. "Sort of like being back in New London, isn't it?"

"And we left a soft cushy job for this," Szabo said. "We really goofed this time."

"Stop complaining," Cole said. "You wanted to go to war, well, you're here, right in the middle of it. Someday you'll be able to tell your grandchildren what a hero you were."

"If we live to tell about it."

"Stop grumbling up there," Walford ordered, "and keep rowing."

Circling around, they allowed the tow to come alongside. Grabbing the ladder, they tied up the lifeboat, climbed aboard and looked around.

"My God," Cole exclaimed. "This thing is like a floating football field. It's bigger than I thought."

Like a group of tourists, they stared high into the darkness at the network of steel cross supports and beams.

"We brought you a long way, baby," Ericson said. "We're not gonna lose you now."

"That's right," Walford said. "Now let's get below and see what's going on. We'll go by way of the bow hatch. It seems to be listing in that direction."

In the hold, they turned on their flashlights and were overwhelmed by the cavernous space that surrounded them. Only the crane's engine in the center of the hold relieved the dank emptiness about them. Other than some lumber, extra lines, and a few steel plates, it was a vast nothingness with a motor in the center. They played their flashlights on the bulkhead and the deck. Sure enough, about 50 feet of the deck on the starboard bow side was under water. As the tow moved, the water sloshed back and forth, producing small waves that broke at their feet. They moved forward until they were knee deep in the water.

"There's the leak," Walford shouted as he played the light on the starboard bulkhead near the bow. "The bulkhead's been pushed in just aft of the bow. It's not much, but enough to sink this thing if nothing's done."

They all held their flashlights on it.

"The plate ahead of it overlaps it somewhat," Walford said. "When the tow's moving forward most of the water bypasses the opening. It's only when we slow down, like now, that the sea starts pouring in."

"You think we can close it up?"

"I don't know. But we have a better chance of doing it while she's moving." He looked at the bulkhead and ran his flashlight over the lumber and metal.

"I know what my father would do," Szabo said. "I worked with him for one back-breakin' year at the Navy yard in Brooklyn. If we can find a piece of sheet metal about 5x5, we might be able to force it closed."

"Okay, Szabo. You're in charge of this operation, so go to it. I'm going to examine the rest of the hull. Call me when you're ready."

Walford found the remainder of the hull sound and, holding a hammer he had picked up, returned to his crew.

"How're we doing?"

"We found everything we need," Szabo said. "2x4s, metal plates, but I can't figure out how to keep the 2x4s from slipping back once they're jammed against the plate."

Walford looked at the bulkhead. "What are those L-shaped hooks sticking out along the hull?"

"I'm not sure," Szabo said. "But I think they're for handling and storing."

"There's our answer," Walford said. "Press the plate home with 2x4s, then slip other 2x4s horizontally along the plate and ram them down into those L's."

"Great idea," Szabo said. "Let's go."

The plate was pressed against the opening by Walford and Rusty, and the rest began pushing a 2x4 against it. At first nothing happened, but slowly the amount of water rushing through the opening seemed to lessen.

"We need a little more fuckin' muscle here," Szabo said. "Sir, can you keep that plate in place by yourself so Rusty can help us push?"

They applied their combined weight with as much force as possible. They lost their footing several times on the slippery deck and were soaking wet.

"Heave," Szabo yelled. "Again! How's it look Mr. Walford?"

"Water still coming in, but it's a great deal better. A few more good shoves might reduce it to a trickle. The pumps will control it after that. Hand me three of those 2x4s. On your next try, I'll ram them home. Okay, now!"

Again and again they heaved, and at last Walford was able to force a 2x4 across the plate and down into the "L" supports. He pounded the ends tight with the hammer and repeated the operation twice more. There were now three 2x4 bars holding the plate tightly against the bulkhead.

"We've done it," Walford shouted. "Great work men, especially you, Szabo. You did a great job."

Szabo flushed at this compliment and everybody cheered and slapped each other on their backs.

They climbed up on deck and sealed the hatch.

"That fresh air sure smells good," Ericson declared.

"It's getting light," Rusty said. "I can see somebody on the fantail, waving."

Walford waved back. "They're slowing down. Into the lifeboat everybody." He looked at their clothes as they scrambled down the ladder. "Jesus Christ, you guys look like something the sea threw up."

## 37

In the dim, smoky haze of morning, the LT 677 moved slowly into the Daugava River estuary, tied securely to the port side of its tow. The area looked deserted and not a working vessel of any kind had appeared. Captain Sugarman decided to dock the tow to the first available pier. Riga was still a mile or two up the river, but the wreckage of ships and the port itself were already plainly visible. Evidence of fierce fighting was everywhere. Burning buildings and a grey pall of mist and smoke combined to give the appearance of twilight rather than mid-morning. Cannon fire coming from the western horizon indicated that the front wasn't that far away.

Guiding the tug between sunken ships was tricky business and would have been impossible at night.

Anderson was at the wheel, the captain, Mr. Herning and Walford stood at the windshield, Rusty was on the port bridge, Cole was on the deck above the wheelhouse, and Szabo and Ericson were on the starboard bridge.

Walford looked at the destruction in amazement. "There's hardly anything standing. We may have trouble finding an undamaged pier."

"And nobody to turn the tow over to," Captain Sugarman noted. "There's not a soul around."

"It looks like a massive earthquake hit this place," Herning said. "This is as bad as anything I've seen. This crane certainly has its work cut out for it."

Rusty entered the wheelhouse. "Mr. Cole reports seeing a pier about a half mile up on the port side that might be usable, sir."

"Keep it in the center of the channel, if possible, Mr. Anderson. The tide doesn't seem too swift. We'll bring her in against it."

"There's a small vessel half under water at the opposite pier," Herning said, "but there may be just enough room for us to squeeze in."

"It's going to be close."

"Yes," the captain said. "Walford, get some men onto the tow and tell them to climb down to the pier at first opportunity. We'll need them to make the tow fast. Keep me notified."

Walford left to round up some of the off-duty crew that were standing around on the fantail.

"A little more to port, Mr. Anderson. That's it, okay. I'll take it from here." Anderson relinquished the wheel to his captain.

They approached the opening between the two piers diagonally. The engine was on dead slow ahead as Captain Sugarman turned slowly parallel to the piers. The water became turbulent after the captain signalled the engine room to activate the engine on the port side of the tug.

"Scraping wreckage on port side," Rusty shouted.

The captain swore. "We can't back out now!"

"Clear of wreckage," Rusty shouted. Almost immediately there was a slight bump indicating contact and Walford's voice could be heard ordering some of his men to climb down onto the pier. The Captain signalled "slow ahead," but still maintained pressure against the pier with the port screw. After several minutes Szabo came into the wheelhouse from the starboard bridge.

"Mr. Walford reports all secure, sir."

"Very good," the captain said. "We've done our job. The crane belongs to the Russians now."


Rusty knocked on the door of the captain's cabin and was ushered to a chair beside his desk. It was his first glimpse inside. and he was surprised to see that Captain Sugarman's cabin was so small. It did contain some comforts which the rest of the crew didn't enjoy. Besides a single bunk against the wall and the desk and two chairs, there was a tiny private toilet and a stall shower. Even the junior officers shared toilets and showers with the rest of the crew.

The captain looked refreshed after sleeping ten hours and having shaved and showered. He was wearing civilian clothes – pants, turtleneck shirt, heavy sweater and was in his stocking feet. He lit his pipe and sat down on the opposite side of the desk.

"What's on your mind, Kurtz?"

"Sir, do you know how long we'll be here?"

Captain Sugarman leaned back and blew a cloud of smoke toward the ceiling. It was clear that he enjoyed these moments free of the stress of the previous days.

"Chief says about a week. Parts aren't available here and we're on our own as far as repairs are concerned. Five days at best. Why do you want to know? There's nothing much to do around here."

"When I first heard the name Riga it sounded familiar to me, but I couldn't place it. Now I know. I remember my grandmother mentioning it."

Sugarman blew a smoke ring into the air and poked his finger through it. "That's interesting, Kurtz. So what's the problem?"

"No problem, sir. I just wondered if I could go ashore and look around. Maybe there's a city hall or something that might have some information about my family."

"If it's still standing," the captain said.

"Maybe the city proper isn't damaged as much as the port area."

"That's possible, but you don't speak any Russian. How do you propose to find your way around?"

"Well, with most of the work left to be done in the engine room, I thought I would ask Sven Ericson to go with me. I think he would, with your permission, of course. We wouldn't be gone long, a day or two."

Captain Sugarman thought for a moment. His great-grandparents came from Russia also, but he had no idea exactly when or from which part. If he was in Kurtz's shoes, he would want to do the same thing.

"Kurtz, our little ship is in pretty good shape except for the engine room. If Ericson will go with you, okay, but I don't want you going alone. The port captain told Herning that this place has changed hands three times in the last six months. I don't want anybody in my crew winding up in a concentration camp. It could be hazardous to your health, especially a nice little Jewish boy like yourself."

Rusty laughed. "Thanks, Captain, I'll be careful. I guess we don't have a street map of Riga on board."

"Kurtz, I never even heard of Riga before this trip. All I know is it's a Soviet port in the Gulf of Riga east of the Baltic Sea, and there's not much left of it. Take some bread, chocolate bars and some money with you. It might open a few doors. Good luck."

"Thanks again, sir."

Rusty and Ericson, carrying small back packs, and picking their way through the rubble, left the port area and headed toward some taller buildings which were still standing amid the destruction around them. Here and there people were emerging. The further from the port area that they walked, the more buildings they saw that somehow escaped being damaged.

An elderly man wearing a police uniform came toward them and uttered a few words.

"He wants to know who we are and where we come from," Sven said.

"Tell him why we're here and ask if they have a city hall somewhere near here."

With some difficulty, Ericson conveyed the message. The policeman rattled off a few sentences, pointing his finger in the direction he wanted them to go.

"He says they love all Americans, but why don't we open up a second front? They feel they are fighting the war all by themselves."

"Why does he think we're here," Rusty asked, "to play chess?"

"I guess they don't get much news here. Only what the government wants them to have."

"Did you get any kind of an address from him?"

"10 Slokas Street, if it's still there. He said about a mile from here."

Picking their way carefully around shell holes, large slabs of concrete, and downed electrical wires, they came to a corner with a street sign leaning against a wall – Slokas Street. The city hall consisted of a two-story building with a surprising number of people going in and out. Women in ragged clothes and babooshkas covering their heads. The men's clothes were no better, except for the fur hats on their heads. Although it wasn't winter yet, the air this far north was raw and the lack of sunlight contributed to the overall discomfort. The building was dark, there being no electricity, but the bureaucratic work of running a city continued.

This time they were fortunate. The woman at the front desk, wearing a heavy coat, spoke a little English mixed with Russian. Ericson told her what they were looking for.

"Not here," she stated. "We too busy, anyway. Go number 16, the Latvians History Building. Maybe open, maybe somebody there. Go. We too busy."

"Number 16," Rusty repeated. "It should be just up the street."

It was a one-story stone building with a sign in Russian over the doorway that confirmed what she had said – Latvian State Historical Archive. The door was open.

The archive was dark and gloomy inside, but unlike the city hall it was devoid of people. There was an empty desk inside the front door, a statue of Lenin behind it, a tattered flag with the hammer and sickle hanging limply from the ceiling and no windows, which made it even gloomier.

Just when it appeared that the building was deserted, an elderly man, short and stooped shouldered came out of a dark room. His wrinkled face broke into a smile when he saw them.

"You're not Russian," he observed in very correct English, which took them by surprise. "I don't get many visitors these days. It's good to see young faces again." His old eyes sparkled over the spectacles perched on his nose and he limped forward with his right hand extended. "Come in," he urged, shaking hands warmly.

"What brings you to Riga at a time like this?"

Rusty related the trip from England and the delivery of the crane to his city.

"Wonderful. We are getting help at last. You are English?"

"American," Rusty said. "My name is Sid Kurtz. My friend is from Denmark, Sven Ericson. We are looking for some information about my family. My grandparents left here to go to America around 1910 and I am curious about where they lived."

"Ah, yes, America. The hope of the world. The future rests on your shoulders. I, too, went to live in your country. I returned after the revolution. I wanted to be part of the new Russia. It was no different than the old. At least now we have a goal to fight for. We finally have something in common with the rest of the world – the defeat of Nazi Germany."

"Amen to that," Rusty said. "You sound like an educated man."

"Self-educated. All my life I have begged and borrowed books to read. America opened my eyes to a world I never knew. A world of free expression and books that I didn't realize existed. When I returned it was like coming from daylight into darkness, such a mistake. Now I live here in the past with the tortured history of my people and pray that things will get better." He sighed heavily. "Enough of ravings from an old man, what can I do for you?"

"My name is Kurtz. It used to be Kurtzman. I thought you might have some record of it."

The old man rubbed his chin. "Perhaps. Kurtzman is a German name, but that's not unusual here. Many Jewish families with German names settled in Russian Latvia. They were hounded out of other countries but were welcomed here many years ago. Now the wheel has turned. The Jewish people know what persecution is. Kurtzman, let us see. Come to the file room with me."

He pulled out an index card drawer and ran his fingers through the cards. "Here we are. There are a few Kurtzmans here. Your grandfather's given name?"

"David."

"Some day we must make new cards. These will be dust soon. After the war perhaps."

Rusty found himself suddenly on edge as the old man called out name after name. His family had travelled 5,000 miles to escape tyranny. He had come back to help erase it. There was something mystical about his being here. Maybe Catherine was right. Fate had everything planned from beginning to end. He was meant to retrace his family's footsteps, back to their roots. He trembled with excitement.

"David," the old man cried triumphantly. "We are in luck. There are two Davids. His wife was Lida."

Rusty's face fell.

"The other David Kurtzman lived in Lutzin, wife, Itkah."

"That's it," Rusty shouted. "My Grandmother."

"Children, Jacob."

"That's my Uncle Jake, I can't believe it."

"Jacob," he continued. "Sam, Lena, Herman, Nathan."

"That's my father!" Rusty couldn't contain himself. "How old was he then?"

"Let us see. The card is dated 1910, a census taking year. He was nine years old."

"That's about right. Amazing. Excuse my breaking in."

"Rhea," the man continued, "and Ellis. That's the end."

"This is wonderful. I wish I could photograph this card. Do you have any equipment here?"

"This city has been ransacked three times by the Germans. Everything of value is gone."

"Then I'll write it down. Wait until everybody back home hears about this. They'll go nuts. Especially Grandmom. I wish she was here with me."

The old man supplied an unused index card and Rusty copied everything down.

"Where is Lutzin from here?" he asked.

"About 75 miles."

"Shit, excuse me, it's too far."

"You wish to go there?"

"If I could, but I can't take a chance of being left behind. Sven, didn't we cross over railroad tracks on the way here?"

"Aye, I think so. There was so much rubble. Yes, I'm sure of it."

"Are trains still operating out of here?"

"Not for three months," the old man said. "The only way to Lutzin is the Daugava River to Hegste – then the train to Rezekne. From there it's a ten miles walk or wagon ride to Lutsin, if the military doesn't stop you."

Rusty tried to concentrate. He'd never have another opportunity. "Are there boats going down to Hegste every day?"

"They try, when the airplanes don't stop them and when they have fuel."

"How long does it take?"

"To Hegste? About five hours if the weather is good."

"How far from Hegste – to what was it – Rezekne?"

"That's correct. About 25 miles, barring air raids."

"Are trains running on a regular schedule?"

"Where do you think you are? In America? There's no such thing as a regular schedule here. Wherever you go you take a chance."

Sven looked at his shipmate. "Rusty, you're not thinking of doing this? It's crazy! We'll never get back on time."

"I'll never have another chance like this, Sven. I know what the captain said, but – you go back to the tug and tell Captain Sugarman I might be here overnight and – "

"Wait just a minute, my friend. If I leave you alone, the captain will skin me alive. I go with you and we face the music together."

Rusty smiled and turned to the old man. "Sir, I'm indebted to you. What's your name?"

"Malik Ouspensa to the Russians." He lowered his voice. "Meyer Lipschutz to you."

Rusty smiled and shook his hand. "Your secret is safe with us."

"There are still a few of us here. We manage to survive somehow."

"Goodbye, sir."

"Goodbye, my young friends. Be careful."


The ferry, Polotsk, was an old fishing boat converted to carry passengers down river to Hegste. About 30 feet long, it looked somewhat like a small version of the LT 677. The Polotsk was crowded, probably overcrowded, with shabbily dressed villagers loaded down with a myriad of cloth bags and old suitcases bulging with their possessions. They were returning to their homes or leaving Riga's wreckage to live elsewhere.

The boat owner, a gruff, unshaven man of middle age had looked suspiciously at Rusty and his companion, but two American dollar bills and a Hershey bar quieted his fears.

The villagers stared at them curiously. One elderly man tried to open a conversation with the few English words he knew, but it was hopeless, so Sven spoke to him in Russian.

When America was mentioned all heads turned toward them and the trip upriver became a question and answer period. Sven was overwhelmed, barely able to keep up with the rapid fire Russian being thrown at him. Sven explained he was originally from Norway, and now a Merchant Seaman serving the U.S. Army.

The questions continued until Sven was forced to hold up his hands in protest and sit down exhausted. Gradually the villagers quieted down and busied themselves by looking at the passing countryside. Here, east of Riga, the channel was free of wreckage. The Polotsk coughed and sputtered its way up the Daugava River, it's fly-wheel engine straining mightily under it's burden.

They glided past farm houses, some destroyed, others appearing untouched. An occasional farmer could be seen in his field, picking and scratching at the land.

One man spoke to Sven who then turned to Rusty. "He says what's the use of farming. The Germans will come back again and take everything."

Rusty looked at this group of war-weary people and thought of the Statue of Liberty. At this moment some people back home were probably complaining about gasoline and food rationing. He was suddenly tired and sat down on the deck next to Sven and leaned against the bulkhead. Soon he was asleep.


Rusty and Sven forced their way onto the two car cattle train that was leaving Hegste for Krezekne, a distance of 25 miles, normally a half-hour journey. This day it took two and a half interminable hours of breakdowns – delays caused by the removal of wreckage from the tracks, and one stop outside of Krezekne to retrieve the bodies of several people who had fallen from the roof as the train negotiated a curve on the tracks.

Krezekne's train station was nothing more than an open space with a wooden platform next to the tracks, its building a pile of burned out rubble and bricks.

Away from the station, the town appeared to fare better than Riga, which was an important supply port. There was destruction, but many buildings were still standing. Fruit and vegetable stands were doing business on the streets.

They stopped at one of the carts, but the shabbily dressed woman spoke no English. However, seeing two young foreigners, she did her best to make a sale. She and Sven spoke for some time.

"She'll tell us how to get to Lutzin, but we have to buy something first. Let's try somebody else."

"No. I could use something to eat. Those apples look good. Offer her a dollar."

She snatched it and handed over two apples, while pouring out directions.

Sven wrote down what he understood. "She say go left, then through center of town, past all the stores. Lutzin is about ten miles east on a dirt road through the forest. She calls it Ludza."

"That's probably the Russian pronunciation. Let's go."

They turned into the main street, nothing more than broken up gravel with brick sidewalks, hurried past rows of stores on both sides. Most were closed or had their fronts blown out, but here and there some merchants were making a brave attempt at reopening. A husky man with leathery skin and white hair was setting up a table on the sidewalk as they went by. He gave them a momentary glance as they passed and then returned to his work.

The business district of Krezekne was presently left behind and Rusty and Sven looked down a narrow dirt road that stretched between rows of trees on either side. It was deserted except for some wrecked German trucks and a disabled tank. The late afternoon sun slanted through the trees and a light breeze rustled the leaves that had survived the numerous battles fought here. They walked mostly in silence, Rusty emotionally affected by the thought that perhaps his Grandfather David and Grandmother Itkah might have traveled over this road for many years. Sven walked quietly beside his friend, enjoying the stillness and beauty of a late summer afternoon.

It was a strange sight – two seaman in dungarees, pea jackets, white sailor caps and backpacks, strolling down an empty dirt road between Krezekne and Lutzin. To Rusty, it seemed unreal, a dream. Sven was content to share his friend's feelings silently, realizing it was a special moment in his life, one he would not soon forget.

The sun was setting far behind them when the road widened into a clearing and several cottages, some damaged, others intact, appeared on either side. Beyond the cottages, on the right, was a small lake where several villagers seemed to be filling buckets with water. They were about to turn toward them when Sven spotted an elderly man and woman sitting on boxes by their front door. Rusty waved to them in a friendly manner. They did not wave back.

"Do you speak English?" Rusty called out as they approached. There was no answer.

"Ask them in Russian, Sven."

The response was the same.

"How do we tell them who we are?" Rusty asked. "We're nearly 100 miles from the ship. They'll never believe us. They might even call the police."

"What police?" Sven asked. "There's nobody here but a few villagers. Wait a minute. Why don't you tell them your name, it might ring a bell."

"Great idea," Rusty said as he stepped closer. These poor people, he thought as he looked at their tattered clothes and frightened faces. "Sven, give them a couple of chocolate bars."

Sven reached out to them but they shrank in terror against the wall.

"Unwrap the bars, Sven, so they can see what it is."

Sven leaned closer so the odor of the chocolate might reach them. They looked at each other, then the man stood up, motioned to his wife to remain where she was. He hesitantly reached out and took the bars with a grimy hand, looked at them in amazement and bit into one. His grizzled face broke into a smile as he handed the other bar to his wife who, following her husband's actions, disposed of the bar quickly. They both came forward and held out their arms.

"Sven, ask them if Kurtzman means anything to them?"

The mention of his family's name had a magical effect. They began chattering in Russian and, taking their hands, led them a little further down the road to a cottage nestled among some trees with a vegetable garden alongside. An old woman was bending over the garden as the neighbors shuffled up to her. They spoke to each other for several minutes before she turned toward Rusty and Sven. She was moderately tall for a Russian woman, about 5'8", slightly bent over with a kerchief around her grey hair. Her wrinkled face had the same blank expression they had seen on most people here. Her hazel eyes were tinged with red from lack of sleep, but they brightened at the sound of Rusty's family name.

"Ask her if she knew the Kurtzman family," Rusty said.

Her voice was soft and tired. "No need, I speak English. I taught school in Minsk but returned during the revolution. It was not healthy to be a teacher in those days. I married Krushenko and have lived here ever since."

"Krushenko," Rusty muttered. "I saw that name somewhere. Yeah, just today on a store front in the town. He's an importer."

She laughed. "The sign is an old one. He imports nothing today. Russia took his money, the Germans his spirit. Today he sells what he can."

Rusty looked at her, their eyes almost level.

"Did you know the Kurtzman family that lived in Lutzin? They left in 1910 or 1912. Itkah and David were the parents."

She laughed again, a pleasant, cheery laugh. "Know them? Of course, I know them. We bought this cottage from them when they left. Why do you ask?"

Rusty took a step closer. "I'm their grandson. David and Itkah Kurtzman are my grandparents. I came here to see where they lived." He explained how they came to be in Russia and how they got here from Riga.

"Then you have retraced their steps to here. That is wonderful." She wiped her hands on her apron. "You must be very tired. Come inside and I'll make some tea. Coffee is impossible to obtain, as is most everything else. You'll find the house changed little. Our two sons are gone, in the army. We haven't heard from them in two years. We keep their room ready. You will rest in it tonight."

"I don't see how. We have to get back to the ship."

"At night? Impossible. You might as well commit suicide. There are thieves and murderers on the roads and a curfew in effect as well. If any soldiers see you, they will shoot. You must not try to get back tonight."

Rusty looked at Sven who shook his shoulders. "I could surely use a good night's rest."

"O.K." Rusty said. "The captain knows where we went. He won't be surprised if we're not back today."

"I just hope they are there when we return," Sven said.

"The house itself hasn't changed much since they left," Mrs. Krushenko said as she waved them inside. "The furnishings are different. My husband imported all manner of merchandise, and the furniture you see is what is left. The Germans fortunately were in such a hurry coming into this area, and in such a hurry to leave, that they only took whatever food they could carry. As you can see the house is undamaged. The stove is the same, large but efficient."

"It's very satisfying just to be here," Rusty said. "It'll be a thrill to tell everybody back home that I was here, and it'll be a special thrill for my grandparents."

Mrs. Krushenko sat them down and brewed a pot of tea and warmed a bowl of goulash that she had prepared for dinner. "My husband may or may not come home for dinner. Sometimes he stays in town for days at a time. He is not the man he used to be, but very few of us in Russia are. The war has taken a heavy toll. Here, I make this bread myself."

Rusty and Sven plunged into the meal and would have gladly eaten second helpings, but politely refused.

"You've been very kind," Rusty said. "Do you think you've seen the last of the Germans?"

"I doubt it," she said. "They don't give up easily. But tell me about America. How are Itkah and David? What are they doing?"

Rusty wiped his mouth and took a sip of the wine she had brought up. He could feel its warmth spread through his body.

"They have a small store where they sell everything from thread and groceries to shoes. They had a much larger store, but it was wiped out by the Depression, just as many other businesses were. I don't know much about it though, because I was only in my teens."

"Your grandfather was a paperhanger, but it didn't bring in much. Itkah was a worker. Every day she was on the road between Rezekne and Lutzin with Aaron and her cart of groceries."

"Aaron?"

"Her famous mule. She'll be happy to hear it lived another ten years. A legend in this area. Itkah loved life. She always wanted children. Did you know that when she married David he already had five children?"

"She told me," Sidney said. "I can't wait to get back and tell her about being here. It's like a dream."

"It's more than a dream. It's a miracle," she said. "The last thing I expected to see was a Kurtzman under this roof again. And Joshua, whose parents were killed by soldiers in the house next to this one. What about him? How did he ever get into America with only one leg?"

"One leg?" Rusty answered, surprised. "I had no idea that he only had one leg. He limped, but it never occurred to me to ask him why. I didn't know his parents had been murdered. He's a wealthy man today. He's a coal and fuel oil supplier and I understand he has government contracts to supply the military for the duration. He's married and has two sons."

Mrs. Krushenko clapped her hands. "I'm so happy for him."

For two hours she plied Rusty with questions about his family and the United States. Her eyes shone as he related the various paths the Kurtzman family had taken.

"And your own parents," she finally asked. "You've hardly spoken of them. How are they?"

Rusty hesitated. It was true, he hadn't mentioned his parents. He was embarrassed. It wasn't intentional. He just didn't give it any thought. Did his parents mean so little to him that he completely forgot about them? Was his life at home so empty that he could skip over it so easily? "My father has his own barbershop and my mother takes care of the house," he finally said.

"No brothers or sisters?"

"I have one sister, Edith. She's five years older than me and works in an office in a clothing factory. She has red hair, too. She's very nice."

"I'm sure she is," Mrs. Krushenko said. "It sounds wonderful. Make sure you give everybody my best wishes when you get back. But you both look exhausted. Excuse me for keeping you up. I'm sure you want to rest. You'll sleep in my son's room. Don't object. I'll wake you. You should get an early start, just in case the Germans come back. They've been chased out of here twice before and have always fought their way back. You don't want to be stranded here."


Rusty lay awake for some time that night, thinking of the strange circumstances that led him to retrace the route of his family.

Sven was breathing heavily beside him, having fallen asleep

almost at the same time his head touched the pillow. A good man, Rusty thought, somebody you can count on. He didn't have to come with him, but he had.

He thought about Mrs. Krushenko and her unfortunate husband, the dirt road from Krezekne, how often his grandparents and his aunts and uncles must have traveled over it in the years that they lived here. He could visualize them helping their parents tend the large plot beside the house. It was indeed a miracle, Rusty thought, traveling thousands of miles and ending up here. He looked around the bedroom. One bureau, a chair on either side of the bed, an outside closet which was nothing more than a large, free standing box with hooks inside to hang clothes on, a single oil or kerosene burning lamp on a small table in the corner and a window that overlooked the vegetable garden.

He felt strangely comfortable here, not only physically, but emotionally, even spiritually. It was an emotion unlike any he had ever experienced in his young life. The feeling of belonging, of being a part of this place where his family came from. He imagined traveling on that road, possibly sitting beside his grandmother as she made the trip between Krezekne and Lutzin. Why was he so certain that he had in fact done so, he wondered. It didn't matter why, it was enough that he was moved to feel it.

His thoughts shifted to home, his mother and father and sister. When he returned he wanted to take this experience with him, this feeling of closeness, almost love for this place. He wanted to feel close to his parents and Edie, to the house on 7th Street. Here he was dealing with the past. The real world was back in Philadelphia. He wondered if his grandparents ever spoke about things like that, the past and the real. They must have. They had lived face to face with reality. What a difficult decision it must have been to turn their backs on their homeland and leave forever. He must talk to them about their life here, and the situation that had driven them to a strange land to start all over again.

His head was swimming. He wanted to share his thoughts with Sven, but his friend was fast asleep. Rusty closed his eyes. Soon he was also asleep, dreaming of Krezekne and Lutzin, his grandmother. "Family," she was saying. "It's all that matters." His sleep was restless. He squirmed and moved as the pictures floated past. His parents and sister, his grandmother, Catherine. Finally, the dreams faded. True sleep overcame him, the sleep of the physically and emotionally drained. His body was still, his eyes motionless.


Something was holding his arm, shaking him awake. It was Mrs. Krushenko. A bright sun flooded the room with light. Sven was out of bed quickly, his years at sea having instilled in him the discipline for instant action. Rusty was slower, needing more time to get this thoughts together. He heard a rumbling in the distance, like thunder, but it was a clear day.

"Quickly, my friends," Mrs. Krushenko whispered, as though what she said might be overheard. "It doesn't sound good. The gunfire is getting closer. Eat your breakfast and go."

The table contained scrambled eggs, homemade bread and hot tea.

"We managed to hide a few hens from the Germans, hence the eggs. Now we must hide them again. Why don't they leave once and for all?"

After breakfast she stuffed several apples into their backpacks and hurried them on their way. She threw her arms around both of them, planting a healthy kiss on their cheeks. "God be with you, if there is such a thing in this land. Go, and tell everyone my heart is with them."

The sun had disappeared behind heavy clouds as they hurried down the road to Krezekne. As they entered the road where it was bordered by trees on each side, Rusty turned and looked back. She still was in the doorway. He waved to her and she raised her arm in response. She looked so alone back there.

"I hope the Germans leave her alone," he said.

"She is very good woman," Sven said. "It's a pity to live one's life in the hell of war."

Rusty turned his back on her. His eyes were moist. "Let's get going," he said. "Those guns seem to be getting closer all the time."

## 38

When Rusty and Sven turned into the port area, they saw the LT 677 still tied up to the same pier. The tow was gone.

"I guess the Russians took possession of it," Rusty said.

"I hope they put it to good use," Sven replied. "We went through a lot to get that thing here."

Captain Sugarman was on the bridge and raised a hand as they approached. They boarded the tug and went right up to him.

"Sorry we stayed overnight, sir," Rusty said. "It was almost dark when we got there and Mrs. Krushenko wouldn't let us travel at night. She said it was too dangerous."

"She was probably right. Who's Mrs. Krushenko?"

"She lives in the house where my grandparents lived with their children, including my father." He related their experience.

Captain Sugarman looked at the two of them. "That's quite a story you'll have to take home with you. Don't worry about coming back late. We still have two days work in the engine room before we're able to get out of here, if we don't get bombed out before that."

Rusty looked out at the pier. "Lucky the Russians moved the tow to a safe place."

"Come up to the top deck," the captain said. "I'll show you something that'll break your heart."

From that vantage point they could see over the top of the pier. The tow had been sunk. The barge platform was under water and the crane was bent over, nearly parallel with the water.

Captain Sugarman looked at the disbelieving faces of his seamen. "The German's must have heard it was here, and sent a single bomber over yesterday. It was pure luck that the tug survived."

Sven was the first to regain his voice.

"God fordomme," he hissed in Norwegian. "All that work for nothing. There's no justice in this world. No justice."

"I'm with you, Sven," Rusty said. "It's just not fair. Almost 5,000 miles for what? To wind up like this? It's unbelievable."

"The German's don't want this port operating," Captain Sugarman stated. "That pilot didn't waste any bombs."

"All that work for nothing," Sven repeated.

Rusty stared at the crane. It was nothing more than a pile of twisted metal. "Well, what now, sir?"

"Now we get back to England as soon as the work below is finished. That's not all. We lost three men in the raid."

"What?"

"Mr. Walford and your friend Cole were on the tow pumping it out. They didn't have a chance."

"George Cole," Rusty half-shouted. He began crying, heavy sobs, uncontrolled, with both hands to his face.

Sven put his arm around his shoulder. "I share your feelings, Rusty. Sometimes it doesn't pay to get too close."

Rusty wiped his eyes and blew his nose. "And Mr. Walford, too," he said, his voice shaking. "He'll never teach another history class."

"Who was the third man?" Sven asked.

"Our Danish pilot, Mr. Herning. He was standing where we are when a piece of metal struck him directly in the forehead."

They were again silent for a moment.

"You two go down and get something to eat, then resume your normal watches. It's better to keep busy than try to sleep."

Down in the mess, Rusty dabbed at his soup. He was hungry, but found it difficult to swallow.

"Poor Cole," he said. "He didn't want to kill anybody so he joined the Merchant Marines. I'll miss him. He was like a big brother. I feel sorry for his parents."

"It could have been worse," Sven said. "If that bomb hit this tug – voom! The whole crew would be dead."

Rusty breathed deeply. "I suppose so. But why Cole of all people? He was a Quaker, anti-war, nonviolent."

"Why anybody?"

Rusty nodded. "Why, indeed."


The next day the firing from the front lines was closer and an occasional shell whistled overhead and exploded among the already wrecked piers. It was 1800 hours and Rusty, Sven and Szabo were summoned to the wheelhouse. Andrew McGonagle, a seaman from one of the other watches, joined them along with 2nd Mate Anderson.

McGonagle was a muscular man about Sven's age with unruly black hair, heavy eye brows, a perpetual frown on his swarthy face and huge hands, hardened from many years of heavy labor.

"McGonagle and you three will be splitting your duties on the way home since the regular deck crew is two men short," Anderson said. "Without a tow we can do away with the acetylene watch, so you'll have more time to do other things, a double wheel watch perhaps and wherever else you're needed."

Another shell passed overhead and again exploded amid the piers. It was a little closer this time.

"How long before we're ready to sail?" McGonagle asked nervously. His voice was gruff.

"Hopefully tomorrow. We don't want to get caught here. Those big guns sound closer and those shells seem to be coming in our direction. I thought at first they were strays, now I'm not so sure. Make certain everything is secure for a fast getaway."

The next morning Captain Sugarman watched a plane pass over high in the sky, circle, and return.

"An observation plane," he muttered. "Ten to one he's reporting our position right now."

Thirty minutes later a shell screamed low over the tug and exploded two piers away. All hands were ordered on deck, except for those working on the engine.

Captain Sugarman stood on the bridge to make himself heard. "Our work on deck is finished. Sooner or later one of those shells is going to get us. We can either go ashore a safe distance and watch this thing go sky-high and pray we don't get captured, or follow another option. We can manually lower the lifeboat and start towing this LT 677 out of the river into the Gulf where we might be unobserved. It'll give us a fighting chance to get back to England, or at least to Sweden. The chief says they should be done in six hours, but it's too dangerous to just sit here waiting. I want eight men not on watch to lower the boat and start rowing. Remember, the further we get from this pier the better chance we have of getting back alive. Now get going, on the double."

It was an hour before the lifeboat was manned and lowered and a heavy line fed down from the bow of the tug.

Rusty was in the wheelhouse with Mr. Anderson and Szabo as the LT 677 itself became a tow, moving slowly away from the pier.

They all looked at the sunken crane as they floated past. Rusty thought of George Cole, his body trapped somewhere at the bottom, to remain there until some day in the future when the crane was raised to the surface for salvage.

His thoughts were interrupted by another shell that passed by to starboard. The explosion ripped away the land end of the pier where the tug had been tied up.

"They're getting the range," Mr. Anderson said.

Captain Sugarman came into the wheelhouse. "The tide's emptying into the gulf. If it flows faster than they can row, we'll run them down. The wheel won't do us much good with the tide behind us. Just keep it positioned straight ahead to reduce the tendency to swing to port or starboard. I don't have any figures on these waters but when we came in the tide seemed to be about four knots. That's a lot of rowing. Kurtz, you, Szabo and McGonagle stand by the anchor and lift it over the side. Drop it as soon as I give the order."

The lifeboat crew maneuvered through the wreckage with Sparks doing duty on the tiller. With the engine down, there was no power for the radio room, so the captain had put him to work. The rowers were barely able to maintain course which meant their speed combined with the tide was moving them at about six or seven knots an hour – fast enough to get them out of the cramped quarters of the harbor and into the more open waters of the estuary.

Another shell passed behind them, followed instantly by a tremendous explosion. A lookout atop the wheelhouse shouted down, "That one got it. We'd be dead ducks if we were still at the pier."

The captain's decision proved a wise one and in another hour the Gulf of Riga stretched before them.

"Call in the lifeboat," shouted the captain. "Stand by to drop anchor!"

Just after this order, Chief Baker came up to the wheelhouse. "We're finished, Captain. Engine room is ready."

"Great work, Chief." He turned toward the bow. "Secure that anchor. All men return to your watch stations. We're getting underway as soon as the lifeboat is aboard. Anderson, turn the wheel over to the deck watch as soon as they've secured the anchor."

The lifeboat maneuvered its way alongside the tug as it drifted into the gulf, where the tide had little effect. The second it cleared the water the order was given for "slow ahead." It was reassuring to feel the vibration of the engine again.

"Sparks," Anderson shouted as soon as his feet touched the deck. "Get into the radio room and find out what's going on in the world."

The lifeboat was secured and the crew went to their normal stations. "Half ahead," followed shortly by "full ahead" was sent down to the engine room. Without the tow the LT 677 was free to show what it could do. The speed was soon up to 20 knots, the first time it had achieved that mark since Charleston.

Szabo was at the wheel, his normally expressionless face lit up by a broad smile. Rusty was on the starboard bridge, Sven on the port bridge as life on LT 677 slowly returned to regular shipboard routine.

Captain Sugarman left the wheelhouse when Anderson came in. "I'm going to sleep, Hank. Eight hours at most, then it's your turn. Take it back out into the Baltic and then toward the Swedish coast. Without the tow, we should be back in England in 2-1/2 days, barring complications. Pass on a well done to the whole crew. They deserve it."

## 39

Rusty stepped off the bus near Picadilly and strolled past the small clubs, music shops and street walkers, deliberately avoiding the Friend's House where Cole had spent his first night off the tug.

He could have stayed on the bus but he wanted to walk. He needed time to arrange his thoughts, to mull over what to say to Catherine. It was three weeks since they had spent the three days together. He needed to know if he was merely another guy. Was she thinking about him? Sven had warned him, but Rusty set it aside – there had to be more to it.

Was it love or infatuation that drew him to this solemn woman with her soft, soothing voice? "It's fate that brought you to me," she had said. He wanted to understand her, talk with her and be held. It was wonderful when they were close. Another world, away from war and ships. He considered the worst case scenario – a pleasant wartime interlude that ended when he left her tiny apartment. Could he accept that? he wondered. And at best, if she did want him, what then? Was he prepared to follow up? There were too many questions – too many decisions.

The sun struggled to break through the smog that seemed to forever hang over London. Life had been simple before he met her. He was on an LT delivering a harbor crane to the war zone. The crane was sunk but they could hardly be faulted for that. After repairs they would go out again. No complicated emotional upheavals. Just follow orders.

And love? How did that fit in? He could turn around with a clear conscience. He made no promises or commitments. But he knew that wouldn't happen. His grandmother would have some answers.

The sun gave up its feeble attempt as he entered Collet's Book Shop. His head throbbed as he looked around. A girl in her teens approached, thin with hair hanging uncombed, wearing a skirt far too short for her bony legs.

"Can I 'elp ya?" Her voice was high and scratchy, the cockney accent heavy and almost unintelligible.

"Is Catherine here?"

"Oo?"

"Catherine. She works here. Brown hair, attractive."

"Ain't no attractive girls 'ere. I just begun 'ere."

How can anybody understand her?, he wondered. And in a book shop.

"Mebbe she's the one 'oose place I took."

"You mean Catherine's not here anymore?"

"If that's 'er name. Ya got a ciggy, Yank?"

"A what?"

"A ciggy, a smoke."

"I don't smoke."

She placed her hands defiantly on her hips. "One a them kind, ey?"

"What?"

"I run inta blokes like ya afore. Ya don't smoke so ya think yer better than little folks like me. Any more blinkin' requests y'r majesty?"

"Forget it." He left the store, thankful that there was no need for further conversation.

Why did Catherine give up her job? he wondered. He continued down Charing Cross to Oxford, then left on Brook to #21. He stopped short. The house was gone. Where it had stood was rubble – bricks, broken furniture, nothing in one piece. Two houses on either side were also wrecked, but it was obvious that #21 had received a direct hit.

Maybe she wasn't home when it happened. She was forced to move, or left London altogether.

A bobby strolled up, swinging his night stick. "Lookin' for someone, mate?"

"Yes, a girl that lived here. I guess she moved out after this."

"You mean, Miss Bowers?"

"That's her! Have you seen her?"

The bobby hesitated. "Only once since that bloody bomb hit, when they pulled her body out. It wasn't pretty."

Rusty swallowed hard. "She's dead?"

"Sorry, mate. She was a decent sort. I didn't know her well, but she was always ready with a few words for me when our paths crossed. Had a quality about her, she did. Kind of dreamy and faraway, like she was thinkin' of somethin' else. You her friend or somethin'?"

"Just a friend. When did it happen?"

"About ten days ago. Hardly a day goes by without one of those blasted things leaving its mark somewhere."

Rusty stepped closer to #21. Nothing much was left. A piece of her Grosvenor Square window, the tattered remains of a familiar bed cover. This was her legacy. Like Cole, Walford and Linus Herning – in the wrong place at the wrong time. She would say it was meant to be. Fate had it all planned, her life, her death. Nobody could escape.

Poor Catherine, he thought. Alone, reaching for the few bits of pleasure that drifted her way. He had been part of it, but for what purpose he knew not. Sven was right. No emotional ties. Get the war over with and move on. He walked down Brook Road and stopped at the corner, looking back at #21. Her fate had caught up with her.

## 40

The cargo vessel, S.S. Admiral Byrd, a 600 foot, 24,000 ton freighter named for the famous Arctic explorer, in convoy with eight other ships, turned southwest out of the English Channel past the Bay of Biscay, then south along the west coast of Portugal. She was loaded with tanks, an assortment of vehicles including half-tracks, jeeps and trucks, as well as artillery pieces, ammunition and a division of soldiers destined for Italy.

It was 1944 and after 4-1/2 years of war, the Germans were feeling the pressure from the south and east. The Russians had built up a huge army far behind the front lines and were now unleashing this power against the Germans, whose dreams of conquering that vast country were dissolving into harsh reality. In the south, they had finally been beaten in the North African desert, and were now fighting desperately to contain the Allies in Italy. With the invasion of France imminent, the end of the 1,000 year Reich seemed at last within reach.

Short of a full crew upon its arrival in England, the Admiral Byrd had put in a request for additional seamen. Rusty, Sven and Szabo, their tug expected to be laid up for three months, volunteered to fill the openings. After losing their tow in Riga and having three crewmen killed in that attack, they desperately wanted to do something positive, something to justify their presence in a war zone.

Rusty needed to get away from England and the memory of that destroyed house on Brook Road. Sven was a career sailor and was not one to spend time on the beach waiting for LT 677 to be ready to go to work again.

Szabo summed everything up in his own style. "So far we ain't done a fucking think to help end this goddamn war. I ain't goin' home to tell everybody that all I done was tow a crane over for target practice by the Germans and watch three shipmates get killed in the bargain."

When the Byrd's master was hospitalized in London with appendicitis, Captain Sugarman left the LT 677 in charge of 2nd Mate Anderson and took over command of the freighter until the tug was ready for sea again.

High above the deck, Sven and Szabo were on the starboard bridge. Rusty was at the wheel with Captain Sugarman. A tall slender black man about the captain's age, his curly hair pebbled with gray, was standing lookout on the port bridge. His skin was as dark as any black man Rusty had ever seen, and his eyes shone out brightly against his complexion. His nose was straight, and with his jutting chin and shiny cheekbones, his profile could have been cut by a professional sculptor. His appearance was striking, one to attract the interest of the most casual observer, and he carried himself straight and with dignity. He looked out of place on the bridge of a ship at sea.

"Do you know anything about him?" Rusty asked the captain.

"Not much," Captain Sugarman answered. "Of course, as master of this ship, I have access to records of everybody in the crew. He's from Alabama, signed on in Charleston and is 58 years old. This is his first ship."

Rusty whistled. "Pretty old to sign on as a merchant seaman."

"He's not much older than me," the captain said.

"But you've been at sea all your life. What makes a black man come out of Alabama to join the Merchant Marines?"

"Don't ask me. Maybe he's patriotic."

"Fat chance," Rusty said. "A patriotic black man from Alabama? That's a good one."

"You're drifting off to port, Kurtz. Pay attention to your course."

"Sorry, sir. 180 degrees south."

"180 degrees south, it is."

Rusty looked out at the small convoy as they sailed parallel to the Portuguese coast on a calm, pleasant day. The sky was clear except for streaks of cirrus clouds high in the atmosphere, and the ship rolled and dipped lazily to the long swells rolling in from the Atlantic.

"How do you like this duty compared to the tug?" Captain Sugarman asked.

"Luxurious," he said. "More room for everything. If you feel like taking a walk, there's 600 feet of deck to do it in. You could put the tug in this wheelhouse."

"It's big, but there something to be said about an LT. It's cozier, easier to handle, and I knew everything that was going on. If somebody pissed in the shower I would hear about it. On a ship this size, a crewman can disappear for hours without anybody knowing where he is."

Szabo came in from the starboard bridge for his wheel watch. "180 degrees south," Rusty said, relinquishing the wheel.

"180 degrees south," Szabo said as he stepped on the platform. "Well, you Rusty nail, this is more fuckin' like it, ain't it? A real ship with real cargo. No fuckin' around with a goddamned tow."

"Szabo," Captain Sugarman said in an exasperated tone, "if you can't clean up your act when you're around me you'll be banned from the wheelhouse. And that goes for when we're back on the tug, too. I don't know where you come from or who you're trying to impress, but as long as I'm captain, you'll have to express yourself without the help of all those four letter words. Understand?" His voice was calm, but the message was clear.

"Yes, sir," Szabo said in a low voice. "I understand, sir."

Rusty withdrew from the wheelhouse quietly. He nearly collided with the black seaman as he exited. "Excuse me," Rusty said. He held out his right hand. "My name's Kurtz, Sid Kurtz, but everybody calls me Rusty."

His hand was smothered by the black man's right hand. His fingers were long, like a piano player's, and strong. He looked down at Rusty. "I'm Solomon Mobuto." His voice was firm and clear. "Everybody calls me Sol." His accent hinted of the Caribbean.

Sol must be seven feet tall, Rusty judged and with his pea jacket and black knit cap securely fitted around his head and pulled down over his forehead, he looked like nothing Rusty had ever seen before.

"Glad to meet you," Rusty said. "I have to go into the hold and check out the cargo. See you later."

"Okay, Rusty," he said with a slight smile. "See you later."

Rusty spent two hours roaming the ship, making certain nothing was loose and likely to shift around if the weather deteriorated. The Sherman tanks were lashed on deck, while down below jeeps, trucks, artillery pieces and huge cases of ammunition occupied every square foot. It was amazing, Rusty thought. The ingenuity and inventiveness that war brought out in people. Millions spent on destroying, a fraction spent on creating. The world was certainly a strange place. He double-checked the fastenings on the masses of equipment surrounding the ammunition – rifles, pistols, machine guns, tank destroyers, shells for the artillery, flame throwers, land mines. If a torpedo hit this ship, there wouldn't be much left. He finished his tour and went up on deck, glad to escape the claustrophobic gloom of the hold. Up here he at least might be blown overboard by any explosions. Down below he wouldn't have a chance. His watch ended with an hour on the port bridge. Sol was nowhere to be seen. Sven was at the wheel with the ship's 2nd Mate, a hulking, sour-faced, bald-headed man, about 40 years old, with a perpetual scowl showing through his beard. His pug nose was lost between bloated round cheeks and bloodshot eyes.

He was 2nd in command to the captain and he never let anybody forget it. He was apparently used to having a free hand in his attitude toward the crew. He and Captain Sugarman had already had a difference of opinion on how to run the ship. Rusty could hear his gruff voice admonishing Sven every time the ship veered off course by as much as a degree, a situation that couldn't be helped due to the wind and waves. He must have been a great kid to play with when he was younger, Rusty thought. How did a man like that get to be a 2nd Mate?

The watch ended at 12:00 noon, an improvement over the 4 to 8 hour watch on the tug, and Rusty went below to the mess for lunch. He helped himself to meatloaf, mashed potatoes, peas and a cup of tea, then joined Sven, Szabo and Solomon Mobuto, who towered over everybody else. There were also several other members of the crew, including the 2nd Mate, who sat down at the end of the table.

Szabo cast a menacing eye toward the bearded mate. "How come we got stuck with this son of a bitch on our watch all of a sudden? What happened to the captain?"

"Upset stomach," Sven said. "His food won't stay down. He should be back in day or two."

"I heard the mate giving it to you in the wheelhouse," Rusty said.

"I ship with guys like that before," Sven said. "They get carried away with their authority. They got to show their power."

"He's showing it all right. What's his name, anyway?"

"Streep," Szabo said. "Jack Streep. I saw his name on the cabin door. He's the only officer that has his fuckin' name on his door."

"He give Solomon bad time, too," Sven said.

Rusty looked at the black man's face. It was expressionless.

"What did he do?"

"Solomon moved the platform away from the wheel so his head wouldn't bump against ceiling. Streep made him put it back, so he spent whole watch bent over. When Solomon asked him again if he could move it, Streep say, 'No black African beanpole tell me what to do.'"

"That dirty bastard," Szabo hissed. "What did Solomon say?"

"He say nothing. He stand whole hour while Streep scream at him every time ship go off course a degree or two. Such language. He make you look like boy scout, Szabo."

Everybody but Solomon laughed.

"He better not fuck with this boy scout," Szabo said, "or he'll wind up with a god-damned medal hanging from his eye."

"Careful, Szabo," Sven warned. "Even in Merchant Marines, it is serious offense to strike an officer. You end up in prison sure."

"It'd be worth it," Szabo said. "I don't take any shit from bastards like that."

Rusty thought it best to change the subject. "Where are you from, Sol?"

Solomon hesitated slightly. "Alabama."

"Where in Alabama?"

Again there was hesitation. "Small village, you never hear it."

"I'm pretty good at geography," Rusty said. "What's the name of that village."

Solomon Mobuto sighed. "Miami," he said.

Everyone stared at him incredulously.

"Miami?" Szabo asked. "When did they move it?"

"Sorry, Sol," Rusty said. "You're a little off. You can tell us where you're really from. We won't say anything."

Solomon looked at them sheepishly. "I am from Africa. I boarded ship in Tanga to help fight for world. If I say I from Tanzania, I fear the Merchant Service don't take me. I too tall and too old for Army, so I sign on ship."

"Tanza-who?" Szabo asked. "Where the hell is that?"

"East Africa, next to Kenya."

"That's not much help."

"Why did you pick Alabama?" Rusty asked.

"When I was boy our elders would talk of the many slaves taken to America in the olden days. They spoke of many names. I remember Alabama."

"But Miami, where did that come from?"

"The ship I sailed on was City of Miami.

"Quite a story," Rusty said. "But why sign up at all? You live in a country far from the war where there's no fighting or bombing. You could have sat out the war, and nobody could say anything bad about you."

Solomon finished his coffee and rested his large hands on the table. "That is true. Most of the tribes in that area are entirely ignorant of the war. They hear little of outside world. We are cattle herders and travel over the countryside and our elders hear everything. They come back with stories of great fighting – of good against evil. They say that evil forces will take over the world if they win. That's why I come here. The Masai are great warriors. I am here to help Africa and the world. At home I too old. I am called Junior Elder and not permitted to fight. Here I can fight. I fight for the good in the world, just as my ancestors did for the Masai many generations ago."

His simple sincerity held the attention of his small audience, and when he spoke of his people, they saw a faraway look come over his face. It was obvious that Solomon was here only physically. His spirit was still in Africa. Szabo broke the silence.

"Is everybody in your tribe as tall as you?"

Solomon roused himself from his private thoughts. "Not everybody, but the Masai are tall people. It has always been so. Other tribes envy our height. They are jealous, but they do not fight us – not anymore. The Masai are great warriors, are feared in the entire Rift Valley and on the slopes of Mt. Merv and Kilimanjaro. The Masai Steppe has been ours since our ancestors moved down from Kenya. Even in the old days, the slave traders never bother us. The Masai were not the weak, submissive people like the others who refused to fight and sold their own into slavery. That is not the Masai. We are our own masters, not sheep to be shackled and whipped, crowded into floating coffins, and sent far away to serve white men we have never seen."

"But, Solomon," Sven interrupted, "this is white man's war. Why you want to fight?

"This everybody's war," Solomon answered. "I am more fortunate than many of my countrymen. I learn to read, write. I read about war. At first, I say it is far away, but then war comes to Africa. The enemy kills both white and black. They hate black. I fight to show that black is not bad, that we are all brothers in this world. We must look after each other."

There was silence for a moment, again broken by Szabo. "You're all right, Solomon. Anybody gives you a hard time, they'll have Szabo to deal with, like that screwball Streep."

"Mr. Streep bad man," Solomon said. "Don't trouble yourself with him. He will be dealt with in the manner of the Masai."

Szabo exchanged glances with Sven and Rusty.

"You know," Szabo muttered, "I almost feel sorry for Streep."


The Admiral Byrd rounded the southern tip of Spain and passed through the narrow channel between Gibraltar and Morocco, then entered the Mediterranean Sea. Now that the Germans were cleared out of North Africa, the passage from the Atlantic was uneventful except for an occasional submarine contact. Even that menace, through the use of expanded air coverage was nothing more than a nuisance. A sub did manage a success here and there, but the days of helpless convoys at the mercy of wolf packs and German planes was a thing of the past. The Allies were rapidly gaining control of the air and seas. Long distance bombers flying out of England and North Africa were attacking the German homeland, while more and more U-boats failed to return from their tours in the Atlantic. Germany was on the defensive, attempting to contain the Russians in the east, and keeping a nervous eye on the coast of France.

Captain Sugarman's stomach returned to normal and he resumed full command of the ship to the enormous relief of the crew, who had been subjected to torrents of orders and abusive language from 2nd Mate Jack Streep. Solomon Mobuto's tall angular form was a particularly convenient target for his venemous attacks. The quiet black man from the Masai Steppes bore the insults in silence and went about his duties as though he heard nothing. This only infuriated Streep still further, and he redoubled his efforts to antagonize him.

At this point, Captain Sugarman returned to full command and Streep's attacks, if not ended, were at least markedly reduced. The ship returned to near normal and Streep's ravings were confined to remote areas of the vessel where the captain was not likely to hear about it, and upon those men who would not report it for fear of incurring his anger even further.

The weather remained favorable as the small convoy sailed south of Cartagena, past the Balearil Islands, and out into the open Mediterranean Sea, keeping a good distance away from occupied France.

Rusty and Sven were sitting on watch, enjoying the warm breeze blowing off the North Africa mainland, and watching the Island of Sardinia pass by to the North, when the sound of wood hitting the metal deck intruded upon their thoughts. It was a measured sound, about one every two seconds, and soon the cause of this noise came into view from between two rows of tanks that were lashed to the deck. It was Solomon Mobuto, dressed in a long native gown that reached down to the deck, giving him the appearance of being taller than he was, with a long walking stick in his right hand that struck the deck with every other step. He could have been in Africa tending his flock as he strode toward them in a dignified manner. His long gown, with a colorful shield emblazoned across the front, flowed in the wind as he stepped in front of them.

"That's one beautiful outfit," Sven said politely. "Is that what you wear at home?"

"It is my tribal dress – a common sight among my people, but only elders can wear the shield. It is a sign that one has passed through the warrior stage and has earned the respect of all his people."

"That's real honor," Rusty said sincerely.

"Thank you," Sol said, obviously pleased at the compliment. "I miss my home so I wear this to make me feel better. The walking stick is a hard wood from the Galam tree, set with bone at each end. It helps one to walk through the fields and is also an excellent weapon. The bone can inflict serious damage."

"I'll bet," Rusty answered. "You take a swing at somebody with that and you can really knock them for a loop."

"Ah, but we rarely swing them. We throw them, like spears. Watch. See the opening on that tank?" He held up his right arm, carefully balanced the heavy stick in his hand, and let it fly. In an instant the stick had covered the 30 foot distance to its target and disappeared inside the observation window of the tank.

"Wonderful!" Sven exclaimed, clapping his hands.

"You said it, Sven," Rusty joined in. "That's what I call a perfect strike."

"What're you doin' dressed like that?" The voice startled them. It was Streep. "You belong in a side show with that get-up on. Get back into your work clothes."

"I am not on watch," Sol said, recovering his walking stick from the tank.

"Don't argue with me, you black beanpole. You'll wear what I tell you to wear. You're not walking around this ship dressed like a goddamned clown!"

"Mr. Streep," Sven said, "there's no law that say he can't wear what he wants when he is off watch."

Streep turned his bloodshot eyes at Sven. "Who asked you, big mouth? You're better off keeping that nose of yours right where it is or you'll find it spread all over that Norwegian face."

"I don't like that," Sven said angrily.

"Oh, you don't like that," Streep said, mimicking Sven's accent. "Well, ain't that just too bad? And maybe you'd like to do somethin' about it?"

He clenched his fists while thick veins bulged in his neck. Sven stood up, ready to defend himself. Streep's thick neck, broad face, and shoulders hunched forward, his muscular arms flexed.

"Come on guys," Rusty said. "We're all part of the same crew. We shouldn't be fighting."

"Ain't we the three musketeers?" Streep growled. "When I finish with your Norwegian friend, I'll take care of you. Kurtz, that's a German name, ain't it? Might even be a Jew name. You one of them Jews that's fillin' up the country so regular Americans can't find jobs or a place to live? Why don't you people go back where you belong?"

"You bigoted maniac," Rusty shouted. "You're worse than Hitler." He leaped from the hatch and swung a wide right fist at Streep's face.

Streep stepped aside with surprising agility and aimed a swift blow at Rusty's head. It never found it's mark. His arm was deflected by a walking stick made from the hard wood of the Galam tree. Streep, his motion interrupted, was thrown off balance and he fell heavily to the deck.

Solomon Mobuto stood over him. "You bad man, Mr. Streep. We do nothing to hurt you. Why are you so angry?"

Streep got up and grabbed the stick but the Masai's grip was firm. Solomon, instead of pulling the stick back, pushed it hard into his stomach, knocking him once again to the deck, surprised and breathless. Sven and Rusty looked on in astonishment.

Once again Solomon Mobuto stood over Streep. "Do not goad me into enforcing the code of the Masai. You will regret it."

Streep jumped up. "It's you three that'll regret it," he said, taken aback by this unexpected resistance. "Now I guess you'll run to your Jew-Captain and squeal about this. You guys better grow eyes in the back of your heads from now on." He turned and strode away, his fists still clenched, but his pride damaged.

"He bad man," Sol said.

"The worst kind," Rusty agreed

"He madder than ever," Sven said. "We have to watch ourselves as long as he on same ship with us."


The Admiral Byrd pulled alongside the pier at Anzio and immediately began the task of unloading its much needed cargo. General Mark Clark had surprised the Germans by landing behind the front lines with the goal of forcing the enemy to pull back and relieve the pressure in the south. Gunfire could be heard in the distance, an indication that fighting was not too far away.

There was no shore leave for any of the crew as they worked around the clock to unload the tanks, artillery and other weapons of war. By noon the next day the Admiral Byrd drifted away from the pier and turning slowly to port, heading back into the Mediterranean Sea. A forecast of bad weather moving toward Italy encouraged Captain Sugarman to leave as soon as the last piece of equipment was set ashore.

No sooner did the Italian mainland drop out of sight than the wind and seas picked up dramatically and the Admiral Byrd was dipping and rolling severely. Without the weight of the cargo the ship was tossed around like a cork. In the mess room, dishes were soon flying about like so many missiles, and those members of the crew attempting to eat were forced to keep a sharp lookout.

Rusty, Sven and Szabo held on tightly while trying to down a quick sandwich and coffee. Szabo was in a foul mood.

"When we get back I'm getting out from under that fuckin' Streep. He's an animal. He came into the wheelhouse the other day madder than shit and started givin' everybody a hard time. The captain came in and I thought they're gonna start swingin' at each other. That guy's sick in the head."

Sol staggered in, barely able to keep his balance as the ship rolled sharply, first to port and then to starboard. He threw his cloak onto the mess table. It was in tatters, cut into strips and torn apart. The Junior Elder emblem was missing completely. His eyes were moist. "Mr. Streep has gone too far. My cloak is my people. An attack on it is an attack on my people." His long hand brushed aside the tear rolling down his face. "It would seem to me that one enemy to fight at a time is enough." He turned and left the mess room.

Except for the straining and creaking of the ship, the mess was silent. Szabo pounded the table with his fist.

"That son of a bitch! I'm for givin' it to him. Between the three of us we could make mincemeat outta him. What d'ya say?"

"I think the time has come," Sven said.

"If you two are willing, then I'm in, too," Rusty said. "But he is an officer. We'll have to take the consequences."

"The whole crew hates his guts," Szabo said. "We'll jump him at night. He'll never know who or what."

"Let us go before we change our minds," Sven said. "It is dark out in the storm and Mr. Streep tours the deck every day about this time."

They clung to the handrails as they climbed up the steps to the main deck. It wasn't raining, but low heavy clouds rushing across the sky turned daylight into dusk, and the screaming wind ripped at the waves sending whitecaps bouncing across the water.

Standing in the lee of a bulkhead, their eyes scanned the deck looking for Streep. Presently a figure appeared by the port rail walking toward the stern. He held the rail with his right hand as he made his way along the heaving deck. His collar was pulled up around his head, but as he passed the unseen crew members, a flash of lightning lit up the familiar scowling red face. He continued on toward the stern and stopped at a lifeboat station. He lifted the cover and looked inside.

"What the hell's he doing?" Szabo hissed.

"I don't know," Rusty said.

"He looking for slackers," Sven whispered. "He find crewman asleep once and give him beating. He hoping to find somebody again."

"Ain't he a pip?" Szabo declared. "Now what's he up to?"

Streep was leaning over the rail looking down at the ocean.

"Looks like he's examining the hull or something," Rusty answered.

"Listen," Sven whispered.

At first they heard nothing but the wind and the sea, then another sound reached their ears. The sound of coughing and gurgling.

"By God, he's seasick!"

"Or drunk," Sven said.

"I'll be a son of a bitch," Szabo said with a half smile. "The bastard's seasick. Who would've thought it?"

"It's not unusual," Sven said. "Some sailors never get sick and others get sick every time a storm comes up. Our friend, Mr. Streep, is one of those. Too bad."

"Yeah, my heart bleeds for him. Come on, now's the time to teach that fucker a lesson."

As they moved out of the shelter of the bulkhead, a strange sound stopped them before they had gone very far. A voice was singing a song, an unfamiliar song in an unfamiliar language. It's mournful tone blended with the wind, and its eerie melody, rising ·higher and sounding like the unhappy cry of a distraught soul sent shivers through their bodies. They turned to look for the source of this melancholy song, but before they could do so, something flew past their heads. It was a long stick, made from the hard wood of the Galam tree, with bone embedded in each end, hurled straight and true, followed by a distinct ugly thud.

When they looked toward the rail, Mr. Streep was gone. The next moment, Solomon Mobuto strode past them, retrieved his walking stick, which lay by the rail, and walked back in dignified silence. He was still humming that strange melody to himself as he disappeared below deck.

Rusty, Sven and Szabo stood stunned by what they had just witnessed. Sven put a finger to his lips and they slowly left the deck and retreated below to their bunks, where they lay for a long time, each lost in their own thoughts.

They said little to each other about that day, and less to the captain when he questioned the crew about Streep's possible fate. Some crew members commented on his seasickness and drinking the day of his disappearance, and there was speculation that he might have lost his footing in the heavy weather.

Captain Sugarman wrote matter of factly in the ship's journal – "Mr. Streep, due to seasickness or drunkenness, or both, during heavy weather while outward bound from Italy, either slipped or was washed overboard while making his rounds aboard the Admiral Byrd. He vanished without a trace and has not been seen since."

No regrets were mentioned and there were no tears shed by the crew. His name would live forever in the long casualty lists of World War II, an achievement he would not have attained had he lived.

**41**

The LT 677 was ready for sea. Most of its needs were met in the British dockyard, but the propeller shaft fashioned by the workmen at the yard broke on its first trial. Along with a new oil pump, it had to be shipped from Charleston.

Feeling gratified that they had at last contributed positively to the war effort, Captain Sugarman, Kurtz, Ericson and Szabo, left the Admiral Byrd and returned to their tug. Joining them was a new member of the crew, brought with them to help fill the vacancies left by the action at Riga – a tall, regal black man from the Masai Steppe of Tanzania in East Africa.

Rumors had spread from the Admiral Byrd's crew that Solomon Mobuto had received a great deal of verbal abuse at the hands of a certain unnamed 2nd Mate, and that particular 2nd Mate had mysteriously disappeared during a sudden Mediterranean storm, never to be found. Rumor also had it that he had unofficially died in the "manner of the Masai." Officially, he was washed overboard. Seaman Mobuto was warily welcomed by the crew of the LT 677, and was treated, if not respectfully, at least carefully.

He looked as much out of place on the tug as he did on the Admiral Byrd, but his bearing and politeness soon won the men over and they accepted him as one of their own. He became a familiar figure walking back and forth on the dock, as well as the confined space of the 135 foot LT 677, with his curious walking stick, and his royal cloak, painstakingly repaired and restored to its original beauty. He was a good worker, never complaining and always willing to lend a hand. After two weeks it seemed as though he was part of the original crew. As on the Admiral Byrd, his bunk was too short for his nearly seven foot frame, and Szabo could be heard grumbling when he was awakened by two large, black feet ruffling through his hair.

On June 1st, 1944, Captain Sugerman assembled the crew of LT 677 in the messroom. Twenty-eight men, seamen and officers, squeezed around the one long table or standing against the bunks along both bulkheads. It was early, barely after sunrise and there was

315

grumbling by those whose sleep was interrupted.

"What's up?" Szabo asked, rubbing his eyes. "Ya think this is it?"

"I tell you," Sven said. "They don't bring so many soldiers to England for sightseeing."

"That's for sure," Rusty agreed. "Everybody knows there's going to be an invasion. How about it, Sol?"

Seaman Mobuto, his back straight, and hands folded in his lap was quiet for a moment. "I think so," he said. "We must do what we must. The sooner the better so we can all return to our families."

Rusty thought of his grandmother. He could still feel the strength of her embrace. "Sol," he said, "Is family the most important thing among your people?"

"Yes," Sol replied. "Both our blood family and tribal family. They are the same. To fail in your duty to one is to fail in your duty to both. Family, duty, honor. The three are tied together. There is no questioning it. We are taught it as children. There is no worse crime than failing your family."

The men around him sat quietly, touched by the simple language of this humble black man from the shadows of Kiliminjaro.

"My grandmother told me the same thing," Rusty said.

"A wise lady," Solomon Mobuto answered.

Captain Sugarman entered dressed in his usual work clothes, dungarees, turtleneck sweatshirt and khaki jacket. He stood at the head of the table.

"Good morning, men. Sorry to shake some of you out of your bunks. I've just spent the night at the British Merchant Service." The room was still, all eyes riveted on their captain. "The whole world, including the enemy, knows what's coming. What they don't know is the time or the place. The weather has a lot to do with it. I can tell you this – with the assistance of another tug, we'll tow a floating dock across the channel onto some beach so ships can unload cargo. The British will lead us in. We're only a small part of a tremendous operation, but if we don't do our job it will cost lives."

He paused to allow what he said to sink in.

"I don't want to go home and dream about men dying because we didn't do our part. I can't stress strongly enough how important it is that nothing goes wrong. Every port is choked with men and material. Every ship with a gun will be firing. Nobody turns back. We'll leave it to the historians to decide if we did our best. There will be no more leave. Everybody's confined to the vessel until we go in. That's all for now."


A 12:00 noon on June 5, the LT 677, as it had done with the crane, hooked its cable to the floating dock and waited. A brisk breeze blew a light rain in from the misty channel. Rusty sat at the mess table with Szabo and Sven.

"I'm getting the jitters," he said. "Five days on this tug doing nothing is too much. I'm claustrophobic."

"Amen to that," Szabo muttered. "No place to go. Nothin' to do. No girls. It's fuckin' not human."

"Take it easy, boys," Sven cautioned. "It won't be long now. Remember, there are thousands waiting, just like we are. We'll be moving soon, you bet."

"Not much consolation, Sven," Rusty said. "I'm tired of this war. I hate it. The waiting, the killing. I dreamed of Cole last night, rotting in that crane. I wish he was here."

"Yah, that would be good," Sven answered.

"He was a nice guy," Szabo said.

Rusty swallowed hard. "His family won't ever be able to bury him," he said.

They were quiet, each with his own memories of the peaceable Quaker.

"Where's Sol?" Szabo asked, anxious to steer the conversation in another direction.

"I see him all dressed up standing on the port lookout," Sven said. "In the rain."

"What's he doing?"

"I ask him. He say he prays for his family."

"In Africa?"

"No. On this tug. He say we are family now."

"One thing about war," Rusty said, "you meet a lot of interesting people."

The weather was still prohibitive on June 5th when the decision was passed down from the high command - "Overlord postponed one day."

Outside the harbor, ships were rocking at their anchor chains and the troops fought the debilitating effects of seasickness and boredom. They looked at the menacing clouds racing in low from the Atlantic and the wind-whipped whitecaps visible out on the channel. They felt the stinging rain that fell occasionally, and the odor of men vomiting added to their misery, making the prospects of facing enemy fire on the beaches a welcome relief. They had long ago been resigned to fighting and dying. Now they just wanted to get it over with.

The ships' radios crackled with suspicious phrases and cliche-ridden sentences. But among the useless clatter, the code words for "go" finally were heard throughout the fleet. The orders were to set sail the night of June 5th, carrying out landings on assigned beaches 06:30 the morning of June 6th. "Good luck to all," came at the end.

Anchor chains rattled, ships slid silently from their docks and the armada left England and started across the channel.

Slowly the harbor emptied as the ships left. Some would not return. The tugs suddenly found themselves alone, and the emptiness was in sharp contrast to the activity of several hours ago.

On the LT 677, Rusty and Sven stood at the starboard rail and watched the ships disappear into the darkness.

"What do you think?" Rusty asked. "Will they get ashore?"

Sven was lost in his thoughts, and Rusty had to repeat the question.

"They have to," Sven said. "We can't go on fighting forever. The world will destroy itself."

As they spoke, 12 bombers passed overhead, going in the same direction as the ships. Soon the sky was covered with planes. There seemed no end to them.

Captain Sugarman's voice interrupted their thoughts. "Cast off all lines. We're getting under way."

"That was fast," Rusty said. He felt a chill at what lay ahead. He wondered if he would come back. He thought of Catherine. "If it's meant to be," she would have said. I have no control over it, he thought. My life is in other hands, just like thousands of others. It doesn't pay to worry about it. Let's get it over with. He went to help with the lines.

LT 775 and 677 moved out of Portsmouth Harbor into the choppy waters of the English Channel, 775 on the portside and 677 on the starboard, each connected to the tow by their cables, which had been run out to 100 yards. The tugs maneuvered until they were only about 25 yards apart, and the cables fanned out until they formed a large triangle with the front of the tow. The artificial dock was not much different in size from the crane, except for its height. The deck was higher and when sunk in place would be like an iceberg, more below water than above.

On the tug cable duty was again instituted and the acetylene torch was reactivated, with two seamen standing one-hour watches.

Rusty and Sven drew the first cable watch and looked out over the stern at their new toy.

"At least it won't be five weeks before we get rid of it," Sven said.

"Five hours is more like it," Rusty said. "It's only about 30 miles across. Hey, who're those guys on the tow?" Although the channel was boiling and a stiff wind was blowing, there was no rain falling and the tow was visible in the darkness.

"Szabo and someone from the 775," Sven answered. "It's their job to open the flood gates on both sides at the same time so she settles on the bottom without capsizing. Szabo volunteered to do it."

The two figures stood on the tow like shadowy statues before disappearing below.

"Szabo the volunteer," Rusty murmured.

At the change of watch, Rusty and Sven reported topside, Rusty at the wheel, Sven on lookout.

"Keep her aimed at the red light on that trawler's stern," Captain Sugarman ordered. "That's our guide across the channel."

"Yes, sir," Rusty answered as he turned the wheel a bit to the left.

The British trawler ahead of them, having fished off the French coast for years, was leading them through the shifting currents and difficult tides that ran between the Atlantic Ocean and the North Sea. Finding the correct beach at night by themselves would have been impossible. It was far better to follow men with years of experience in these waters than to plunge into unfamiliar seas at night.

There were also the mines. For weeks, British minesweepers had been scooping up mines, clearing invisible highways for the invasion forces to follow. A little to the left or right could be deadly. The captain had charts, but the low power red light on the stern of the trawler was much more comforting. Off to port, keeping directly abreast of them was the LT 775 and behind both tugs was the floating dock, a huge dark shadow looming high overhead. Farther back were LT 701 and 705 with their tow. Later, small cargo ships would be following the same course, hoping the docks will be in place.

The predicted brief period of clearing weather had come and gone, staying just long enough to get the men ashore and allow protective air cover. Out in the channel the heavy clouds had closed in again, shutting off the early morning daylight. It was raining moderately, cutting down visibility but not enough to block out the vital red light. The wind was blowing from the southwest, directly up the channel, and the tow kept veering to port, forcing the LT 775 to drift off a bit lest she collide with 677. The sea was kicking up too, not the long, regular swells of the Atlantic, but sharp, choppy waves that rocked the tugs unevenly, causing that unsettled feeling to return to some seamen.

It was nearly midday as they approached the French coast, still hidden by dark clouds and rain. The occasional sound of gunfire, both from ships and ashore, indicated that the men on the beaches were not having an easy time. Fighter planes passed by, flying low to stay under the cloud cover.

Rusty and Sven, wearing foul weather gear, were now on the port bridge and 2nd Mate Anderson and seaman McGonagle were on the starboard bridge. Captain Sugarman was in the wheelhouse where he could see directly ahead, hear reports from both bridges, watch over the man at the wheel, and stay in contact with the engine room.

A sudden, heavy rain squall reduced visibility to zero and blotted out the trawler.

"Keep the wheel on the present course. Do not deviate."

Rusty peered into the darkness. "I can't see a thing. If this rain doesn't let up how'll we know if we're too close to shore?"

"We don't," Sven said. "But we must be there by now. We've been underway for six hours."

The gunfire was louder, audible above the driving rain.

"I wonder if that trawler is still there? If it doesn't clear soon we might run right up on the beach."

"Maybe they are in low power radio contact with us. That way we know where they are."

A whooshing sound passed overhead and a tremendous explosion sent tons of water washing over the tow.

"That was close!" Rusty shouted excitedly. "Must have been a wild one." Seconds later, another geyser of water shot into the air just ahead of them.

"I don't think they are so wild. It looks like they have our range."

"But how do they know we are here? I still can't make out the trawler's light."

"Maybe that low power radio is not so low power," Sven said.

Rusty looked at him. "Damn it, Sven, we have no way of protecting ourselves."

"The captain say we cannot turn back."

This time there was no whooshing sound. A brilliant flash from the port side lit up the wheelhouse, followed by an ear-splitting blast. Pieces of metal rattled against the hull of 677 and one jagged lump of metal smashed through the glass of the port wheelhouse door, zipped behind the head of the man at the wheel and exited through the window of the starboard door.

Instinctively everybody ducked. When they recovered and looked off to port they saw the LT 775 reduced to a burning wreckage, some parts of it blown away and smoking. It sank within minutes, leaving the job of towing the dock into place up to the LT 677, which was pulled off course by the loss of its partner.

Captain Sugarman grabbed the engine room phone.

"Chief, the other tug's been knocked out. I'll need everything you've got. Stand by!"

He stuck his head through the broken window. "Kurtz, get on the fantail. Until visibility improves you'll have to run back and forth to the wheelhouse to let me know where the tow is. Get moving!"

Rusty rushed down to join Solomon Mobuto, who was standing at the acetylene watch.

"Where's the tow?" Rusty shouted.

Sol pointed off to port diagonally from the tug. Without the second tug to keep it stabilized, the tow was now drifting at a crazy angle, its only link to 677 being the cable attached to its starboard bow keeper. Delivering it to its determined location now looked like a long shot.

Captain Sugarman was running between both outside bridges, hoping to see where they were in relation to the other vessels and the shoreline.

"Captain," Rusty said breathlessly, "the tow's all right, but it's at about a 45 degree angle to the stern."

"That's okay. Keep me advised of any change. Anderson, I'm afraid that we're right at the beach but there's no way to tell."

"That firing's getting louder but I don't hear the sound of waves breaking."

"I don't think you would. This is the channel, not the Atlantic. What waves there are would be too small to make much noise."

"What do we do then?" Anderson asked.

Captain Sugarman didn't answer. He was thinking of the worst case scenario. If they flooded the dock in water too deep, it would be useless, and a menace to any ships coming in behind them. It would also give him the distinction of losing two tows within a year. Even though the first was not his fault, he was the man in command and the Army brass of the A.T.S. would make note of that fact.

He had to find out how much water was beneath them. And those two men out there. He had completely forgotten about them.

"Anderson, unless this fog lifts we have to find a way to figure out the depth of the water. I have an idea. First, reel in the tow to 50 yards, then come up on the bow with a few men and loosen the anchor." He signalled the engine room to "slow ahead."

The anchor swung freely from the starboard bow of the tug as they moved slowly through the dense fog. The firing on shore was clearer than before, and the warships off the coast were hurling shell after shell at the enemy defenses.

"Let go!" Captain Sugarman shouted. The cable rattled and the anchor plunged into the water with a large splash. The cable remained taut as the anchor sank further down. Suddenly, the chain slackened, it was on the bottom.

"How much chain went out?" Captain Sugarman shouted.

"Twenty-six feet," Anderson answered

"Raise the anchor to just above the water line."

The motor roared to life, reeling in the chain until the anchor was barely scraping the surface. Five minutes went by.

"Drop it again," the captain ordered.

The chain seemed to slacken earlier than before.

"How much this time?" he asked.

"Twenty-two feet."

"It's shoaling fast," Captain Sugarman said. "Tell them to open the flood cocks on the tow, quickly!"

Voices were heard shouting from the stern. The two figures on deck disappeared below and soon it was clear that the tow was settling lower in the water.

"Captain!" Sol's voice come from the stern. "Look there!"

Captain Sugarman rushed to the stern where Sol and Rusty were pointing into the water. Three American soldiers floated on the surface, their arms outstretched, one still holding his rifle. The crew silently stared down at the bodies. Several men made the sign of the cross. One seaman cried audibly, others swallowed hard and fought back the tears. Two of the bodies floated face down, the third was on his back, as if asleep.

The captain's voice broke the silence. "Bring them aboard and wrap them in canvas. We'll turn them over to the Army when we get back."

At that moment, they suddenly came out of the fog bank into the brightness of daylight. They were about 200 yards from the beach where men were still coming ashore from landing craft and running toward the shelter of the cliffs. Smoke was pouring from the massive concrete bunkers built by the Germans, but the shells from the battleships, cruisers and planes had put most out of action. Here and there a brave gun crew managed to fire back at the hundreds of ships in the channel, but it was a feeble gesture. The Allies had succeeded in getting a foothold.

It took 30 minutes for the dock to settle on the bottom. Orders were given to disconnect the towing cable and retrieve the two men aboard. They prudently crept closer to the tow to allow the two seamen to climb down a ladder and leap onto the tug. A sudden hail of bullets swept the tow's deck. Both men dropped. At first it appeared that they were trying to hide from the gunfire, but Rusty heard a familiar voice shouting, "Mom, I'm hit!" It was Szabo.

"Captain," Rusty screamed hysterically. "Szabo's been shot! We've got to get him off that tow!"

"Kurtz, I can see him crawling over to the edge! Get to the bow with Mobuto. Maybe he can reach up to the deck and grab him."

"Sol," Rusty yelled, "we need you up on the bow. Szabo's lying wounded on that deck!"

Solomon Mobuto ran in long, leaping strides to the bow and in one jump was on the rail reaching up to the deck. His hand found an arm and he pulled with all his strength. Szabo's limp form rolled off the edge of the deck and fell into Solomon's arms. It seemed that the Masai would fall under the weight, but he recovered his balance and gently handed him down to Rusty and several other crewmen clustered about. They laid him on the deck where he lay motionless.

When they opened his torn pea jacket it was clear that John Szabo never had a chance. His shirt was red with blood. His chest had been shattered by machine gun bullets. He wasn't breathing. Rusty dropped to his knees, his eyes wet. Off in the distance he heard Captain Sugarman's voice.

"Help Mobuto with that other body! Easy now! Okay, Solomon, get aboard! We're getting out of here!"

Freed of its tow, LT 677 leaped forward and reentered the fog bank hanging over the channel. The coast of France disappeared behind them and the sound of gunfire gradually faded away. LT 677 was returning to England, its mission a success, but with five dead men lying on the deck – three soldiers, a seaman from LT 775 and John Szabo.

Rusty sat beside his friend and looked down at the rough hewn face with black, curly hair hanging across his forehead.

"Stupid idiots," Rusty said, cradling his friend's body. "We could have stayed in New London, but no, we had to be heroes. We wanted to fight. This wouldn't have happened if we had stayed in New London. It wasn't worth it, John! It wasn't worth it!"

Rusty got off the BMT at 57th Street and walked six blocks to Sheldan Street, an area typical of many neighborhoods in Brooklyn – rows of four story walk-ups on both sides of a paper-strewn street, with fire escape ladders on the outside and basement apartments at the bottom.

When the war ended, the frantic rush to get home from overseas taxed transportation to the limit. After receiving his release papers from the A.T.S. office in London, he had hoped to catch a flight back to the States, but he soon found that priorities and influence pushed him onto a two week waiting list. When the opportunity opened up to ship home on a troop transport with the 2nd Armored Division, he took it.

The 2nd Armored, at least on this vessel, was comprised of mostly southerners, lean and tough veterans of many tank battles on the fields of France and Germany. Their casual drawl, which European women adored, and innate sense of humor, were in marked contrast to the seriousness of the battles they had fought. Despite their joking and laughter, Rusty could feel their no-nonsense attitude. These were men you didn't take liberties with. He was glad that they were on his side.

Rusty looked at the addresses – 20015, 20017, 20019. If the records at A.T.S. in London were correct, this was the house: 20019, Apt.A2.A2 was in the basement. He looked at the name on the mailbox, John and Elizabeth Szabo. He heard slow footsteps approaching the door in response to his ringing.

The door was partially opened by a short, elderly, grey-haired man, thin and slightly stooped over. His wrinkled face was pale, and his dark eyes peered suspiciously through thick lenses.

"My name is Sid Kurtz. John and I served on the LT 677 together," he paused, uncomfortably. "I thought I'd just stop in to say hello."

The door opened wider. "You Rusty?" The old man's voice was strained as if it was an effort for him to speak.

"That's what everybody calls me."

"Please come in, son." He stepped aside, closed the door and led

Rusty down a hallway to a door in the rear. The air was rank with the strong odor of cigarette smoke.

The door opened into a parlor with a throw rug on the floor, an old sofa, two padded rocking chairs, and a piano against one wall. An open area on the left led into a kitchen, and two doors on the right were probably bedrooms. Rusty barely noticed this. At the moment his attention was riveted on the woman rocking slowly near the piano. Her upper body moved back and forth deliberately to keep the rocker going and she took no notice of the visitor. Her hair was grey and every time she rocked forward, several strands would fall unhindered over her forehead. There was a half-smile on her small round face, and her smooth skin showed vestiges of a once attractive woman. Her eyes looked neither to left or right, but stared constantly at a picture on the piano. It was John Szabo, standing on the parade ground at New London. Rusty swallowed hard.

"Don't bother talking to her. She won't hear you, at least she makes out like she don't. She's been like this since we got the news." The man sat down in the other rocker and lit a cigarette, adding more smoke to an already hazy room.

"I'm sorry," Rusty said. "Does she ever say anything?"

"Yeah, she comes out of it once in a while, but she don't make too much sense. He was our only child."

Rusty was at a loss. What could he say? How could he understand what it was like to lose an only child? Maybe it would have been better not to come, he thought, not to remind them of their loss. They might resent that he was still alive while their son was dead. He was ashamed to be alive.

He started to get up. "Maybe I should leave. It was a mistake to come here and open up fresh wounds."

"Don't go!" she shouted. "Please don't go. I want to hear all about John."

The urgency of her plea surprised him and he quickly sat down, not wanting to excite her further.

"Take it easy, Elizabeth," the old man urged. "He's not goin' anywhere, are you?"

"No, no. Of course not. I didn't mean to upset you."

"She's right though, We both want to hear about John. What else do we have? We were married late in life, Liz and me – never married before and with no children. When John was born, I was 50 and the wife was 45. Pretty old for starting a family. We both had our doubts about it, but after he came we never had any regrets. We poured out our love on him like a flood. He was the center of our lives. We couldn't do enough for him. Course we wasn't well to do, but he never went without. What we couldn't give him in material stuff, we more than made up for in love and attention. He would sit between us on that sofa where you are, in the best pajamas that our money could buy, with his black curly hair, and we would take turns reading to him until he fell asleep. Then we'd carry him into our room and put him in the crib. We had that second bedroom but she wouldn't think of it. He'll be away from us when he gets older,' she would say. 'I want him close to me for as many years as possible.' God, they grow up quick. It seems no time that he was on the street running around with those roughnecks. But he was a good boy. And now..." He suddenly had a fit of coughing. Rusty waited politely for it to pass. When it did, the old man lit another cigarette. "And now he's away for good."

His wife was crying softly.

"I'm not a religious man," Mr. Szabo continued, "but that thing in the Bible about the Lord giving and the Lord taking away, I guess I got to go along with that. What else is there?"

What else indeed, Rusty thought. This gloomy place was depressing him. He felt closed in, and his chest hurt from the tension and the smoke. He was wondering how to make a reasonably inoffensive exit.

"Now tell us about John," the old man said. "From the beginning."

"Please," she asked. "From the beginning."

So Rusty started from the beginning. From New London to New York and then to the LT 677. Finally he told about the invasion. When he told of the bullets that raked the deck of the tow, he heard the sharp intake of a breath. When he repeated John's words, "Mom, I'm hit," she started crying again and the old man put out his cigarette and stared straight ahead. The room was silent. Rusty looked at them. They seemed far away – like ghostly figures in a dream. He wasn't really here. But her voice brought him back to reality.

"I want you to stay over with us, Rusty," she said. "Just for tonight. That's what John would want. It'll be nice to have you in his room."

That was the farthest thing from Rusty's mind. He had no wish to spend the night in John Szabo's room, but looking at the two lonely faces in front of him, he couldn't refuse.

John's room was neat, with a bureau and a night table on each side of the bed. His clothes still hung in the closet, untouched. She offered him a pair of her son's pajamas but he drew the line.

"I have my own, thank you." He wouldn't wear a dead man's clothes. He would have enough trouble sleeping as it was.

He lay in bed thinking about Mr. and Mrs. Szabo, buried alone in this basement apartment, spending the remainder of their lives grieving for their son. His heart went out to them. A few years of happiness, and then it was over. He wished he might somehow help them, but short of bringing John back, there was nothing he could do.

After a fitful sleep, he was awakened by the smell of coffee brewing. He quickly dressed and went into the parlor. Some daylight was forcing its way from the alleyway through the one window, giving the room a less disheartening appearance. The rocker by the piano was empty. He peeked into the kitchen. Mrs. Szabo was fussing about with bread and eggs and her husband was setting the small wooden table. She looked much better today, taller than he had expected. Her hair was combed neatly back and a touch of makeup and lipstick had done wonders.

"Sit down, you two. I'm making toast and scrambled eggs this morning."

Mr. Szabo joined Rusty at the table. "I got up and found her like this in the kitchen. Your visit's shaken her out of it, at least for a while."

"I'm glad it helped," Rusty said.

Breakfast turned out to be rather pleasant. John's parents seemed less morose today and more animated. They talked about their lives before they were married. She, a gentle librarian and he a rough mechanic, an unlikely match. Their very different lives had attracted them to each other. Their courtship had been passionate and short, leading to marriage in just six months. They made small talk about their faults and how they used to joke about them before marriage, and how irritating they became after. They suddenly seemed like normal people.

After breakfast they asked to walk with him to the subway stop. It was a beautiful morning for Brooklyn, warm, not yet humid, with sunlight slanting across the street. People were on their way to work or shopping, while some women were sweeping the sidewalk and washing down the marble steps.

At the subway stop, he turned to them one last time.

"When I came yesterday, I regretted it," he said. "Now I'm glad."

She stepped forward and put her arms around him. "Thank you so much for coming. We hope to see you again sometime. God bless you." She kissed his cheek.

Mr. Szabo shook his hand. "Good luck to you, son."

Rusty looked at them, smiled weakly and disappeared down the subway steps. Halfway down, he stopped and quickly ran back to the top. John's parents were walking down the street hand in hand. Rusty's eyes were wet.

"I wish you were here to see them, John," he whispered.

The train ride from New York to Philadelphia was too short. He needed more time to sort things out. He had too much on his mind. When he had left home he knew what lay ahead. Now it was different. The war was over and the enemy was gone. It had been difficult, but in a sense it was easy. The goal was clear.

What about now, he wondered. What is the goal? To go home to a divided house, where a lone man and a lone woman cannot live side by side in harmony? He had witnessed too much to live with that. He didn't watch men die to come home to his parent's petty squabbles.

If he saw his father still leaving the house after closing the shop it would be too much. If he still saw his mother begging him for food money or crying because she was unhappy, that would be it. He would pack up and go. He didn't leave a big war to come home to a little one. All he wanted now was peace and quiet. He would search until he found it.

He thought about Edie. He had left her to endure it alone. She couldn't go off to war to get away from it. She had no escape route. It wouldn't be fair to leave her in the middle. It was cowardly and he suddenly felt ashamed. What would his grandmother do? Edie was family, his sister, and he owed her something. He couldn't turn his back on her. He would go home – for the time being anyway.

The train pulled into North Philadelphia Station and he walked, duffle bag on his shoulder, to Broad and Columbia, where he took a #3 trolley car heading east to 7th Street. It turned north to Montgomery where he got off. Store lights were lit up and down the block.

He stood outside Bloom's Candy store and watched Mrs. Bloom behind the counter washing dishes. He knew she would be glad to see him, but that could wait. Home came first. Better to get that over with. He walked the one block up 7th Street, passing the bakery where he had bought pretzels from Mrs. Silver. His father's barbershop was still there, across the street on the northwest corner of Berks Street. It seemed like a hundred years since he had last seen it. He set down his duffle bag and leaned against the wall of Dave's Fruit Store. He wanted to look at the barbership for a while before going in.

He stood alone in the dark, given only a casual glance by an occasional passerby. The store was brightly lit as usual. His father liked it that way. He wanted it to stand out so people would see it.

He was standing at the first chair giving a customer a haircut while another barber was at the second chair. Two men sat along the 7th Street window waiting their turn. He looked keenly at his father. It was like looking at a stranger. He really didn't know the man. He couldn't remember having one conversation with him. It was an odd feeling going home to a stranger. His mother was simpler. A good homemaker. The meals were always ready, the house was always clean.

He'd been told that she carried him from doctor to doctor during a series of illnesses throughout his childhood, but he had no memory of her holding him. He didn't know his family. He had no insight into their feelings and emotions. It was like starting all over again.

Was he that way, too? Uncommunicative, unemotional, without warmth? Maybe it was time he reviewed his own shortcomings, he thought. Maybe he was holding back. Was he making his parents and sister convenient excuses for this emptiness in his life? Perhaps it was time for him to be more assertive, more caring, more feeling, but he wasn't sure how to start. Should he just walk in and say, "Things are going to be different from now on?" It wouldn't be that easy.

Then he saw his mother, wearing her ever-present apron, come into the store from the breakfast room. She sat down in the nearest chair and waited, looking directly at her husband. Rusty knew what that meant. She needed money for tomorrow's supplies. She sat there for five minutes before his father took notice of her. He opened the register and took out a few bills, walked to where she was sitting and dropped the money into her lap. One bill fell on the floor. She leaned over, picked it up and went back into the breakfast room.

So things haven't changed after all, he thought. I need more time. A taxicab was passing and he started to raise his hand to hail it, but he stopped. Where would he go? To some hotel by himself with nobody to talk to? He needed somebody to talk to, about anything, baseball, the weather, the stars. Maybe Yussel was home. They could sit on the breadbox again. Life had been simple then. He suddenly felt thirsty, in need of a refreshing drink. Maybe he'd go back to Bloom's for a soda. He thought of Sylvia at Brook's Luncheonette and wondered if she was still there. She was nice, and she liked him. She said she'd wait for him, even if she didn't mean it. He had promised to look her up when he came back. That was it. He'd go home later, but first he'd visit Sylvia. Maybe she'd make him a free milkshake.

He shouldered his duffel bag and walked along Berks Street toward 8th stopping at his grandparent's small store. He stared through the window – everything was dark. They're either asleep or out, he thought. Turning left on 8th street he walked past the brick row houses down to Montgomery Avenue. Brook's Luncheonette was still on the corner. Setting the duffel bag down on the step he opened the door and went in. The store was the same. A few teens sipping on ice cream sodas and banana splits. The nickelodeon was silent. It seemed like yesterday when Yussel and he sat there the night before leaving.

"Rusty Kurtz!" Sylvia looked up from behind the counter. "You came back after all. You here for a milkshake or to see me?"

Her voice – its youthful exuberance with a hint of laughter – brought his mood up. "A little of both, I guess."

"At least I have a fifty percent chance. It's nice to see you again – and all in one piece."

He sat down on the stool searching for something to say. "Things haven't changed around here. You're still in the same spot where I left you."

"I don't get around much." She looked closely at him.

"You don't look happy about being back. Something bothering you?"

"No," he lied.

"I'm sorry about your grandmother," Sylvia said.

"What?"

"Your grandmother. I heard she died."

Rusty stared blankly at her. His eyes moistened and he choked back a sob. Sylvia's face was a mixture of pity and embarrassment.

"You didn't know? Oh, Rusty. I'm so sorry. I didn't have any idea."

Grandmother Itkah's last words came back to him. He thought of

Sol. Family – the only thing that matters.

He ran a hand across his cheeks. "When did she die?"

"About six months ago. It never occurred to me that you didn't know."

"The mail must've passed me on the way." He reflected for a moment. "Well, that's one more I can add to the list."

"What list?"

"You wouldn't know any of them. People I got to know and began to care for. Anderson, Walford, Cole, John Szabo, Catherine."

"Catherine?"

"Yes, a girl I met in London. I was lonely and we were both vulnerable."

"Did you make love? Never mind. I have no right to ask that. You were far from home. I had no ties on you."

"It doesn't matter," he said. "She's dead, just like the others. All of them. Sometimes I wonder why them and not me?"

"Why anybody?" Sylvia said.

"I suppose so," he said. "In the wrong place at the wrong time."

"You didn't know about your grandmother. Then you haven't been home?"

"My duffle bag's outside on the step."

"Why haven't you been home?"

"To answer a question with a question, why should I go home when I can come to Brook's Luncheonette and get a free milkshake?"

She flashed that wonderful smile that brought his mood up. She sure was a pretty girl. It didn't take a minute for a thick chocolate milkshake to magically appear on the counter.

"Seriously, Rusty. It's not fair to your parents. They're probably on pins and needles."

"It's possible," he said.

She looked at him closely. "I'm off in 15 minutes. If you want to we can take a walk and talk about things. If you want to."

Rusty savored another mouthful of the milkshake. "Okay," he finally said. "I'll finish this and wait outside."

They strolled up 8th Street as they had three years ago, the night before he left for New London.

"You know, Sylvia, going to war is sad, but coming home should be happy. For me, it's just the opposite."

"Why's that?" She slid her hand into his. It felt secure.

"My home life. Mom and Pop don't like each other. They hardly talk. After I got off the trolley I stood there a while looking at the store. I thought maybe things had changed since I left. They're still the same."

"You didn't even go in. How could you tell?"

"I could tell. I don't know if I can face it again. I was just a kid when I left."

"You were 18. That's not a kid."

"It's funny," he said. "You come home after three years and expect everything to be different. It's really a shock to see that nothing's changed after all."

They stopped at Berks Street as a #3 trolley clattered across the intersection.

"Rusty, can I say something?"

They crossed over to the far sidewalk. It was a pleasant night and some people were sitting in folding chairs or lounging on the steps. A radio was playing classical music.

"I have two sisters and three brothers. We can't do anything about our parents either. You think we haven't tried?"

"What happened?"

"We were told to mind our own business."

"That's quite an answer."

"What I'm getting at is you can't change the whole world. The only thing you can do is try to make a better life for yourself. If people want to hurt each other, there's not much you can do except learn from their mistakes."

He took the star from under his shirt.

"The Star of David," Sylvia said.

"My grandmother gave it to me before I left. She felt it would protect me."

"And it has."

"But she's dead," Rusty said. "What kind of trade-off is that? I'm having trouble figuring things out."

"She was an old lady. Her time had come."

Catherine would have said the same thing, he thought.

"You're a smart girl, Sylvia. You know what else my grandmother told me before I left?"

"What?"

"She told me to take care of my family."

"What's wrong with that?"

"Nothing."

"Maybe I can help you."

Rusty looked sideways at her. Brown eyes, nearly straight nose, hair swept up in back. There was something solid about her, dependable.

"You find any boyfriends while I was away?"

"About a hundred." She smiled. "I was comparison shopping."

"How'd I come out?"

"One hundred and one."

They looked at each other and laughed. He didn't have to ask her to be his girl. He just held her hand a little tighter.